Fuzzy Sets
and Fuzzy
Decision-Making

Hong Xing Li
and Vincent C. Yen

CRC Press

Boca Raton   New York   London   Tokyo

Library of Congress Cataloging-in-Publication Data

Li, Hong-Xing, 1953-
    Fuzzy sets and fuzzy decision-making / Hong-Xing Li, Vincent C. Yen.
        p.   cm.
    Includes bibliographical references and index.
    ISBN 0-8493-8931-3 (hard)
    1. Fuzzy sets.   2. Decision-making.   I. Yen, Vincent C.   II. Title.
QA248.L487 1995
003′.7—dc20   95-1571
                                                                               CIP

© 1995 by CRC Press, Inc.

No claim to original U.S. Government works
International Standard Book Number 0-8493-8931-3
Library of Congress Card Number 95-1571
Printed in the United States of America 1 2 3 4 5 6 7 8 9 0
Printed on acid-free paper

Contents

To our families
Qian Xuan and Li ke Yu
Yung-Hsih Yen, Bessie Y. Yen,
and Ruth C. Yen

Preface

Since the founding of the theory of fuzzy sets by L. A. Zadeh in 1965, it has seen three decades of development and applications. The scope of developments and applications ranges from theoretical to practical, and from natural sciences and engineering to humanity, medicine, and artificial intelligence. The broad array of applications demonstrates the value of the theory.

Fuzzy set theory has made applications in the field of management science and/or decision science, and consequently a branch of study called the fuzzy decision-making is in existence. One important question in the fuzzy decision-making is "What is its theoretical basis?" The answer to this question is not completely available at this time. In this book, we try to lay a foundation of fuzzy decision-making by means of the concept of factor spaces that was first proposed by P. Z. Wang in 1981, and was subsequently applied to knowledge representation in artificial intelligence. We will show through our framework that many interesting methods of fuzzy decision-making can be developed and we illustrate them with examples.

This book contains ten chapters. Chapter 1 provides a basic knowledge of fuzzy set theory. New concepts such as pan-Venn-diagrams, nested sets, and representation theorem based on the nested sets are given. Chapter 2 introduces the concept of factor spaces and its theory. This includes state spaces, operations and relations between factors, concept description and concept ranking, etc. Chapter 3 covers the basics of fuzzy decision-making. First, by means of Zadeh's extension principle, the feedback extension of a concept is proposed and made operational for decision-making because of the capability of approximating the extension of a concept by its feedback extensions. Next, G-envelope and π-closure of the extension of a concept are introduced; they can simplify the approximation process. In order to measure how close the approximation is we define the feedback rank and the degree of coincidence of a concept. Then we proceed to consider a very important problem: How can we represent the intension of a concept? Traditional mathematics always solve problems from the view of "extensions" since it is hard to describe a problem from the view of "intensions". So, starting with a rough representation of the intension of a concept, we then study the precision of the representation by means of the ϵ-essential factors. We show that the intension of a concept can be represented by the extension of the concept, and vice versa. This establishes the basic framework of fuzzy decision-making and its operational procedures. Detailed examples are given.

Chapter 4 provides many effective methods for the determination of membership functions. Chapter 5 introduces the concept of multifactorial analysis that is a basic tool in multifactorial fuzzy decision-making. A detailed discussion is also given on multifactorial functions, their basic properties, and their generation methods. Finally, we give a general model of multifactorial decision-making. Chapter 6 is about the variable weights analysis where we explore the principle of variable weights and its basic forms. Chapter 7 discusses multifactorial fuzzy decision-making with multiple objectives. Chapter 8 studies the degree analysis, i.e., based on set-valued statistics, that is an important branch of fuzzy decision-making. Chapter 9 offers many effective methods for improving fuzzy operators that will enhance the effectiveness of fuzzy decision-making. Chapter 10 introduces multifactorial fuzzy decision-making based on G. Shafer's theory of evidence.

We believe that methods of operations research or management science, especially linear programming can be studied in the framework of factor spaces, and such studies will generate enriched content and additional methods.

Hong-Xing Li
Vincent C. Yen

Acknowledgments

We would like to express our gratitude to the National Laboratory for Fuzzy Information Processing and Fuzzy Computing at Beijing Normal University, Beijing, China, and to Professor Rishi Kumar, Dean, College of Business Administration, Wright State University, Dayton, Ohio, for their support in the preparation of this book.

We also want to thank Ruth C. Yen, for her computer expertise and efforts on the drawings of figures in this book.

In addition, we would like to thank the editorial board of CRC Press for their interest in our book and continuing assistance throughout the preparation.

1

The Basics of Fuzzy Set Theory

1.1 Fuzzy Phenomena and Fuzzy Concepts

Fuzzy concepts derive from fuzzy phenomena that commonly occur in the natural world. For example, "rain" is a common natural phenomenon that is difficult to describe precisely since it can "rain" with varying intensity anywhere from a light sprinkle to a torrential downpour. Since the word "rain" does not adequately or precisely describe the wide variations in the amount and intensity of any rain event, rain is considered a "fuzzy" phenomenon.

The concepts formed in human brains for perceiving, recognizing, and categorizing natural phenomena are often fuzzy concepts. Boundaries of these concepts are vague. The classifying (dividing), judging, and reasoning emerging from them also are fuzzy concepts. For instance, "rain" might be classified as "light rain", "moderate rain", and "heavy rain" in order to describe the degree of "raining". Unfortunately, it is difficult to say when rain is light, moderate, or heavy. The concepts of light, moderate, and heavy are prime examples of fuzzy concepts themselves and are examples of fuzzy classifying. If it is raining today, you can call it light rain, or moderate rain, or heavy rain based on the relative amount of rainfall: This is fuzzy judging. If you are predicting a good, fair, or poor harvest based on the results of fuzzy judging, you are using fuzzy reasoning.

The human brain has the incredible ability of processing fuzzy classification, fuzzy judgment, and fuzzy reasoning. The natural languages are ingeniously permeated with inherent fuzziness so that we can express rich information content in a few words.

Historically, as reflected in classical mathematics, we commonly seek "precise and crisp" descriptions of things or events. This precision is accomplished by expressing phenomena in numerical values. However, due to fuzziness, classical mathematics can encounter substantial difficulties. People in ancient Greece discussed such a problem: How many seeds in a pile constitute a heap? Because "heap" is a fuzzy concept, they could not find a unique number that could be judged as a heap.

In fact, we often come into contact with fuzziness. There exist many fuzzy concepts in everyday life, such as a "tall" man, a "fat" man, a "pretty" girl, "cloudy" skies, "dawn", and "dusk", etc. We may say that fuzziness is absolute, whereas crispness or preciseness is relative. The so-called crispness or preciseness is only separated from fuzziness by simplification and idealization. The separation is significant because people can conveniently describe, in some situations, by means of exact models with pure mathematical expressions. But the knowledge domain is getting increasingly complex and deep. The complication has two striking features: (1) There are many factors associated with problems of interest. In practice, only a subset of factors is considered, and the originally crisp things are transformed into fuzzy things. (2) The degree of difficulty in dealing with problems is increased and the fuzziness is accumulated incrementally, with the result that the fuzziness cannot be neglected. The polarity between fuzziness and preciseness (or crispness) is quite a striking contradiction for the development of today's science. One of the effective means of resolving the contradiction is fuzzy set theory, a bridge between high preciseness and high complexity.

1.2   Naive Thoughts of Fuzzy Sets

People routinely use the word "concept". For example, the object "man" is a concept. A concept has its intension and extension; by intension we mean attributes of the object, and by extension we mean all of the objects defined by the concept. The extension of the concept "set" has been interpreted as the set formed by all of the objects defined by the concept. That is, sets can be used to express concepts. Since set operations and transformations can express judging and reasoning, modern mathematics becomes a formal language for describing and expressing certain areas of knowledge.

Set theory was founded in 1874 by G. Cantor, a German mathematician. One of the important methods used by Cantor in creating sets is the comprehension principle, which means that for any p, a property, all the objects with and only with p can be included together to form a set denoted by the symbol

$$A = \{a \mid p(a)\}$$

where A expresses the set and "a" an object in A. Generally, "a" is referred to as an element or a member of A. The expression $p(a)$ represents the element, a satisfies p, and { } represents all the elements that satisfy p subsumed to form a set. In logic, the comprehension principle is stated as

$$(\forall a)(a \in A \Leftrightarrow p(a))$$

Cantor's set theory has made great contributions to the foundations of mathematics. Unfortunately, it has also given rise to some restrictions on the use of mathematics. In fact, according to Cantor's claim, the objects that form the set are definite and distinct from each other. Thus, the property p used to form the set must be crisp: for any object, it must be precise whether the property p is satisfied or not. This is the application of the law of the excluded middle. From this law, the concept (e.g., property, proposition) expressed as a set is either true or false. Reasoning only with true or false forms a kind of bivalent logic. However, concepts in human brains hardly have crisp extensions. For example, the concept "tall man" (property p) cannot form a set based on Cantor's set theory because, for any man, we cannot unequivocally determine if the man satisfies the property p (i.e., tall man).

A concept without a crisp extension is a fuzzy concept. We now ask if a fuzzy concept can be rigidly described by Cantor's notion of sets or the bivalent (true/false or two-valued) logic. We will show that the answer is negative via the "baldhead paradox". Since one single hair change does not distinguish a man from his bald-headed status, we have the following postulate:

Postulate: If a man with n (a natural number) hairs is baldheaded, then so is a man with $n + 1$ hairs.

Based on the postulate, we can prove the following paradox:

Baldhead Paradox. Every man is baldheaded.

PROOF By mathematical induction,
 1) A man having only one hair is baldheaded.
 2) Assume that a man with n hairs is baldheaded.
 3) By the postulate, a man with $n + 1$ hairs is also baldheaded.
 4) By induction, we have the result: every man is baldheaded. ∎

The cause of the paradox is due to the use of bivalent logic for inference, whereas in fact, bivalent logic does not apply in this case.

Qualitative and quantitative values are closely related to each other. As the quantity changes so does the quality. In the baldheaded example, one cannot define a man as baldheaded because one cannot establish an absolute boundary by means of the number of hairs. But the tiny increase or decrease in the number of hairs (changes in quantity) does influence the change in quality, which cannot be described in words like "true/yes" or "false/no".

"True" and "false", regarded as logical values, can be respectively denoted by 1 (=100%) and 0 (=1–100%). Logical values are a kind of measure for the degree of truth. The "baldhead paradox" shows us that it is not enough to use only two values, 1 and 0, for fuzzy concepts; we have to use other logical values between 1 and 0 to express different degrees of truth. Therefore, in order to enable mathematics to describe fuzzy phenomena, it is of prime importance to reform Cantor's set concept, namely, to define a new kind of set called a fuzzy set.

In a practical problem, a set is always regarded as an extension of a concept, so a topic under discussion may always be limited to the same "scope". For example, if the topic of discussion is the concept "man", then the scope is limited to "people", and it is not necessary to consider other objects that have no relation to the concept. Let all people be denoted by U. All men selected from U form a set A in U (a subset of U), which is the extension of the concept "man".

All objects of a "concept" under discussion form a **universe**, and are often denoted by capital letters, (e.g., U, V). Each object in the universe is called an element, denoted by corresponding lower case letters (e.g., u, v). A portion of elements in U is a set, which is denoted by capital letters (e.g., A, B). A universe U may be imagined as a "square frame". The elements of U are "points" without mass and size. A set A on U may be represented by a "circular ring" in the "square frame". The relationship is depicted as a Venn diagram in Figure 1.1.

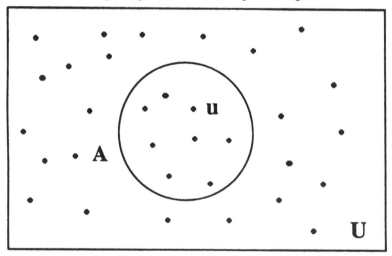

FIGURE 1.1
A Venn diagram containing a universe, a set and its elements.

For any element u and a set A in U, u either belongs to A (denoted by $u \in A$) or does not belong to A (denoted by $u \notin A$). If $u \in A$, (u lies inside the circle), then the relationship between u and A is denoted by 1; if $u \notin A$, (u lies outside of the circle), then the relationship is denoted by 0. In order to define fuzzy sets, the absolute membership relation for elements belonging to a set should be extended to multimembership with grades between 0 and 1.

We can illustrate fuzzy sets by using a graphing method similar to Venn diagrams. First, universe U is taken to be a rectangle in a Euclidean plane. The elements of U are some points in the rectangle (not necessarily all points of the rectangle) (see Figure 1.2).

For any point x (which may not necessarily belong to U) in the rectangle, the rays emitted from that point to all directions cover the whole rectangle. Every

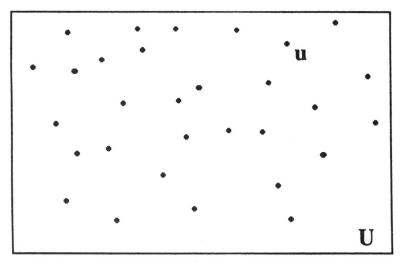

FIGURE 1.2
A universe and its elements.

point in U must be situated on such a ray (see Figure 1.3). Let A be a fuzzy set.

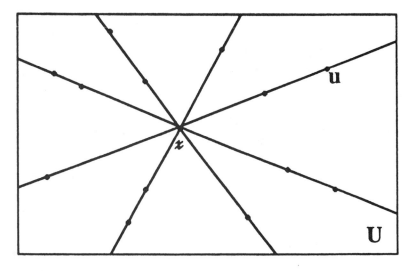

FIGURE 1.3
Rays and elements of universe.

Then A can be graphically represented as a "circle" with a unit width of boundary, a concentric circular ring (see Figure 1.4). For any $u \in U$, u could be in one of the three situations: (1) If u is situated inside of the inner circle, then its grade of

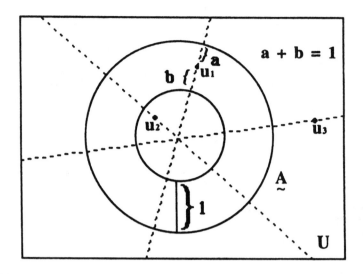

FIGURE 1.4
A fuzzy set.

membership is 1, denoted by A $(u) = 1$, which means that u absolutely belongs to A (see u_2 in Figure 1.4). (2) If u is outside of the outer circle, then its grade of membership is 0, denoted by A $(u) = 0$, which means that u does not belong to A (see u_3 in Figure 1.4). And (3) if u is in the annular region, then the depth "a", $0 \leq a \leq 1$, of the ray u into the large circle from the outside is exactly the grade of the membership (see u_1 in Figure 1.4). The diagrammatic sketch of Figure 1.4 is called a **pan-Venn-diagram**.

1.3   Definition of Fuzzy Sets

DEFINITION 1   *A* **fuzzy set** *A on the given universe U is that, for any $u \in U$, there is a corresponding real number $\mu_A(u) \in [0, 1]$ to u, where $\mu_A(u)$ is called the grade of membership of u belonging to A.*

This means that there is a mapping,

$$\mu_A : U \to [0, 1], \qquad u \mapsto \mu_A (u)$$

and this mapping is called the **membership function** of A.

Just as Cantor sets can be completely described by characteristic functions, fuzzy sets can also be described by membership functions. If the range of μ_A admits only two values 0 and 1, then μ_A degenerates to a usual set characteristic function.

$$A = \left\{ u \in U \mid \mu_A (u) = 1 \right\}$$

Therefore, Cantor sets are special cases of fuzzy sets.

All of the fuzzy sets on U will be denoted by $\mathcal{F}(U)$, and the power set of U in the sense of Cantor is denoted by $\mathcal{P}(U)$. Obviously, $\mathcal{F}(U) \supset \mathcal{P}(U)$. When $A \in \mathcal{F}(U) \setminus \mathcal{P}(U)$, A is called a proper fuzzy set; there exists at least one element $u_0 \in U$ such that $\mu_A (u_0) \notin \{0, 1\}$.

Note: For convenience, we will make no distinction between a fuzzy set A and its membership function μ_A, namely, $A(u) = \mu_A (u)$, for all $u \in U$.

Example 1

As shown in Figure 1.5, the universe U consists of five pieces: $a, b, c, d,$ and e. The circle piece "a" is a fuzzy concept on U and is denoted by A. The membership function of A is defined as $A(a) = 1$, $A(b) = 0.75$, $A(c) = 0.5$, $A(d) = 0.25$, and $A(e) = 0$. ☐

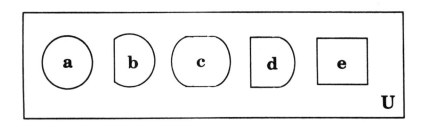

FIGURE 1.5
$U = \{a, b, c, d, e\}$.

Example 2

Zadeh defines the fuzzy sets "young" and "old", denoted by Y and O, respectively,

over the universe $U = [0, 100]$ as follows: ▯

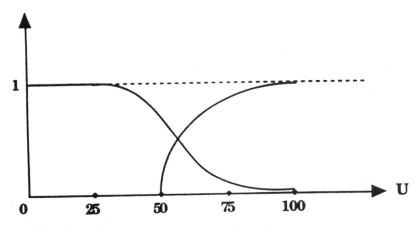

FIGURE 1.6
Membership functions of "young" and "old".

Example 3

Let $U = \{1, 2, ..., 9\}$ and A be the set of "natural numbers close to 5". The

membership function of A is defined as follows: ▯

$A(u)$	0	0.2	0.6	0.9	1.0	0.9	0.6	0.2	0
u	1	2	3	4	5	6	7	8	9

Example 4

Let U be the set of real numbers and A be the set of "real numbers considerably

larger than 10". Then a membership function of A is defined as $A(u) = 0$, $u < 10$,

and

$$A(u) = \left[1 + (u - 10)^{-2}\right]^{-1}, \qquad u \geq 10$$

▯

There are at least three forms for representing a fuzzy set. We will use Example 1

to illustrate these forms.

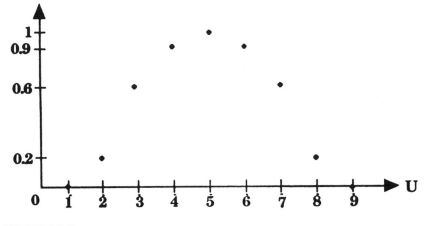

FIGURE 1.7
Natural numbers close to 5.

1) Zadeh's form. $\underset{\sim}{A}$ is represented by

$$\underset{\sim}{A} = \frac{1}{a} + \frac{0.25}{b} + \frac{0.5}{c} + \frac{0.25}{d} + \frac{0}{e}$$

where the numerator of each fraction is the grade of the membership of the corresponding element in the denominator, and the plus sign (+) is simply a notation without the usual meaning of addition. When the grade of membership for some element is zero, then that element may be omitted from the expression. For example, the term $\frac{0}{e}$ in the last expression may be omitted.

2) $\underset{\sim}{A}$ is represented by a set of ordered pairs. The first entry of the pair is an element of the universe, and the second entry of the pair is the grade of membership of the first entry. In this form, $\underset{\sim}{A}$ is represented as

$$\underset{\sim}{A} = \{(a, 1), (b, 0.75), (c, 0.5), (d, 0.25), (e, 0)\}$$

3) $\underset{\sim}{A}$ is represented by a vector called the fuzzy vector.

$$\underset{\sim}{A} = (1, 0.75, 0.5, 0.25, 0)$$

Note: Both Zedah's form and the ordered pairs representation may be extended to an infinite universe U by the following forms:

$$\underset{\sim}{A} = \int_{u \in U} \underset{\sim}{A}(u) / u$$

$$\underset{\sim}{A}= \left\{ \left(u, \underset{\sim}{A}\,(u) \right) \mid u \in U \right\}$$

where the $\int$ sign is not an integration in the usual sense; rather it is a notation that represents the grade of membership of u in a continuous universe U. For example, $\underset{\sim}{A}$ in Example 4 can be expressed by

$$\underset{\sim}{A}= \int_{u \in \Re} \left[1 + (u - 10)^{-2} \right]^{-1} / u$$

$$\underset{\sim}{A}= \left\{ \left(u, \left[1 + (u - 10)^{-2} \right]^{-1} \right) \mid u \in \Re \right\}$$

where $\Re$ is the set of all real numbers.

1.4   Basic Operations of Fuzzy Sets

Let $\underset{\sim}{A}$ and $\underset{\sim}{B}$ be members of $\mathcal{F}\,(U)$. We now define the basic fuzzy set operations on $\underset{\sim}{A}$ and $\underset{\sim}{B}$, such as inclusion, equality, union, and intersection, and the complement $\underset{\sim}{A}^c$ of $\underset{\sim}{A}$ as follows:

$$\underset{\sim}{A} \supset \underset{\sim}{B} \Longleftrightarrow (\forall\, u \in U) \left(\underset{\sim}{A}\,(u) \geq \underset{\sim}{B}\,(u) \right)$$

$$\underset{\sim}{A}= \underset{\sim}{B} \Longleftrightarrow \underset{\sim}{A} \supset \underset{\sim}{B} \text{ and } \underset{\sim}{A} \subset \underset{\sim}{B} \text{, or equivalently, } (\forall\, u \in U) \left(\underset{\sim}{A}\,(u) = \underset{\sim}{B}\,(u) \right)$$

$$\underset{\sim}{C}= \underset{\sim}{A} \cup \underset{\sim}{B} \Longleftrightarrow (\forall\, u \in U) \left(\underset{\sim}{C}\,(u) = \underset{\sim}{A}\,(u) \vee \underset{\sim}{B}\,(u) \right)$$

$$\underset{\sim}{C}= \underset{\sim}{A} \cap \underset{\sim}{B} \Longleftrightarrow (\forall\, u \in U) \left(\underset{\sim}{C}\,(u) = \underset{\sim}{A}\,(u) \wedge \underset{\sim}{B}\,(u) \right)$$

$$\underset{\sim}{C}= \underset{\sim}{A}^c \Longleftrightarrow (\forall\, u \in U) \left(\underset{\sim}{C}\,(u) = 1 - \underset{\sim}{A}\,(u) \right)$$

where $\vee$ and $\wedge$ are max and min operators, respectively.

The union and intersection operations can be extended to any index set T:

$$\left(\bigcup_{t \in T} \underset{\sim}{A}_t \right) (u) = \bigvee_{t \in T} \underset{\sim}{A}_t\,(u)$$

$$\left(\bigcap_{t \in T} A_{\sim t} \right)(u) = \bigwedge_{t \in T} A_{\sim t}(u)$$

where $\vee$ and $\wedge$ means sup and inf, respectively.

The operations of fuzzy sets can be illustrated by a graph of their membership functions as shown in Figure 1.8, Figure 1.9, and Figure 1.10.

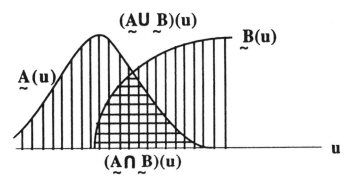

FIGURE 1.8
Membership functions and union and intersection of two fuzzy sets.

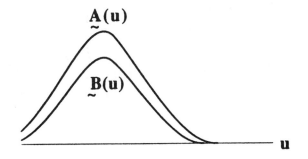

FIGURE 1.9
Subset relationship of fuzzy sets.

Note: Like Cantor sets, the operations of fuzzy sets can be expressed by pan-Venn diagrams. These are shown in Figure 1.11 and Figure 1.12.

From Figure 1.11 we see that:

$$\left(A_{\sim} \cup B_{\sim} \right)(u) = A_{\sim}(u) \vee B_{\sim}(u) = a \vee b = b$$

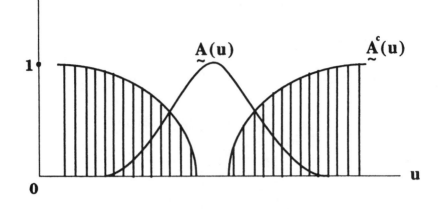

FIGURE 1.10
The membership function of a complement fuzzy set.

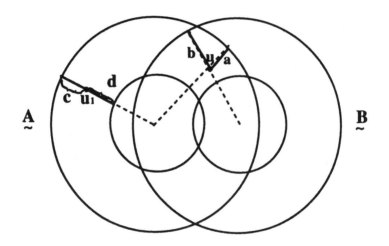

FIGURE 1.11
The union, intersection, and complement of fuzzy sets.

$$\left(\underset{\sim}{A} \cap \underset{\sim}{B} \right)(u) = \underset{\sim}{A}(u) \wedge \underset{\sim}{B}(u) = a \wedge b = a$$

$$\underset{\sim}{A}^{c}(u_1) = 1 - \underset{\sim}{A}(u_1) = 1 - c = d$$

From Figure 1.12 we see that $\underset{\sim}{A}(u) = a \geq b = \underset{\sim}{B}(u)$.

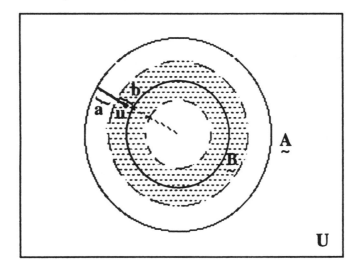

FIGURE 1.12
A fuzzy subset.

Example 5

Let the fuzzy sets young ($\underset{\sim}{Y}$) and old ($\underset{\sim}{O}$) be defined as in Example 2. Then the fuzzy sets "young or old" ($\underset{\sim}{Y} \cup \underset{\sim}{O}$), "young and old" ($\underset{\sim}{Y} \cap \underset{\sim}{O}$), and "not young" ($\underset{\sim}{Y}^c$) are defined as follows: □

$$\left(\underset{\sim}{Y} \cup \underset{\sim}{O}\right)(u) = \begin{cases} 1, & 0 \le u \le 25 \\[2mm] \left[1 + \left(\frac{u-25}{5}\right)^2\right]^{-1}, & 25 < u \le 51 \\[2mm] \left[1 + \left(\frac{u-50}{5}\right)^{-2}\right]^{-1}, & 51 < u \le 100 \end{cases}$$

$$\left(\underset{\sim}{Y} \cap \underset{\sim}{O}\right)(u) = \begin{cases} 1, & 0 \le u \le 25 \\[2mm] \left[1 + \left(\frac{u-50}{5}\right)^{-2}\right]^{-1}, & 25 < u \le 51 \\[2mm] \left[1 + \left(\frac{u-25}{5}\right)^2\right]^{-1}, & 51 < u \le 100 \end{cases}$$

$$\underset{\sim}{Y}^c(u) = \begin{cases} 0, & 0 \le u \le 25 \\[2mm] 1 - \left[1 + \left(\frac{u-25}{5}\right)^2\right]^{-1}, & 25 < u \le 100 \end{cases}$$

The union, intersection, and complement operations of fuzzy sets have the following properties:

1. Idempotency.

$$A \cup A = A, \qquad A \cap A = A$$

2. Commutativity.

$$A \cup B = B \cup A, \qquad A \cap B = B \cap A$$

3. Associativity.

$$\left(A \cup B \right) \cup C = A \cup \left(B \cup C \right), \qquad \left(A \cap B \right) \cap C = A \cap \left(B \cap C \right)$$

4. Absorption.

$$\left(A \cap B \right) \cup A = A, \qquad \left(A \cup B \right) \cap A = A$$

5. Distributivity.

$$A \cap \left(B \cup C \right) = \left(A \cap B \right) \cup \left(A \cap C \right);$$

$$A \cup \left(B \cap C \right) = \left(A \cup B \right) \cap \left(A \cup C \right)$$

6. Bipolarity.

$$A \cup U = U, \qquad A \cap U = A, \qquad A \cup \Phi = A, \qquad A \cap \Phi = \Phi$$

7. Reflexivity.

$$\left(A^c \right)^c = A$$

8. De Morgan's Law.

$$\left(A \cup B \right)^c = A^c \cap B^c, \qquad \left(A \cap B \right)^c = A^c \cup B^c$$

Note that the complementary law of Cantor sets does not apply to the fuzzy sets, i.e.,

$$A \cup A^c \neq U, \qquad A \cup A^c \neq \Phi$$

In fact, for any $u_0 \in U$ and $0 < A(u_0) < 1$, we have

$$A(u_0) \vee \left(1 - A(u_0)\right) \leq 1 \text{ and } A(u_0) \wedge \left(1 - A(u_0)\right) > 0$$

Hence,

$$\left(A \cup A^c\right)(u_0) \neq 1 \text{ and } \left(A \cap A^c\right)(u_0) \neq 0.$$

Let U and V be two universes. $A \in \mathcal{F}(U)$ and $B \in \mathcal{F}(V)$ can be two fuzzy sets in U and V. Then we can form a new fuzzy set $A \times B \in \mathcal{F}(U \times V)$ whose membership function is defined by: $\forall (u, v) \in U \times V$,

$$\left(A \times B\right)(u, v) = A(u) \wedge B(v).$$

This is called the **direct product** (or Cartesian product) of A and B.

1.5 The Resolution Theorem

In an actual application, people often like to make a crisp decision, even though the decision is based on fuzzy concepts. Therefore, we need to establish a "bridge" between fuzzy sets and Cantor sets. For a Cantor set $A \in \mathcal{P}(U)$, an element $u \in U$ is an element of A only when $\chi_A(u) = 1$, where χ_A is the characteristic function of A. However, for a fuzzy set, such a "threshold" is too high; it must be lowered to a real number $\lambda \in [0, 1]$. For a given $\lambda \in [0, 1]$, u is said to be an element of A if and only if $A(u) \geq \lambda$. In other words, for each $\lambda \in [0, 1]$, a crisp Cantor set is formed with the property that each element in that set has a grade (confidence level) of λ or higher.

Let $A \in \mathcal{F}(U)$, $\lambda \in [0, 1]$. Define crisp sets

$$A_\lambda = \left(A\right)_\lambda = \left\{u \in U \mid A(u) \geq \lambda\right\}$$

and

$$A_{\bar{\lambda}} = \left(\underset{\sim}{A}\right)_{\bar{\lambda}} = \left\{u \in U \mid \underset{\sim}{A}(u) > \lambda\right\}.$$

These two sets A_λ and $A_{\bar{\lambda}}$ are called the λ**-cut** and **strong** λ**-cut** of $\underset{\sim}{A}$, respectively.

Sets formed by the λ-cut and strong λ-cut have the following properties:

1. $\left(\underset{\sim}{A} \cup \underset{\sim}{B}\right)_\lambda = A_\lambda \cup B_\lambda,$ $\left(\underset{\sim}{A} \cap \underset{\sim}{B}\right)_\lambda = A_\lambda \cap B_\lambda;$

2. $\left(\underset{\sim}{A} \cup \underset{\sim}{B}\right)_{\bar{\lambda}} = A_{\bar{\lambda}} \cup B_{\bar{\lambda}},$ $\left(\underset{\sim}{A} \cap \underset{\sim}{B}\right)_{\bar{\lambda}} = A_{\bar{\lambda}} \cap B_{\bar{\lambda}};$

3. $\left(\bigcup_{t \in T} \underset{\sim}{A}^{(t)}\right)_\lambda \supset \bigcup_{t \in T} A_\lambda^{(t)};$

4. $\left(\bigcup_{t \in T} \underset{\sim}{A}^{(t)}\right)_{\bar{\lambda}} = \bigcup_{t \in T} A_{\bar{\lambda}}^{(t)};$

5. $\left(\bigcap_{t \in T} \underset{\sim}{A}^{(t)}\right)_{\bar{\lambda}} \subset \bigcap_{t \in T} A_{\bar{\lambda}}^{(t)};$

6. $\left(\bigcap_{t \in T} \underset{\sim}{A}^{(t)}\right)_\lambda = \bigcap_{t \in T} A_\lambda^{(t)};$

7. $A_{\bar{\lambda}} \subset A_\lambda;$

8. If $\lambda \leq \eta$ then $A_\lambda \subset A_\eta$ and $A_{\bar{\lambda}} \supset A_\eta \supset A_{\bar{\eta}};$

9. $A_{\bigvee_{t \in T} \lambda_t} = \bigcap_{t \in T} A_{\lambda_t};$

10. $A_{\overline{\bigwedge_{t \in T} \lambda_t}} = \bigcup_{t \in T} A_{\lambda_t};$

11. $\left(\underset{\sim}{A}^c\right)_\lambda = A_{\overline{1-\lambda}}^c;$

12. $\left(\underset{\sim}{A}^c\right)_{\bar{\lambda}} = A_{1-\lambda}^c;$

13. $A_0 = U,$ $A_1 = \Phi.$

Let $\underset{\sim}{A} \in \mathcal{F}(U)$. We call A_1 (where $\lambda = 1$) the **kernel** of $\underset{\sim}{A}$, and it is denoted by ker $\underset{\sim}{A}$. $A_{\bar{0}}$ (where $\lambda = 0$) is the **support** of $\underset{\sim}{A}$, and is denoted by supp $\underset{\sim}{A}$. The difference set $A_{\bar{0}} \setminus A_1$ is called the **boundary** of $\underset{\sim}{A}$ (see Figure 1.13).

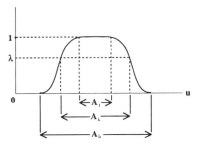 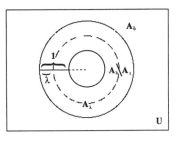

FIGURE 1.13
The kernel, support, and boundary of a fuzzy set.

Example 6

Let $A = \{(a, 1), (b, 0.75), (c, 0.5), (d, 0.25), (e, 0)\}$. Then

$$A_1 = \{a\}, \quad A_{0.7} = \{a, b\}, \quad A_{0.5} = \{a, b, c\}, \quad A_{0.2} = \{a, b, c, d\}, \quad A_0 = U.$$

and

$$A_{\overline{1}} = \Phi, \quad A_{\overline{0.7}} = \{a, b\}, \quad A_{\overline{0.5}} = \{a, b\}, \quad A_{\overline{0.2}} = \{a, b, c, d\}, \quad A_0 = \{a, b, c, d\}.$$

☐

For any real number $\lambda \in [0, 1]$ and fuzzy set $A \in \mathcal{F}(U)$, a new fuzzy set λA can be defined by the membership function

$$\left(\lambda A\right)(u) \overset{\triangle}{=} \lambda \bigwedge A(u), \qquad u \in U$$

The new fuzzy set λA defined in this way is called the **scalar product** of A. It is easy to show that the following properties hold for the scalar product of fuzzy sets.

1) $\lambda_1 \leq \lambda_2 \implies \lambda_1 A \subset \lambda_2 A$;

2) $A \subset B \implies \lambda A \subset \lambda B$.

The following resolution theorems reveal that a fuzzy set may be decomposed into λ-cut sets.

THEOREM 1
[First Resolution] If $\underset{\sim}{A} \in \mathcal{F}(U)$, then

$$\underset{\sim}{A} = \bigcup_{\lambda \in [0,1]} \lambda A_\lambda.$$

PROOF   We need only to prove that $\forall u \in U$,

$$\underset{\sim}{A}(u) = \bigvee_{\lambda \in [0,1]} (\lambda \wedge A_\lambda(u))$$

Since

$$\underset{\sim}{A}(u) = \begin{cases} 1 , & 0 \le \lambda \le \underset{\sim}{A}(u) \\ 0 , & \underset{\sim}{A}(u) \le \lambda \le 1 \end{cases} .$$

we have that

$$\bigvee_{\lambda \in [0,1]} (\lambda \wedge A_\lambda(u))$$

$$= \left(\bigvee_{0 \le \lambda \le \underset{\sim}{A}(u)} (\lambda \wedge A_\lambda(u)) \right) \bigvee \left(\bigvee_{\underset{\sim}{A}(u) \le \lambda \le 1} (\lambda \wedge A_\lambda(u)) \right)$$

$$= \bigvee_{0 \le \lambda \le \underset{\sim}{A}(u)} \lambda = \underset{\sim}{A}(u) .$$

∎

Similarly, we can prove

THEOREM 2
[Second Resolution] If $\underset{\sim}{A} \in \mathcal{F}(U)$, then

$$\underset{\sim}{A} = \bigcup_{\lambda \in [0,1]} \lambda A_{\bar{\lambda}}.$$

Let $\underset{\sim}{A} \in \mathcal{F}(U)$. Define the mapping:

$$H : [0, 1] \to \mathcal{P}(U) , \qquad \lambda \mapsto H(\lambda)$$

that $H(\lambda)$ satisfies

$$(\forall \lambda \in [0, 1]) \left(A_{\overline{\lambda}} \subset H(\lambda) \subset A_\lambda \right).$$

The next resolution theorem will show that $\underset{\sim}{A}$ can be formed by $\{ H(\lambda) \mid \lambda \in [0, 1] \}$.

THEOREM 3
[Third Resolution] If $\underset{\sim}{A} \in \mathcal{F}(U)$, then

$$\underset{\sim}{A} = \bigcup_{\lambda \in [0,1]} \lambda H(\lambda).$$

PROOF   By definition of $H(\lambda)$, we have

$$A_{\overline{\lambda}} \subset H(\lambda) \subset A_\lambda \quad \Longrightarrow \lambda A_{\overline{\lambda}} \subset \lambda H(\lambda) \subset \lambda A_\lambda$$

$$\Longrightarrow \underset{\sim}{A} = \bigcup_{\lambda \in [0,1]} \lambda A_{\overline{\lambda}} \subset \bigcup_{\lambda \in [0,1]} \lambda H(\lambda) \subset \bigcup_{\lambda \in [0,1]} \lambda A_\lambda = \underset{\sim}{A}$$

$$\Longrightarrow \underset{\sim}{A} = \bigcup_{\lambda \in [0,1]} \lambda H(\lambda).$$

∎

PROPOSITION 1
The mapping H defined previously has the following properties:

1) $\lambda < \eta \Longrightarrow H(\lambda) \supset H(\eta)$;
2) $A_\eta = \bigcup_{\lambda \in [0,\eta)} \lambda H(\lambda)$, $\quad \eta \in (0, 1]$;
3) $A_{\overline{\eta}} = \bigcup_{\lambda \in (\eta,1]} \lambda H(\lambda)$, $\quad \eta \in [0, 1)$.

PROOF
1)
$$\lambda < \eta \Longrightarrow H(\lambda) \supset A_{\overline{\lambda}} \supset A_\eta \supset H(\eta) \Longrightarrow H(\lambda) \supset H(\eta).$$

2) On one hand, for every $\lambda \in [0, \eta)$, we have

$$H(\lambda) \supset A_{\overline{\lambda}} \supset A_\eta \quad \Longrightarrow \bigcup_{\lambda \in [0,\eta)} \lambda H(\lambda) \supset A_\eta.$$

On the other hand, $H(\lambda) \subset A_\lambda$; this implies that

$$\bigcap_{\lambda \in [0,\eta)} H(\lambda) \subset \bigcap_{\lambda \in [0,\eta]} A_\lambda = A \bigvee_{\lambda \in [0,\eta)} \lambda = A_\eta.$$

Therefore 2) is valid.

3) This is similar to the proof for 2).   ∎

We now see that a fuzzy set can be represented by a family of classical sets $\{A_\lambda\}_{\lambda \in [0,1]}$ (or $\{A_{\bar{\lambda}}\}_{\lambda \in [0,1]}$ or $\{H(\lambda)\}_{\lambda \in [0,1]}$), and that these sets are revelations of $\underset{\sim}{A}$ at different levels of λ. As λ increases or decreases, sets A_λ (or $A_{\bar{\lambda}}$, or $H(\lambda)$) will contract or expand; that is $\underset{\sim}{A}$ behaves like having an elastic boundary (see Figure 1.13).

1.6   A Representation Theorem

Like resolution theorems, the representation theorem is also a basic theorem in fuzzy set theory. The theorem offers another viewpoint of linking fuzzy sets to classical sets. First, we define the mapping:

$$H : [0,1] \longrightarrow \mathcal{P}(U), \qquad \lambda \longmapsto H(\lambda)$$

If the mapping H satisfies

$$\lambda < \eta \Longrightarrow H(\lambda) \supset H(\eta), \qquad \forall \lambda, \eta \in [0,1]$$

then H is called a **nested set** on U.

The set of all nested sets on U is denoted by $\Psi(U)$. We define union ($\cup$), intersection ($\cap$), and complement (c) operations on $\Psi(U)$ as follows:

$\cup : \Psi(U) \times \Psi(U) \longrightarrow \Psi(U)$
$\qquad (H_1, H_2) \longmapsto H_1 \cup H_2$

$$(H_1 \cup H_2)(\lambda) = H_1(\lambda) \cup H_2(\lambda)$$

$\cap : \Psi(U) \times \Psi(U) \longrightarrow \Psi(U)$
$\qquad (H_1, H_2) \longmapsto H_1 \cap H_2$

$$(H_1 \cap H_2)(\lambda) = H_1(\lambda) \cap H_2(\lambda)$$

$$c : \Psi(U) \longrightarrow \Psi(U)$$

$$H \longmapsto H^c : H^c(\lambda) = (H(1-\lambda))^c$$

More generally, these operations can be extended to an arbitrary index set T:

$$\bigcup_{t \in T} H_t : \left(\bigcup_{t \in T} H_t \right)(\lambda) = \bigcup_{t \in T} H_t(\lambda),$$

and

$$\bigcap_{t \in T} H_t : \left(\bigcap_{t \in T} H_t \right)(\lambda) = \bigcap_{t \in T} H_t(\lambda).$$

THEOREM 4

[Third Representation] Let the mapping φ be defined as

$$\varphi : \Psi(U) \longrightarrow \mathcal{F}(U), \quad H \longmapsto \varphi(H) = \bigcup_{\lambda \in [0,1]} \lambda H(\lambda)$$

then φ is a homomorphic surjection from $(\Psi(U), \cap, \cup, c)$ to $(\Psi(U), \cap, \cup, c)$ and satisfies

$$1) \ (\varphi(H))_\eta = \bigcap_{\lambda \in [0,\eta)} H(\lambda), \quad \eta \in (0,1];$$

$$2) \ (\varphi(H))_{\overline{\eta}} = \bigcup_{\lambda \in (\eta,1]} H(\lambda), \quad \eta \in [0,1);$$

$$3) \ (\varphi(H))_{\overline{\eta}} \subset H(\eta) \subset (\varphi(H))_\eta, \quad \eta \in [0,1].$$

PROOF For any $H \in \Psi(U)$,

$$\varphi(H) = \bigcup_{\lambda \in [0,1]} \lambda H(\lambda) \in \mathcal{F}(U)$$

is uniquely determined. Hence φ is an injection. On the other hand, for any $A \in \mathcal{F}(U)$, define $H(\lambda) = A_\lambda$; then $H \in \Psi(U)$ and H satisfy

$$\varphi(H) = \bigcup_{\lambda \in [0,1]} \lambda A_\lambda = A.$$

Thus, φ is a surjection.

We now prove 3). First we show that $H(\eta) \subset (\varphi(H))_\eta$ holds.

$$\text{For } u \in H(\eta) \Longrightarrow H(\eta)(u) = 1 \text{ (namely } \chi_{H(\eta)}(u) = 1)$$

$$\Longrightarrow \varphi(H)(u) = \bigvee_{\lambda \in [0,1]} (\lambda \wedge H(\lambda)(u))$$

$$\geq \eta \wedge H(\eta)(u) = \eta \wedge 1$$

$$\Longrightarrow u \in (\varphi(H))_\eta$$

Next, we show that $(\varphi(H))_{\bar{\eta}} \subset H(\eta)$ holds.

$$\text{For } u \notin H(\eta) \Longrightarrow H(\eta)(u) = 0$$

$$\Longrightarrow (\forall \lambda \in [\eta, 1]) (H(\lambda)(u) = 0)$$

$$\Longrightarrow \varphi(H)(u) = \bigvee_{\lambda \in [0,\eta)} (\lambda \wedge H(\lambda)(u))$$

$$\leq \bigvee_{\lambda \in [0,\eta)} \lambda = \eta$$

$$\Longrightarrow u \notin (\varphi(H))_{\bar{\eta}}$$

This proves 3).

Based on the proposition of the last section, it is easy to show that 1) and 2) are true. We now prove in three steps that φ is a homomorphic function.

(a) Prove that φ preserves the set union operation.

Let $\underset{\sim}{A}^{(t)} = \varphi(H_t)$ and $\underset{\sim}{A} = \varphi\left(\bigcup_{t \in T} H_t\right)$. For any $\eta \in [0, 1]$, we have

$$A_{\bar{\eta}} = \bigcup_{\lambda \in [0,\eta)} \left(\bigcup_{t \in T} H_t\right)(\lambda) = \bigcup_{\lambda \in (\eta,1]} \left(\bigcup_{t \in T} H_t(\lambda)\right)$$

$$= \bigcup_{t \in T} \left(\bigcup_{\lambda \in (\eta,1]} H_t(\lambda)\right) = \bigcup_{t \in T} A_{\bar{\eta}}^{(t)} = \left(\bigcup_{t \in T} \underset{\sim}{A}^{(t)}\right)_{\bar{\eta}}$$

From the second resolution theorem, we know that $A = \bigcup\limits_{t \in T} A^{(t)}$; therefore,

$$\varphi \left(\bigcup_{t \in T} H_t \right) = \bigcup_{t \in T} \varphi(H_t).$$

(b) Prove that φ preserves the set intersection operation.

Let $A^{(t)} = \varphi(H_t)$ and $A = \varphi\left(\bigcap\limits_{t \in T} H_t \right)$. For any $\eta \in [0, 1]$, we have

$$A_\eta = \bigcap_{\lambda \in [0, \eta)} \left(\bigcap_{t \in T} H_t \right)(\lambda) = \bigcap_{\lambda \in [0, \eta)} \left(\bigcap_{t \in T} H_t(\lambda) \right)$$

$$= \bigcap_{t \in T} \left(\bigcap_{\lambda \in [0, \eta)} H_t(\lambda) \right) = \bigcap_{t \in T} A_\eta^{(t)} = \left(\bigcap_{t \in T} A^{(t)} \right)_\eta.$$

From the first resolution theorem, we know that $A = \bigcap\limits_{t \in T} A^{(t)}$; therefore,

$$\varphi \left(\bigcap_{t \in T} H_t \right) = \bigcap_{t \in T} \varphi(H_t).$$

(c) Prove that φ preserves the set complementary operation.

Let $A = \varphi(H)$, $B = \varphi(H^c)$ and $\lambda' = 1 - \lambda$. For any $\eta \in [0, 1]$, we have

$$B_\eta = \bigcap_{\lambda \in [0, \eta)} H^c(\lambda) = \bigcap_{\lambda \in [0, \eta)} (H(1 - \lambda))^c = \left(\bigcup_{1 - \lambda \in (1-\eta, 1]} H(1-\lambda) \right)^c$$

$$= \left(\bigcup_{\lambda' \in (1-\eta, 1]} H(\lambda') \right)^c = \left(A_{\overline{1-\eta}} \right)^c = \left\{ u \in U \mid A(u) > 1 - \eta \right\}^c$$

$$= \left\{ u \in U \mid A(u) \le 1 - \eta \right\} = \left\{ u \in U \mid 1 - A(u) \ge \eta \right\}$$

$$= \left\{ u \in U \mid A^c(u) \ge \eta \right\} = \left(A^c \right)_\eta.$$

From the first resolution theorem, we have $\underset{\sim}{B} = \underset{\sim}{A^c}$; therefore,

$$\varphi\left(H^c\right) = \left(\varphi\left(H\right)\right)^c .$$

This completes the proof that φ is a homomorphic function from $\Psi\left(U\right)$ to $\mathcal{F}\left(U\right)$.

∎

Resolution theorems illustrate that a fuzzy set can be expressed by a nested set, and the representation theorem shows that any nested set, indeed, corresponds to a fuzzy set.

Since φ is a surjection from $\Psi(U)$ to $\mathcal{F}(U)$, by means of φ, we can define an equivalence relation "$\sim$" as

$$\left(\forall H_1,\ H_2 \in \Psi\left(U\right)\right)\left(H_1 \sim H_2 \Longleftrightarrow \varphi\left(H_1\right) = \varphi\left(H_2\right)\right).$$

Let the equivalent class that H belongs to be denoted by $\overline{H}$. We get the quotient set induced by the equivalent relation as

$$\Psi'\left(U\right) = \Psi\left(U\right)/\sim = \left\{\overline{H} \mid H \in \Psi\left(U\right)\right\}.$$

In $\Psi'\left(U\right)$, we define the set operations of $\cup$, $\cap$, and "c" as follows.

$$\overline{H_1} \cup \overline{H_2} = \overline{H_1 \cup H_2}, \qquad \bigcup_{t\in T} \overline{H_t} = \overline{\bigcup_{t\in T} H_t}$$

$$\overline{H_1} \cap \overline{H_2} = \overline{H_1 \cap H_2}, \qquad \bigcap_{t\in T} \overline{H_t} = \overline{\bigcap_{t\in T} H_t}$$

$$\left(\overline{H}\right)^c = \overline{H^c}$$

We have the following:

COROLLARY 1
The mapping $\varphi' : \Psi'\left(U\right) \longrightarrow \mathcal{F}\left(U\right)$ *defined by* $\overline{H} \longmapsto \varphi'\left(\overline{H}\right) = \varphi\left(H\right)$ *is an isomorphism from* $\left(\Psi'\left(U\right),\ \cup,\ \cap,\ c\right)$ *to* $\left(\mathcal{F}\left(U\right),\ \cup,\ \cap,\ c\right)$.

From the corollary, a fuzzy set is exactly an equivalence class and, conversely, an equivalence class can be regarded as a fuzzy set.

Let $F \in \Psi\left(U\right)$. The nested set F is called a **dizzy set** on U if it satisfies

$$F\left(0\right) = U, \qquad F\left(\bigvee_{t\in T} \lambda_t\right) = \bigcap_{t\in T} F\left(\lambda_t\right) \tag{1.1}$$

where $\lambda_t \in [0, 1]$ and $t \in T$. The set of all dizzy sets is denoted by $\Gamma(U)$.
Let $\overline{F} \in \Psi(U)$. A nested set $\overline{F}$ is called an **open dizzy set** if it satisfies

$$\overline{F}(1) = \emptyset, \qquad \overline{F}\left(\bigwedge_{t \in T} \lambda_t\right) = \bigcup_{t \in T} \overline{F}(\lambda_t) \qquad (1.2)$$

The set of all open dizzy sets on U is denoted by $\overline{\Gamma}(U)$.

Example 7

Let $A \in \mathcal{F}(U)$ and define two mappings: ▯

$$F : [0, 1] \longrightarrow \mathcal{P}(U), \qquad \lambda \longmapsto F(\lambda) = A_\lambda$$

and

$$F : [0, 1] \longrightarrow \mathcal{P}(U), \qquad \lambda \longmapsto \overline{F}(\lambda) = A_{\overline{\lambda}}$$

It is obvious that $F \in \Gamma(U)$ and $\overline{F} \in \overline{\Gamma}(U)$.

PROPOSITION 2

For any $\overline{H} \in \Psi'(U)$, we have

1) there uniquely exists a dizzy set $F_H \in \overline{H}$ such that

$$F_H(\eta) = \bigcap_{\lambda \in [0, \eta)} H(\lambda), \qquad \eta \in (0, 1]$$

2) there uniquely exists an open dizzy set $\overline{F_H} \in \overline{H}$ such that

$$\overline{F}_H(\eta) = \bigcup_{\lambda \in (\eta, 1]} H(\lambda), \qquad \eta \in [0, 1).$$

PROOF   We only prove 1). The proof of 2) is similar.

From the third representation theorem, we know $\varphi(H) \in \mathcal{F}(U)$. The existence of $F_H \in \Gamma(U)$ that satisfies

$$F_H(\eta) = (\varphi(H))_\eta = \bigcap_{\lambda \in [0, \eta)} H(\lambda), \qquad \eta \in (0, 1]$$

and its uniqueness is obvious. We prove that $F_H \in \overline{H}$. In fact,

$$(\varphi(F_H))_\eta = \bigcap_{\lambda \in [0,\eta)} F_H(\lambda) = \bigcap_{\lambda \in [0,\eta)} \left(\bigcap_{v \in [0,\eta)} H(v) \right)$$

$$= \bigcup_{\lambda \in [0,\eta)} H(\lambda) = (\varphi(H))_\eta$$

Hence $F_H \in \overline{H}$, and this proves 1).   ∎

Note: If H, $H' \in \Psi(U)$, then the following conditions are equivalent.
1) $H \sim H'$;

2) $(\forall \eta \in [0,1]) \left(\bigcap_{\lambda \in [0,\eta)} H(\lambda) = \bigcap_{\lambda \in [0,\eta)} H'(\lambda) \right)$;

3) $(\forall \eta \in [0,1]) \left(\bigcup_{\lambda \in (\eta,1]} H(\lambda) = \bigcup_{\lambda \in (\eta,1]} H'(\lambda) \right)$.

THEOREM 5
(1) $\left(\Psi'(U), \cup, \cap, c \right) \cong \left(\Gamma(U), \cup, \cap, c \right)$;
(2) $\left(\Psi'(U), \cup, \cap, c \right) \cong \left(\overline{\Gamma}(U), \cup, \cap, c \right)$.

PROOF   Define the following mappings:

$$f : \Psi'(U) \longrightarrow \Gamma(U), \qquad \overline{H} \longmapsto f\left(\overline{H}\right) = F_H$$

and

$$\overline{f} : \Psi'(U) \longrightarrow \overline{\Gamma}(U), \qquad \overline{H} \longmapsto f\left(\overline{H}\right) = \overline{F}_H.$$

It is easy to verify that both f and $\overline{f}$ are isomorphic mappings.   ∎

COROLLARY 2
[First Representation Theorem]

$$(\Gamma(U), \cup, \cap, c) \cong (\mathcal{F}(U), \cup, \cap, c)$$

PROOF   Let $g = \varphi' \circ f^{-1}$, where φ' and f are defined as before. Then it is easy to show that

$$g : \Gamma(U) \longrightarrow \mathcal{F}(U), \qquad F \longmapsto g(F) = \bigcup_{\lambda \in [0,1]} \lambda F(\lambda)$$

is an isomorphic mapping from $\Gamma(U)$ to $\mathcal{F}(U)$. ∎

COROLLARY 3
[Second Representation Theorem]

$$\left(\overline{\Gamma}(U),\ \cup,\ \cap,\ c\right) \cong \left(\mathcal{F}(U),\ \cup,\ \cap,\ c\right)$$

PROOF   Let $\overline{g} = \varphi' \circ \overline{f}^{-1}$, where φ' and $\overline{f}$ are defined as before. Similar to the above proof,

$$\overline{g} : \overline{\Gamma}(U) \longrightarrow \mathcal{F}(U), \qquad \overline{F} \longmapsto \overline{g}\left(\overline{F}\right) = \bigcup_{\lambda \in [0,1]} \lambda \overline{F}(\lambda)$$

is an isomorphic mapping from $\overline{\Gamma}(U)$ to $\mathcal{F}(U)$. ∎

Clearly, the first and second representation theorems are special cases of the third representation theorem.

1.7   Extension Principles

Extension principles are important principles that have broad applications.

Let X and Y be two universes. Given a mapping $f : X \longrightarrow Y$, the extension principle tells us how to induce a mapping $\underset{\sim}{f} : \mathcal{P}(X) \longrightarrow \mathcal{P}(Y)$ by means of the mapping f.

First, we review the extension principle from the classical set theory. Let $f : X \longrightarrow Y$ be a mapping. The extension of f, still denoted by f, may be induced as

$$f : \mathcal{P}(X) \longrightarrow \mathcal{P}(Y), \qquad A \longmapsto f(A) = \{f(x) \mid x \in A\}.$$

An inverse mapping f^{-1} can also be induced by f :

$$f^{-1} : \mathcal{P}(X) \longrightarrow \mathcal{P}(Y), \qquad B \longmapsto f^{-1}(B) = \{x \in X \mid f(x) \in B\}.$$

We call $f(A)$ the image of A, and $f^{-1}(B)$ the inverse image of B (see Figure 1.14a, b).

The characteristic functions of A, B, $f(A)$, and $f^{-1}(B)$ have the following properties:

Fuzzy Sets and Fuzzy Decision-Making

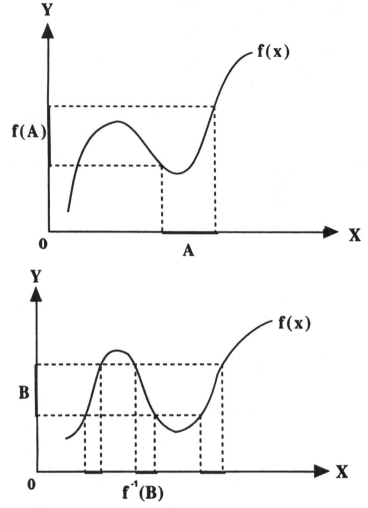

FIGURE 1.14
The classical extension principle.

1)

$$f(A)(y) = \bigvee_{f(x)=y} A(x), \qquad y \in Y; \qquad (1.3)$$

2)

$$f^{-1}(B)(x) = B(f(x)), \qquad x \in X, \qquad (1.4)$$

and images and their inverse images satisfy

a) $f^{-1}(f(A)) \supset A$ [" $\supset$ " *becomes* " $=$ " *when f is an injection*] and
b) $f(f^{-1}(B)) \subset B$.   [" $\subset$ " *becomes* " $=$ " *when f is a surjection*].

The classical extension principle is now generalized below.

Extension Principle 1   The mapping $f : \mathcal{F}(X) \longrightarrow \mathcal{F}(Y)$ can be induced from the mapping $f : X \longrightarrow Y$ by defining

$$\underset{\sim}{A} \longrightarrow \underset{\sim}{f}\left(\underset{\sim}{A}\right) = \bigcup_{\lambda \in [0,1]} \lambda f\left(\underset{\sim}{A}\right), \qquad \forall \underset{\sim}{A} \in \mathcal{F}(X). \qquad (1.5)$$

The mapping $\underset{\sim}{f}$ induced by f is called the **fuzzy transformation** from X to Y. Similarly, $\underset{\sim}{f}^{-1}$ may be induced by f by defining

$$\underset{\sim}{f}^{-1} \colon \mathcal{F}(Y) \longrightarrow \mathcal{F}(X), \qquad B \longmapsto \underset{\sim}{f}^{-1}(B) = \bigcup_{\lambda \in [0,1]} \lambda f^{-1}\left(\underset{\sim}{B}\right). \qquad (1.6)$$

The mapping $\underset{\sim}{f}^{-1}$ induced by f is called the **fuzzy inverse transformation** of f.

The following theorem will show that $\underset{\sim}{A}, \underset{\sim}{B}, \underset{\sim}{f}\left(\underset{\sim}{A}\right)$ and $\underset{\sim}{f}^{-1}(B)$ have properties similar to those of a) and b).

THEOREM 6
Given a mapping $f : X \longrightarrow Y$,

1) if $\underset{\sim}{A} \in \mathcal{F}(X)$, then for any $y \in Y$,

$$\underset{\sim}{f}\left(\underset{\sim}{A}\right)(y) = \bigvee_{f(x)=y} \underset{\sim}{A}(x) \qquad (1.7)$$

$\left(\text{when } \{x \in X \mid f(x) = y\} = \emptyset, \text{ then set } \underset{\sim}{f}\left(\underset{\sim}{A}\right)(y) = 0 \right);$
2) if $\underset{\sim}{B} \in \mathcal{F}(Y)$, then for any $x \in X$,

$$\underset{\sim}{f}^{-1}(B)(x) = \underset{\sim}{B}(f(x)). \qquad (1.8)$$

PROOF

$$\underset{\sim}{f}\left(\underset{\sim}{A}\right)(y) = \bigvee_{\lambda \in [0,1]} (\lambda \wedge f(A_\lambda)(y))$$

$$= \bigvee \{\lambda \in [0, 1] \mid y \in f(A_\lambda)\}$$

$$= \bigvee \{\lambda \in [0, 1] \mid (\exists\, x \in A_\lambda)\, (y = f(x))\}$$

$$= \bigvee_{f(x)=y} \{\lambda \in [0, 1] \mid x \in A_\lambda\}$$

$$= \bigvee_{f(x)=y} \left(\bigvee_{\lambda\in[0,1]} (\lambda \wedge A_\lambda(x)) \right) = \bigvee_{f(x)=y} \underset{\sim}{A}(x)$$

This proves 1). For 2),

$$\underset{\sim}{f^{-1}}(B)(x) = \bigvee_{\lambda\in[0,1]} \left(\lambda \wedge f^{-1}(B_\lambda)(x) \right)$$

$$= \bigvee \left\{ \lambda \in [0, 1] \mid x \in f^{-1}(B_\lambda) \right\}$$

$$= \bigvee \{\lambda \in [0, 1] \mid f(x) \in B_\lambda\}$$

$$= \bigvee_{\lambda\in[0,1]} (\lambda \wedge B_\lambda(f(x))) = \underset{\sim}{B}(f(x))$$

This shows 2) is valid. ∎

THEOREM 7
[Extension Principle 2] Given a mapping $f : X \longrightarrow Y$,

1) if $\underset{\sim}{A} \in \mathcal{F}(X)$, then

$$\underset{\sim}{f}\left(\underset{\sim}{A}\right) = \bigcup_{\lambda\in[0,1]} \lambda\, f(A_\lambda); \qquad (1.9)$$

2) if $\underset{\sim}{B} \in \mathcal{F}(Y)$, then

$$\underset{\sim}{f^{-1}}(B) = \bigcup_{\lambda\in[0,1]} \lambda\, f^{-1}\left(B_{\bar\lambda}\right). \qquad (1.10)$$

PROOF Using a proof similar to the one for the last theorem, we can easily verify that

$$\left(\bigcup_{\lambda \in [0,1]} \lambda\, f\left(A_{\overline{\lambda}}\right) \right)(y) = \bigvee_{f(x)=y} \underset{\sim}{A}(x) = \underset{\sim}{f}\left(\underset{\sim}{A}\right)(y)$$

$$\left(\bigcup_{\lambda \in [0,1]} \lambda\, f^{-1}\left(B_{\overline{\lambda}}\right) \right)(x) = \underset{\sim}{B}\left(f(x)\right) = \underset{\sim}{f^{-1}}(B)(x).$$

Hence the theorem is proved. ∎

THEOREM 8
[Extension Principle 3] Given a mapping $f : X \longrightarrow Y$,

1) if $\underset{\sim}{A} \in \mathcal{F}(X)$, then

$$\underset{\sim}{f}\left(\underset{\sim}{A}\right) = \bigcup_{\lambda \in [0,1]} \lambda\, f\left(H_A(\lambda)\right), \qquad (1.11)$$

where $H_A \in \Psi(X)$ and $A_{\overline{\lambda}} \subset H_A(\lambda) \subset A_{\lambda}$;
2) if $\underset{\sim}{B} \in \mathcal{F}(Y)$, then

$$\underset{\sim}{f^{-1}}(B) = \bigcup_{\lambda \in [0,1]} \lambda\, f^{-1}\left(H_B(\lambda)\right), \qquad (1.12)$$

where $H_B \in \Psi(Y)$ and $B_{\overline{\lambda}} \subset H_B(\lambda) \subset B_{\lambda}$.

PROOF The proof is omitted since it is not difficult. ∎

THEOREM 9
(The Extension Principle for Composite Mappings)

Let $f : X \longrightarrow Y$ and $g : Y \longrightarrow Z$. The composite mapping of f and g is defined by

$$g \circ f : X \longrightarrow Z, \text{ such that } (g \circ f)(x) = g(f(x)).$$

1) If $A \in \mathcal{F}(X)$, then

$$\left(g \circ f \right) \left(\underset{\sim}{A} \right) = \underset{\sim}{g} \left(\underset{\sim}{f} \left(\underset{\sim}{A} \right) \right) = \bigcup_{\lambda \in [0,1]} \lambda g \left(f \left(A_\lambda \right) \right) \tag{1.13}$$

2) If $D \in \mathcal{F}(Z)$, then

$$\left(g \circ f \right)^{-1} \left(\underset{\sim}{D} \right) = \underset{\sim}{f}^{-1} \left(\underset{\sim}{g}^{-1} \left(\underset{\sim}{D} \right) \right) = \bigcup_{\lambda \in [0,1]} \lambda \, f^{-1} \left(g^{-1} \left(D_\lambda \right) \right) \tag{1.14}$$

PROOF   We will only prove 1) because 2) can be shown in a similar manner. Since

$$(g \circ f)(A_\lambda) = \{ z \in Z \mid (\exists x \in A_\lambda)((g \circ f)(x) = g(f(x))) \}$$

$$= \{ z \in Z \mid (\exists x \in A_\lambda)(f(x) = y, \; g(y) = z) \}$$

$$= \{ z \in Z \mid (\exists y \in f(A_\lambda))(g(y) = z) \}$$

$$= g(f(A_\lambda))$$

then

$$\left(g \circ f \right) \left(\underset{\sim}{A} \right) = \bigcup_{\lambda \in [0,1]} \lambda \, (g \circ f)(A_\lambda) = \bigcup_{\lambda \in [0,1]} \lambda g \left(f(A_\lambda) \right).$$

By the extension principle 1 and the representation theorem,

$$\underset{\sim}{f} \left(\underset{\sim}{A} \right) = \bigcup_{\lambda \in [0,1]} \lambda f(A_\lambda), \quad and \quad \left(\underset{\sim}{f} \left(\underset{\sim}{A} \right) \right)_{\overline{\lambda}} \subset f(A_\lambda) \subset \left(f \left(\underset{\sim}{A} \right) \right)_\lambda$$

By the extension principle 3, we have

$$\underset{\sim}{g} \left(\underset{\sim}{f} \left(\underset{\sim}{A} \right) \right) = \bigcup_{\lambda \in [0,1]} \lambda g \left(f(A_\lambda) \right) = \left(g \circ f \right) \left(\underset{\sim}{A} \right).$$

This completes the proof.   ■

PROPOSITION 3

1) $f^{-1}\left(f\left(\underset{\sim}{A}\right)\right) \supset \underset{\sim}{A}$;   *The "⊃" becomes "=" when f is an injection;*

2) $f\left(f^{-1}\left(\underset{\sim}{B}\right)\right) \subset \underset{\sim}{B}$;   *The "⊂" becomes "=" when f is a surjection.*

PROOF   Since

$$f^{-1}\left(f\left(\underset{\sim}{A}\right)\right)(x) = f\left(\underset{\sim}{A}\right)(f(x)) = \bigvee_{f(t)=f(x)} \underset{\sim}{A}(t) \geq \underset{\sim}{A}(x),$$

clearly, when f is an injection, the "≥" becomes "=". Hence 1) is true. Next, since

$$f\left(f^{-1}\left(\underset{\sim}{B}\right)\right)(y) = \bigvee_{f(x)=y} f^{-1}\left(\underset{\sim}{B}\right)(x) = \bigvee_{f(x)=y} \underset{\sim}{B}(f(x))$$

$$= \begin{cases} \underset{\sim}{B}(y), & (\exists x)(f(x)=y) \\ 0, & (\forall x)(f(x) \neq y) \end{cases}$$

$$\leq \underset{\sim}{B}(y).$$

Obviously, when f is a surjection "≤" becomes "=" . This proves 2).   ∎

References

[1] Bellman, R. and Giertz, M., On the analytic formalism of the theory of fuzzy sets, *Information Sciences*, 5, 1973, 149–156.

[2] Dubois, D. and Prade, H., *Fuzzy Sets and Systems*, Academic Press, New York, 1980.

[3] Li, H.-X., *Interesting Talks on Fuzzy Mathematics*, Sichuan Education Press, Sichuan, 1987. (In Chinese.)

[4] Li, H.-X., *Fuzzy Mathematics Methods in Engineering and Its Applications*, Tianjin Scientific and Technical Press, Tianjin, 1993. (In Chinese.)

[5] Li, H.-X. and Wang, P.-Z., *Fuzzy Mathematics*, National Defense Press, Beijing, 1994. (In Chinese.)

[6] Terano, T., Asai, K., and Sugeno, M., *Fuzzy Systems Theory and Its Applications*, Academic Press, San Diego, 1992.

[7] Wang, P.-Z., *Fuzzy Set Theory and Its Applications*, Shanghai Science Press, Shanghai, 1983. (In Chinese.)

[8] Wang, P.-Z., *Fuzzy Sets and the Falling Shadow of Random Sets*, Beijing Normal University Press, 1985. (In Chinese.)

[9] Wang, P.-Z., *Fuzzy Engineering — Principles and Methods*, China Productivity Center, Taipei, 1993. (In Chinese.)

[10] Zadeh, L. A., Fuzzy Sets, *Information and Control*, 8, 1965, 338–353.

[11] Zadeh, L. A., Fuzzy sets as a basis for a theory of possibility, *Fuzzy Sets and Systems*, 1, 1978, 3–28.

[12] Zimmermann, H. J., *Fuzzy Sets Theory and Its Applications*, Kluwer-Academic Publications, Hingham, 1984.

2

Factor Spaces

The original definition of "factor spaces" was proposed by Pei-Zhuang Wang [7] in 1981. He used factor spaces to explain the source of randomness and the essence of probability laws. In 1982, he gave an axiomatic definition of factor spaces [8]. Thereafter, he has applied factor spaces to the study of artificial intelligence (see [9]). Li Hongxing has been devoted to the development of the theory of factor spaces since 1990 [10] and the authors have applied factor spaces to fuzzy decision making since 1991 [3]. This chapter introduces the basic concepts and methods of factor spaces.

2.1 What are "Factors"?

The word "Factor" is a primary term in the factor space theory. Although it is difficult to state its definition, we illustrate its meaning from three different points of view.

2.1.1 Attributivity

When we have a bumper harvest in a good year, we want to know what causes it or what contributed to it. For example, the appropriate amount of rainfall could be a key factor for the bumper harvest. In dealing with factors, we need to differentiate them from states and characteristics. The rainfall mentioned above is a factor; the measurement of it as 50 milliliters is its state; and "appropriate" or "copious" is its characteristic (not factor).

In general, a factor is designated by a noun, a state by a numeral, and a characteristic by an adjective. The factor "temperature", for instance, is a noun; $36°C$, $100°C$, etc. are its states; "hot", "cold", etc., are its characteristics. A factor may be viewed as a common symbol, sign, or code of its states and characteristics. A state is a sign or symbol that represents a special instance of a factor. A characteristic is a rough sign or symbol that describes the factor.

When a state or a characteristic of a factor is used as the condition of producing certain results or effects, we say that the results or effects are attributable to the factor, not the state or the characteristic. This is because attributing a result to a factor is more essential than attributing it to states or characteristics. For example, if we had only observed that the bumper harvest came after an appropriate amount of rainfall, we could not conclude that the harvest was attributable to the amount of rainfall. However, we do recognize from past experience that an appropriate amount of rainfall is a key factor to the harvest. When a crop receives an appropriate level of rainfall, it will result in a good harvest; otherwise, it will result in a poor harvest. Since the rainfall influences the harvest, it is possible to establish a causal relationship between the two factors.

As we have stated, there are two layers of implications in attributivity: One is to seek causes from effects, that is, to find causal factors that may be related to the effects; the other is to identify the states or characteristics of that factor found to be significant. The former layer is basic, whereas the latter one is more essential, although abstract.

2.1.2   Analyticality

Thought is closely related to concepts. Concepts are often formed by means of comparisons among a set of objects. However, comparison requires objects to have both differences and common features; otherwise different objects cannot always be compared. For example, the concept of men and women can be formed by comparison under the common feature, sex. The different colors, red, green, yellow, etc. have the common feature called "color" that help to form concepts of each type of color. These common features are just factors, and they are the common labels of a class of states or a group of characteristics. Terms such as age, height, and profession are examples of factors. Thus factors can be viewed as an analytical way of recognizing the real world.

2.1.3   Describility

Like a point in Cartesian space, an object can be regarded as residing in a space constructed by factors. For example, John Doe has his personal data: age is 26 years old, sex is male, and profession is engineering, etc. In a sense John is being determined by specifying the states of each factor relevant to him. By specifying a sufficient number of factors, John can be uniquely determined and described by them. In other words, John can be viewed simply as a point in abstract coordinate space, and that space can represent any object, just as the Cartesian coordinates can for physical systems. One of the important tasks in constructing such an abstract coordinate system is to specify the terms such as age, sex, title, characteristics, interest, etc. which are factors. We can view this abstract coordinate space as the generalized coordinate space whose dimensions are factors.

2.2   The State Space of Factors

An object may not have significance to an arbitrary factor. For example, it is meaningless to talk about the sex of a stone. An object u is relevant to a factor f (in the direction from u to f); this means that there exists a state $f(u)$ of f corresponding to u.

Let U be a set of objects and V be a set of factors. We call $(U, V]$ a **left-matched pair** if it satisfies the condition that for any $u \in U$, V contains all factors relevant to u.

For a given left-matched pair $(U, V]$, a **relation** R between U and V is defined as follows:

$R(u, f) = 1$ if u is relevant to f. For simplicity, we consider R only as an ordinary (non-fuzzy) relation in this book. Define

$$D(f) = \{u \in U \mid R(u, f) = 1\}$$

$$V(u) = \{f \in U \mid R(u, f) = 1\}$$

A factor $f \in V$ can be regarded as a mapping, acting on an object u and resulting in $f(u)$. That is,

$$f : D(f) \rightarrow X(f), \quad u \longmapsto f(u)$$

where $X(f) = \{f(u) \mid u \in U\}$ is called the **state space** of f, and any element in $X(f)$ is called a **state** of f.

According to the nature of state spaces, factors can be classified into four major categories:

2.2.1   Measurable Factors

Factors such as time, length, mass, height, weight, etc. are measurable factors. Usually their state spaces are subsets, such as intervals, of one-dimensional or n-dimensional Euclidean spaces. For example, X(height)= $[0, 200]$, where the unit is in centimeters. Sometimes, for practical purposes, the state space of a measurable factor is represented as a discrete subset of an interval. Thus, height is given with the range $\{1, 2, 3, \cdots, 200\}$.

2.2.2   Nominal Factors

Factors such as profession, nationality, race, religion, etc. are qualitative in nature. These factors are called nominal factors whose state spaces are sets of terms. For instance,

$$X(title) = \{professor, engineer, lawyer, \cdots\}$$

2.2.3   Degree (Ordinal) Factors

Factors such as ability, feasibility, quality, degree of satisfaction, degree of necessity, etc. are called degree factors. Their state space usually is the interval [0, 1]. For example,

$$X \text{ (degree of satisfaction)} = [0, 1]$$

2.2.4   Switch Factors

Factors such as success, eligibility, permission, etc., whose state space simply contains two values {*yes, no*}, are called switch factors. In general, the values of a state space may be represented by any two appropriate symbols relevant to the context. For instance,

$$X \, (lifeness) = \{life, lifeless\}$$

Although the name of a switch factor is a noun, for convenience sake, other forms of naming are also used. These are: (1) a name with a question mark, and (2) two state values linked with a hyphen. For example, X(life?)={*yes, no*}, and X(life-lifeless)={*life, lifeless*}.

2.3   Relations and Operations Between Factors

Some basic factor relations and operations on factors are now defined and illustrated.

2.3.1   The Zero Factor

The symbol θ is called the empty state if for any state x, the set containing x and θ, and/or the ordered pair formed by x and θ, will be the same before the inclusion of θ. That is,

$$\{x, \theta\} = \{x\}, \quad and \quad (x, \theta) = x = (\theta, x) \tag{2.1}$$

The symbol **0** is called the zero factor if

$$X \, (0) = \{\theta\} . \tag{2.2}$$

That is, the only state of the zero factor is the empty state. The importance of the zero factor in the factor space theory is similar to the empty set in set theory.

From the above properties, we have, for any factor f,

$$X(f) \times X(0) = X(f) = X(0) \times X(f) \tag{2.3}$$

From here on, we assume that the zero factor is always a member of V in any left pair $(U, V]$, i.e., $0 \in V$.

Recall that for a given left pair $(U, V]$, a factor $f \in V$ is the same as a mapping $f : D(f) \longrightarrow X(f)$. For the convenience of discussion in subsequent chapters, we extend the domain of f to the whole set U as shown here.

$$f : U \longrightarrow X(f), \qquad u \longmapsto \begin{cases} f(u), & u \in D(f) \\ \theta, & u \in U \setminus D(f) \end{cases}$$

2.3.2   Equality of Factors

A factor f is equal to a factor g if f and g are equal in the sense of mappings. That is, $D(f) = D(g)$, $X(f) = X(g)$, and $f(u) = g(u)$ for any $u \in D(f)$.

2.3.3   Subfactors

It is possible that the states of a factor g is a subset of the states of another factor f. For example, if we define f to be the plane coordinates and g to be the abscissas (or ordinates), then a state of f is a point (x, y) in the plane that determines the state of g, which is x on the abscissa (or y on the ordinate). Here, the state space of g is represented as a subspace of the state space of f.

A factor g is called a **proper subfactor** of f, denoted by $f > g$, if there exists a set Y satisfying $Y \neq \Phi$ and $Y \neq \{\theta\}$, and

$$X(f) = X(g) \times Y \tag{2.4}$$

A factor g is called a **subfactor** of f, denoted by $f \geq g$, if $f > g$ or $f = g$.

Note 1. The condition $Y \neq \{\theta\}$ in the above definition is indispensable; otherwise by (2.4) we can derive $f < g$ for any f, which is inconceivable.

Note 2. It is obvious that the zero factor is a subfactor of any factor according to (2.3).

Note 3. Generally, the order of the direct product of the state spaces of two factors in the factor space theory is immaterial; that is, $X(f) \times X(g)$ and $X(g) \times X(f)$ are equivalent. Hence (2.4) can also be written as

$$X(f) = Y \times X(g).$$

2.3.4   Conjunction of Factors

A factor h is called the **conjunction of factors** f and g, denoted by

$$h = f \wedge g \tag{2.5}$$

if h is the greatest common subfactor of f and g; that is, if $f \geq h$ and $g \geq h$, and for any factor e, such that $f \geq e$ and $g \geq e$, then $h \geq e$.

A factor g is the **conjunctive factor** of a family of factors $\{f_t\}_{(t \in T)}$, denoted by $g = \bigwedge_{t \in T} f_t$, if g is the greatest common subfactor of f_t $(t \in T)$. In other words, $(\forall t \in T)(f_t \geq g)$ and for any factor h, $(\forall t \in T)(f_t \geq h)$ implies $g \geq h$.

Note: It is not difficult to see that $h = f \wedge g$ if and only if $X(h)$ is the greatest common subspace of $X(f)$ and $X(g)$. That is, if $X(h)$ is a common subspace of $X(f)$ and $X(g)$, and if Y is also a common subspace of $X(f)$ and $X(g)$, then Y is a subspace of $X(h)$. Similarly, $g = \bigwedge_{t \in T} f_t$ if and only if $X(g)$ is the greatest common subspace of $X(f_t)$, $t \in T$.

Example 8

Let f be the length and the width of cuboids and g be the width and the height of cuboids. Then $h = f \wedge g$ is the width of cuboids.   ☐

2.3.5   Disjunction of Factors

A factor h is called the **disjunction of factors** f and g, denoted by

$$h = f \vee g \tag{2.6}$$

if $h \geq g$ and for any factor e such that $e \geq f$ and $e \geq g$ implies $e \geq h$.

A factor $g = \bigvee_{t \in T} f_t$ is the **disjunctive factor** of a family of factors $\{f_t\}_{(t \in T)}$, if $(\forall t \in T)(g \geq f_t)$ and for any factor h such that $(\forall t \in T)(h \geq f_t)$, then $h \geq g$.

Note 1. It is easy to conclude that $h = f \vee g$ if and only if $X(h)$ contains subspaces of $X(f)$ and $X(g)$, and it is the smallest of such spaces. A similar conclusion applies to $g = \bigvee_{t \in T} f_t$.

Note 2. For a given left pair $(U, V]$, disjunctive factors can be determined by conjunctive factors. For example, $h = f \vee g$ if and only if

$$h = \bigwedge \{e \in V \mid e \geq f, \, e \geq g\} \tag{2.7}$$

Conversely, conjunctive factors can also be determined by distinctive factors:

$$f \wedge g = \bigvee \{e \in V \mid e \leq f, \, e \leq g\} \tag{2.8}$$

Example 9
Let f be the abscissas of points of a plane and g be the ordinates of these points. Then $h = f \vee g$ are coordinates of the plane. ⬚

2.3.6 Independent Factors

A family of factors $\{f_t\}_{(t\in T)}$ is called **independent** if it satisfies the following condition:

$$(\forall s, t \in T)\,(f_s \wedge f_t = \mathbf{0}) \tag{2.9}$$

Obviously, the subfactors of independent factors are independent, and the zero factor is independent of any factors.

2.3.7 Difference of Factors

A factor h is called the **difference factor** between factor f and factor g, denoted by $h = f - g$, if

$$(f \wedge g) \vee h = f \quad and \quad h \wedge g = \mathbf{0} \tag{2.10}$$

Example 10
Let f be coordinates of a plane and g be abscissas of points of that plane. Then $h = f - g$ are ordinates of points of the plane. ⬚

2.3.8 Complement of a Factor

Let F be a class of factors considered in a problem. Define $\mathbf{1}$ to be the **complete factor** with respect to F if every factor in F is a subfactor of it. For any factor $f \in F$, define

$$f^c = \mathbf{1} - f \tag{2.11}$$

to be the **complementary factor** of f with respect to $\mathbf{1}$.

2.3.9 Atomic Factors

A factor f is called an **atomic factor** if f does not have proper subfactors except for the zero factor.

Let F be the class of factors of a problem. The set of all atomic factors in F is called the family of atomic factors, which is denoted by π. Clearly, π is independent. Also, we can easily prove that if a family of factors $\{f_t\}_{(t\in T)}$ is independent, then

$$X\left(\bigvee_{t\in T} f_t\right) = \prod_{t\in T} X(f_t) \tag{2.12}$$

If the family of atomic factors exists in the class of factors F, then any factor f in F can be viewed as a disjunction of some subset of π. In other words, the set of all factors in F is equivalent to the power set of π. In notation, we have

$$F = \mathcal{P}(\pi) = \{S \mid S \subset \pi\}$$

$$X(f) = \prod_{g \in f} X(g), \quad and \quad X(1) = \prod_{f \in \pi} X(f).$$

The power set π is a Boolean algebra, whose interesting properties have inspired us to set forth an axiomatic approach to the factor space theory.

2.4   Axiomatic Definition of Factor Spaces

DEFINITION 2   *For a given left pair (U, V) and $F \subset V$, the family $\{X(f)\}_{(f \in F)}$ is called a factor space on U if it satisfies the following axioms:*

(F-1) $F = F(\vee, \wedge, c, \mathbf{1}, \mathbf{0})$ is a complete Boolean algebra;
(F-2) $X(\mathbf{0}) = \{\theta\}$;
(F-3) If $\forall T \subset F$ and $(\forall s, t \in T)(s \neq t \Rightarrow s \wedge t = \mathbf{0})$, then

$$\bigvee_{f \in T} f = \prod_{f \in T} f \tag{2.13}$$

where the right-hand side of the equality is the direct product of the mappings of f in T, since factors can be regarded as mappings.

We call F the set of factors, $f\ (\in F)$ a factor, $X(f)$ the state space of f, $\mathbf{1}$ the complete factor, and $X(\mathbf{1})$ the complete space. As the following example shows, a factor space may be constructed from an appropriate family of Euclidean spaces.

Example 11

Let n be a natural number. Define $S_n = \{1, 2, \cdots, n\}$, and $F = \mathcal{P}(S_n) = \{f \mid f \subset S_n\}$. For any $f \in F$, set

$$X(f) = \prod_{i \in f} X(i)$$

where $X (i)$ is a set for all $i \in f$. Further define $\prod_{i \in \Phi} X (i) = \{\Phi\}$, $0 = \Phi$, and $\theta = \Phi$. It readily follows that $\{X (f)\}_{(f \in F)}$ is a factor space. In particular, when $X (i) = \Re$ (the set of real numbers), then $\{X (f)\}_{(f \in F)}$ is a family of Euclidean spaces with dimensions n or less; for n=3, $\{X (f)\}_{(f \in F)}$ can be viewed as a Cartesian coordinate system with variable dimensions. ▯

Example 12
For a given left pair $(U, V]$, let F be a subset of V and closed with respect to the infinite disjunction, infinite conjuction, and different operations of factors. If we put

$$1 = \bigvee_{f \in F} f, \quad and \quad f^c = 1 - f \quad (f \in F)$$

then $\{X (f)\}_{(f \in F)}$ is a factor space. ▯

Example 13
Let S be a set and $F = \{S, \Phi\}$. Thus F is a complete Boolean algebra with **1**=S and **0**=Φ. If $X (S)$ can be determined, then $\{X (S), \{\Phi\}\}$ forms a factor space with $\theta = \Phi$. Since $\{\Phi\}$ is unnecessary, the factor space degenerates to the state space $X (S)$. ▯

The concept of the state space used in this book is a generalization of the same concept used in control theory, the "characteristics space" or "parameter space" in pattern recognition, and the "phase space" in physics, and so forth. The last example shows that a state space can be viewed as a factor space, or a special case of a factor space. The superiority of factor spaces over the terminologies in the other fields as just mentioned is that a factor space exists not only with a fixed state space, but also with a family of state spaces of variable dimensions. "Variable dimensions" is the key idea in factor spaces.

PROPOSITION 4
Let $\{X (f)\}_{(f \in F)}$ be a factor space. For any $f, g \in F$,

$$X (f \vee g) = X (f - g) \times X (f \wedge g) \times X (g - f) \tag{2.14}$$

PROOF For F is a Boolean algebra, we have

$$f \vee g = (f - g) \vee (f \wedge g) \vee (g - f).$$

Since $(f - g)$, $(f \wedge g)$, and $(g - f)$ can easily be shown to be independent from each other, the result follows from (2.13). ∎

2.5 Describing Concepts in a Factor Space

The "concept" is one of the most important bases for thinking and knowledge building in human reasoning. Generally, concepts may be classified in three forms (see Figure 2.1):

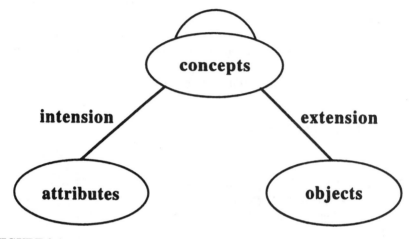

FIGURE 2.1
Description of concepts.

1. Intension: Indicating the essence and attributes of a concept.
2. Extension: Indicating the aggregate of objects according to a concept.
3. Conceptual structure: Using relations between concepts to illustrate a concept.

Traditional set theory can represent a crisp concept in extension form. Fuzzy set theory can express general concepts (either crisp or fuzzy) in extension form. Both theories, however, have not considered the question of how to "select and transform" the universes of interest—the key to describing concepts and analysis. In other words, the open question is how to represent the intension of a concept by means of mathematical methods. Our research on this question is based upon the factor space theory.

Assume $C = \{\alpha, \beta, \gamma, \cdots\}$ to be a group of concepts under the common universe U. Let V be a family of factors such that U and V form a left pair $(U, V]$. Also, let F be a set of factors of V such that F is sufficient, i.e., satisfying

$$(\forall u_1, u_2 \in U)(\exists f \in F)(f(u_1) \neq f(u_2)) \qquad (2.15)$$

The triple $(U, C, F]$ or $\left(U, C, \{X(f)\}_{(f \in F)}\right]$ is called a description frame of C. Two properties follow immediately:

1) $(\forall f, g \in F)\,(f \geq g \Rightarrow (f = g \times (f - g), g \wedge (f - g) = 0))$;
2) $(\forall f \in F)\,(1 = f \times f^c)$.

THEOREM 10

For a given description frame $(U, C, F]$, the complete factor $\mathbf{1}$ must be an injection.

PROOF   Since $(U, C, F]$ is a descriptive frame, for any $u_1, u_2 \in U$, there exists a factor $f \in F$ such that $f(u_1) \neq f(u_2)$. By the properties stated above, we have

$$\mathbf{1}(u_1) = \big(f(u_1), f^c(u_1)\big) \neq \big(f(u_2), f^c(u_2)\big) = \mathbf{1}(u_2)$$

This means the $\mathbf{1}$ is an injection.   ∎

Note 1. Since a factor $f : U \longrightarrow X(f) = \{f(u) \mid u \in U\}$ is always a surjection, this implies that the complete factor $\mathbf{1}$ is a bijection.

Note 2. The "sufficiency" mentioned previously means that for any two distinctive objects u_1, and u_2, there exists at least one factor f in F, such that their state values are different in f.

Let $(U, C, F]$ be a description frame and $\alpha \in C$. The extension of α in U is a fuzzy set $\underset{\sim}{A}$ $(\in \mathcal{F}(U))$ on U, where $\underset{\sim}{A}$ is a mapping:

$$\underset{\sim}{A}: U \to [0, 1], \qquad u \mapsto \underset{\sim}{A}(u)$$

$\underset{\sim}{A}(u)$ is called the degree of membership of u with respect to α or $\underset{\sim}{A}$. When $\underset{\sim}{A}(u) = 1$, we say that u definitely accords with α, or u completely belongs to $\underset{\sim}{A}$; while $\underset{\sim}{A}(u) = 0$, u definitely does not accord with α, or u does not belong to $\underset{\sim}{A}$. When $\underset{\sim}{A}(U) = \{0, 1\}$, $\underset{\sim}{A}$ degenerates to a crisp set and its α is called a crisp concept. For a given concept group C, every state space $X(f)$ is called a representation universe; $X(1)$, in particular, is called the complete representation universe. A factor space is, therefore, just a family of representation universes of C.

According to Zadeh's extension principle, we have

DEFINITION 3   For a given description frame $(U, C, F]$, let $\alpha \in C$ whose extension is $\underset{\sim}{A} \in \mathcal{F}(U)$. For any $f \in F$, define

$$f\left(\underset{\sim}{A}\right) : X(f) \longrightarrow [0, 1], \qquad x \mapsto f\left(\underset{\sim}{A}\right)(x) = \bigvee_{f(u)=x} \underset{\sim}{A}(u).$$

Then $f\left(\underset{\sim}{A}\right)$ *is a fuzzy subset of the representation universe* $X(f)$, *namely*

$f\left(\underset{\sim}{A}\right) \in \mathcal{F}(X(f))$, *and,* $f\left(\underset{\sim}{A}\right)$ *is called the representation extension of* α *in the representation universe of* $X(f)$.

DEFINITION 4   *Let* $\{X(f)\}_{(f \in F)}$ *be a factor space on* U. *Assume* $f, g \in F$ *such that* $f \geq g$ *define*

$$\downarrow_g^f : X(f) \to X(g), \quad (x, y) \longmapsto \downarrow_g^f(x, y) = x, \qquad (2.16)$$

where $X(f) = X(g) \times X(f - g)$, $x \in X(g)$, *and* $y \in X(f - g)$.

We call $\downarrow_g^f$ the projection from f to g. By the extension principle, $\downarrow_g^f$ can be extended to

$$\downarrow_g^f : \mathcal{F}(X(f)) \to \mathcal{F}(X(g)), \quad \underset{\sim}{B} \longmapsto \downarrow_g^f\left(\underset{\sim}{B}\right) = \downarrow_g^f \underset{\sim}{B}$$

$$\downarrow_g^f \underset{\sim}{B} : X(g) \longrightarrow [0, 1],$$

$$x \longmapsto \left(\downarrow_g^f \underset{\sim}{B}\right)(x) = \bigvee_{\downarrow_g^f(x,y)=x} \underset{\sim}{B}(x, y) = \bigvee_{g \in X(f-g)} \underset{\sim}{B}(x, y).$$

We call $\downarrow_g^f \underset{\sim}{B}$ the projection of $\underset{\sim}{B}$ from f to g.

PROPOSITION 5

Let $(U, C, F]$ *be a description frame. For any* $f, g \in F$, *and* $f \geq g$, *if* $\underset{\sim}{A}$ *is the extension of* $\alpha \in C$, *then*

$$\downarrow_g^f f\left(\underset{\sim}{A}\right) = g\left(\underset{\sim}{A}\right). \qquad (2.17)$$

PROOF   Since g is the composite mapping of f and $\downarrow_g^f$, the conclusion holds by the extension principle of composite mappings.   ∎

DEFINITION 5   *Let* $\{X(f)\}_{(f \in F)}$ *be a factor space on* U. *Assume that* $f, g \in$

F with $f \geq g$, and any $\underset{\sim}{B} \in \mathcal{F}(X(g))$, define

$$\uparrow_g^f \underset{\sim}{B} \colon X(f) \longrightarrow [0,1], \quad (x,y) \longmapsto \left(\uparrow_g^f \underset{\sim}{B} \right)(x,y) = \underset{\sim}{B}(x) \qquad (2.18)$$

where $X(f) = X(g) \times X(f-g)$, $x \in X(g)$, $y \in X(f-g)$.

Notice that $\uparrow_g^f \underset{\sim}{B}$ is a fuzzy subset of $X(f)$, i.e., $\uparrow_g^f \underset{\sim}{B} \in \mathcal{F}(X(f))$; we call it the cylindrical extension of $\underset{\sim}{B}$ from g to f.

PROPOSITION 6
For any factor space $\{X(f)\}_{(f \in F)}$, and any $f, g, h \in F$ such that $f \geq g \geq h$, we have

1) if $\underset{\sim}{B} \in \mathcal{F}(X(f))$, then

$$\downarrow_h^g \left(\downarrow_g^f \underset{\sim}{B} \right) = \downarrow_h^f \underset{\sim}{B} \qquad (2.19)$$

2) if $\underset{\sim}{B} \in \mathcal{F}(X(h))$ then

$$\uparrow_g^f \left(\uparrow_h^g \underset{\sim}{B} \right) = \uparrow_h^f \underset{\sim}{B} \qquad (2.20)$$

3) if $\underset{\sim}{B} \in \mathcal{F}(X(g))$ then

$$\downarrow_g^f \left(\uparrow_g^f \underset{\sim}{B} \right) = \underset{\sim}{B} \qquad (2.21)$$

4) if $\underset{\sim}{B} \in \mathcal{F}(X(f))$ then

$$\uparrow_g^f \left(\downarrow_g^f \underset{\sim}{B} \right) \supset \underset{\sim}{B} \qquad (2.22)$$

PROOF 1) Notice that $\downarrow_h^f = \downarrow_h^g \circ \downarrow_g^f$. By the extension principle on composition of mappings, we have (2.19).

2) Since $f \geq g \geq h$, this implies

$$X(f) = X(f-g) \times X(g-h) \times X(h).$$

For any

$$(x, y, z) \in X(f - g) \times X(g - h) \times X(h),$$

we have

$$\left(\uparrow_g^f \left(\uparrow_h^g B\right)\right)(x, y, z) = \left(\uparrow_h^g B\right)(y, z) = B(x)$$

$$\left(\uparrow_h^f B\right)(x, y, z) = B(x)$$

Hence (2.20) is proved.

3) For any $x \in X(g)$, we have

$$\left(\downarrow_g^f \left(\uparrow_g^f B\right)\right)(x) = \bigvee_{y \in X(f-g)} \left(\uparrow_g^f B\right)(x, y) = \bigvee_{y \in X(f-g)} B(x) = B(x)$$

This proves (2.21).

4) Since $X(f) = X(g) \times X(f - g)$, then for any $(x, y) \in X(f)$, we have

$$\left(\uparrow_g^f \left(\downarrow_g^f B\right)\right)(x, y) = \left(\downarrow_g^f B\right)(x) = \bigvee_{y' \in X(f-g)} B(x, y') \geq B(x, y)$$

Hence (2.22) follows. ∎

The next theorem establishes an equality condition for the expression (2.22).

THEOREM 11

Let $\{X(f)\}_{(f \in F)}$ be a factor space on U. Assume $f, g \in F$ such that $f \geq g$ and $B \in \mathcal{F}(X(f))$. Then $\uparrow_g^f \left(\downarrow_g^f B\right) = B$ if and only if

$$(\forall (x, y) \in X(g) \times X(f - g))\left(B(x, y) = B(x)\right) \tag{2.23}$$

PROOF   Since the "if" part is clearly valid, we prove the "only if" part.
Suppose (2.23) is not true. Then there exists y_1 and $y_2 \in X(f - g)$ such that $B(x, y_1) > B(x, y_2)$. Thus, for any $y \in X(f - g)$,

$$B(x, y_2) < B(x, y_1) \leq \bigvee_{y \in X(f-g)} B(x, y) = \left(\downarrow_g^f B\right)(x) = \left(\uparrow_g^f \left(\downarrow_g^f B\right)\right)(x, y).$$

In particular, when $y = y_2$, we deduce a contradiction. This completes the proof. ■

Note: Figure 2.2 illustrates the equality (2.23) in that the cut set of $\underset{\sim}{B}$ at y is unconcerned with the variations of y in $X(f - g)$. That is, the variations of the factor $f - g$ have nothing to do with $\underset{\sim}{B}$. In other words, the information of $\underset{\sim}{B}$ is completely contained in the factor g.

$\underset{\sim}{A}(u)$	0	0.2	0.6	0.9	1	0.9	0.6	0.2	0
u	1	2	3	4	5	6	7	8	9

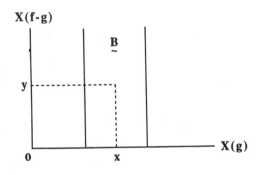

FIGURE 2.2
Illustration of theorem 11.

A factor space has many properties with respect to the projection and cylindrical extension of factors. Their properties are given in the following propositions.

PROPOSITION 7

Let $f, g \in F$ and $\left\{ \underset{\sim}{B}^{(t)} \right\}_{(t \in T)}$ be a family of fuzzy subsets in $X(g)$. If $f \geq g$ then

1) $\uparrow_g^f \left(\bigcup_{t \in T} \underset{\sim}{B}^{(t)} \right) = \bigcup_{t \in T} \left(\uparrow_g^f \underset{\sim}{B}^{(t)} \right)$

2) $\uparrow_g^f \left(\bigcap_{t \in T} \underset{\sim}{B}^{(t)} \right) = \bigcap_{t \in T} \left(\uparrow_g^f \underset{\sim}{B}^{(t)} \right)$

PROOF   For any $(x, y) \in X(f) = X(g) \times X(f - g)$, we have

$$\left(\uparrow_g^f \left(\bigcup_{t \in T} \underset{\sim}{B}^{(t)} \right) \right)(x, y) = \left(\bigcup_{t \in T} \underset{\sim}{B}^{(t)} \right)(x)$$

$$= \bigvee_{t \in T} \underset{\sim}{B}^{(t)}(x) = \bigvee_{t \in T} \left(\uparrow_g^f \underset{\sim}{B}^{(t)} \right)(x, y)$$

$$= \left(\bigcup_{t \in T} \left(\uparrow_g^f \underset{\sim}{B}^{(t)} \right) \right)(x, y)$$

So 1) is true. Similarly, we can prove 2).   ∎

PROPOSITION 8

Let $f, g \in F$, $\underset{\sim}{B} \in \mathcal{F}(X(g))$ and $\underset{\sim}{B}^c$ be the complement of $\underset{\sim}{B}$ in $X(g)$. Then

$$f \geq g \Longrightarrow \uparrow_g^f \underset{\sim}{B}^c = \left(\uparrow_g^f \underset{\sim}{B} \right)^c$$

PROOF   Since $f \geq g$ implies that $X(f) = X(g) \times X(f - g)$, then for any $(x, y) \in X(f)$, we have

$$\left(\uparrow_g^f \underset{\sim}{B}^c \right)(x, y) = \underset{\sim}{B}^c(x) = 1 - \uparrow_g^f \underset{\sim}{B}(x, y) = \left(\uparrow_g^f \underset{\sim}{B} \right)^c(x, y).$$

This completes the proof.   ∎

PROPOSITION 9

Let $f, g \in F$, and $\left\{ \underset{\sim}{B}^{(t)} \right\}_{(t \in T)}$ be a family of fuzzy subsets of $X(f)$. For any $\underset{\sim}{B} \in \mathcal{F}(X(f))$, if $f \geq g$, then

1) $\downarrow_g^f \left(\bigcup_{t \in T} \underset{\sim}{B}^{(t)} \right) = \bigcup_{t \in T} \left(\downarrow_g^f \underset{\sim}{B}^{(t)} \right)$

2) $\downarrow_g^f \left(\bigcap_{t \in T} \underset{\sim}{B}^{(t)} \right) \subset \bigcap_{t \in T} \left(\downarrow_g^f \underset{\sim}{B}^{(t)} \right)$

3) $\downarrow_g^f \left(\underset{\sim}{B}^c \right) \supset \left(\uparrow_g^f \underset{\sim}{B} \right)^c$

PROOF

1) For any $(x, y) \in X(f) = X(g) \times X(f - g)$, we have

$$\left(\downarrow_g^f \left(\bigcup_{t \in T} B^{(t)}_{\sim} \right) \right)(x) = \bigvee_{y \in X(f-g)} \left(\bigcup_{t \in T} B^{(t)}_{\sim} \right)(x, y)$$

$$= \bigvee_{y \in X(f-g)} \left(\bigvee_{t \in T} B^{(t)}_{\sim}(x, y) \right) = \bigvee_{t \in T} \left(\bigvee_{y \in X(f-g)} B^{(t)}_{\sim}(x, y) \right)$$

$$= \bigvee_{t \in T} \left(\downarrow_g^f B^{(t)}_{\sim} \right)(x) = \left(\bigcup_{t \in T} \left(\downarrow_g^f B^{(t)}_{\sim} \right) \right)(x)$$

Hence 1) is proved.

2) For any $(x, y) \in X(f) = X(g) \times X(f - g)$, we have

$$\left(\downarrow_g^f \left(\bigcap_{t \in T} B^{(t)}_{\sim} \right) \right)(x) = \bigvee_{y \in X(f-g)} \left(\bigcap_{t \in T} B^{(t)}_{\sim} \right)(x, y) = \bigvee_{y \in X(f-g)} \left(\bigwedge_{t \in T} B^{(t)}_{\sim} \right)(x, y)$$

$$\left(\bigcap_{t \in T} \left(\downarrow_g^f B^{(t)}_{\sim} \right) \right)(x) = \bigwedge_{t \in T} \left(\downarrow_g^f B^{(t)}_{\sim} \right)(x) = \bigwedge_{t \in T} \left(\bigvee_{y \in X(f-g)} B^{(t)}_{\sim}(x, y) \right)$$

Also notice that for any $y \in X(f - g)$, y satisfies

$$\bigwedge_{t \in T} B^{(t)}_{\sim}(x, y) \leq \bigwedge_{t \in T} \left(\bigvee_{y \in X(f-g)} B^{(t)}_{\sim}(x, y) \right).$$

Hence we have the following inequality:

$$\bigvee_{y \in X(f-g)} \left(\bigwedge_{t \in T} B^{(t)}_{\sim}(x, y) \right) \leq \bigwedge_{t \in T} \left(\bigvee_{y \in X(f-g)} B^{(t)}_{\sim}(x, y) \right).$$

This completes the proof of 2).

3) For any $(x, y) \in X(f) = X(g) \times X(f - g)$, we have

$$\left(\downarrow_g^f B_{\sim} \right)^c (x) = 1 - \left(\downarrow_g^f B_{\sim} \right)(x) = 1 - \bigvee_{y \in X(f-g)} B_{\sim}(x, y)$$

$$\left(\downarrow_g^f B^c_{\sim} \right)(x) = \bigvee_{y \in X(f-g)} B^c_{\sim}(x, y) = \bigvee_{y \in X(f-g)} \left(1 - B_{\sim}(x, y) \right)$$

By comparing the right-hand sides of the above equations, we can conclude that

$$\left(\downarrow_g^f B_{\sim} \right)^c (x) \leq \left(\downarrow_g^f B^c_{\sim} \right)(x).$$

This proves 3). ∎

PROPOSITION 10

Let $\{f_t\}_{(t\in T)}$ be an independent family of factors in F. For any $\underset{\sim}{B}^{(t)}\in \mathcal{F}(X(f_t))$, $t \in T$, if $f = \underset{t\in T}{\bigvee} f_t$ then

$$\bigcap_{t\in T}\left(\uparrow_{f_t}^{f}\underset{\sim}{B}^{(t)}\right) =\prod_{t\in T}\underset{\sim}{B}^{(t)} \qquad (2.24)$$

PROOF   For any w,

$$w \in \prod_{t\in T} X(f_t) = \left\{w \mid w : T \longrightarrow \bigcup_{t\in T} X(f_t),\ w(t) \in X(f_t),\ t \in T\right\},$$

we have

$$\left(\bigcap_{t\in T}\right)\left(\uparrow_{f_t}^{f}\underset{\sim}{B}^{(t)}\right)(w) =\bigwedge_{t\in T}\left(\uparrow_{f_t}^{f}\underset{\sim}{B}^{(t)}\right)(w) =\bigwedge_{t\in T}\underset{\sim}{B}^{(t)}(w(t)) = \left(\prod_{t\in T}\underset{\sim}{B}^{(t)}\right)(w).$$

This completes the proof. ∎

PROPOSITION 11

Let (1) $f, g \in F$ such that $f \geq g$, and (2) $\underset{\sim}{B}$ and $\underset{\sim}{B}^{(n)}\in \mathcal{F}(X(f))$, $n = 1, 2, 3, \cdots$.

$$\text{If } \underset{\sim}{B}^{(n)} \nearrow \underset{\sim}{B},\ \text{ then } \left(\downarrow_{g}^{f}\underset{\sim}{B}^{(n)}\right) \nearrow \left(\downarrow_{g}^{f}\underset{\sim}{B}\right).$$

PROOF   Since

$$\underset{\sim}{B}^{(n)} \nearrow \underset{\sim}{B} \Longrightarrow \bigcup_{n=1}^{\infty} \underset{\sim}{B}^{(n)}=\underset{\sim}{B}$$

$$\Longrightarrow \downarrow_{g}^{f}\underset{\sim}{B}=\downarrow_{g}^{f}\left(\bigcup_{n=1}^{\infty} \underset{\sim}{B}\right) = \bigcup_{n=1}^{\infty}\left(\downarrow_{g}^{f}\underset{\sim}{B}^{(n)}\right)$$

$$\Longrightarrow \left(\downarrow_{g}^{f}\underset{\sim}{B}^{(n)}\right) \nearrow \left(\downarrow_{g}^{f}\underset{\sim}{B}\right)$$

The proof is complete. ∎

DEFINITION 6 *Let $(U, C, F]$ be a description frame. For any $\alpha \in C$, let $\underset{\sim}{A}$ be its extension and write $\underset{\sim}{B} = 1\left(\underset{\sim}{A}\right)$. When $\underset{\sim}{B} \neq X(1)$ and Φ, we call a factor $f \in F$ sufficient with respect to α if it satisfies*

$$\uparrow_f^1 \left(\downarrow_f^1 \underset{\sim}{B} \right) = \underset{\sim}{B} \tag{2.25}$$

Every factor that is independent of f is called a surplus with respect to α. When $\underset{\sim}{B} = X(1)$ or Φ, every factor $f \in F$ is regarded as both sufficient and a surplus with respect to α simultaneously.

PROPOSITION 12
Let $(U, C, F]$ be a description frame, $f, g \in F$, such that $f \geq g$, and $\alpha \in C$. If g is sufficient with respect to α, so is f. If f is a surplus with respect to α, so is g.

PROOF The proof is omitted since it is simple. ∎

DEFINITION 7 *Let $(U, C, F]$ be a description frame. Let $\alpha \in C$ whose extension is $\underset{\sim}{A}$ and $1\left(\underset{\sim}{A}\right) \notin \{X(1), \Phi\}$. Define*

$$r(\alpha) = r\left(\underset{\sim}{A}\right) = \bigwedge \{f \in F \mid f \text{ is sufficient with respect to } \alpha\}$$

to be the rank of the concept α. When $1\left(\underset{\sim}{A}\right) = X(1)$, or Φ, we set $r(\alpha) = r\left(\underset{\sim}{A}\right) = 0$.

Note: The rank of a concept α is a factor, which is the greatest lower bound of the sufficient factors (in the sense of conjunction operator). Those factors that are greater than $r(\alpha)$ are sufficient with respect to α, but those factors that are less than $r(\alpha)$ are not sufficient. The complementary factor of $r(\alpha)$ is the least upper bound of the surplus factors (in the sense of disjunction operator), which means that the factors less than it are surpluses with respect to α, but the factors greater than it are not surpluses.

PROPOSITION 13
Every pair of opposite concepts has the same rank; namely, for any $\underset{\sim}{B} \in \mathcal{F}(X(1))$,

we have

$$r\left(\underset{\sim}{B}^c\right) = r\left(\underset{\sim}{B}\right) \tag{2.26}$$

PROOF   The proof is straightforward and, hence, omitted.   ∎

PROPOSITION 14

Let $(U, C, F]$ be a description frame. Also, let $A^{(1)}$ and $A^{(2)}$ be the extensions of two concepts $\alpha, \beta \in C$, respectively. Then the following inequalities hold:

$$1)\ r\left(\underset{\sim}{A}^{(1)} \bigcup \underset{\sim}{A}^{(2)}\right) \leq r\left(\underset{\sim}{A}^{(1)}\right) \bigvee r\left(\underset{\sim}{A}^{(2)}\right)$$

$$2)\ r\left(\underset{\sim}{A}^{(1)} \bigcap \underset{\sim}{A}^{(2)}\right) \leq r\left(\underset{\sim}{A}^{(1)}\right) \bigvee r\left(\underset{\sim}{A}^{(2)}\right)$$

PROOF   The proof is simple and, thus, omitted.   ∎

PROPOSITION 15

Let $\{X\,(f)\}_{(f \in F)}$ be a factor space on U and $f,\ g \in F$ such that $f \geq g$. For any $\underset{\sim}{B} \in \mathcal{F}\,(X\,(f))$ and $\underset{\sim}{D} \in \mathcal{F}\,(X\,(g))$, we have

1) $\forall\,(x, y) \in X\,(f) = X\,(g) \times X\,(f - g)$,

$$\left(\downarrow_g^f \underset{\sim}{B}\right)(x) = \bigvee_{y \in X(f-g)} \underset{\sim}{B}\,(x, y) \tag{2.27}$$

2) $\uparrow_g^f \underset{\sim}{D} = \underset{\sim}{D} \times X\,(f - g)$

PROOF   We omit the proof since it is not difficult.   ∎

We now consider this problem: Is the rank of a concept itself sufficient? Alternatively, we are asking: Given a description frame $(U, C, F]$ and an $\alpha \in C$ with $\underset{\sim}{A}$ as its extension, is the following true?

$$\uparrow_{r(\alpha)}^1 \left(\downarrow_{r(\alpha)}^1 1\left(\underset{\sim}{A}\right)\right) = 1\left(\underset{\sim}{A}\right) \tag{2.28}$$

The answer is positive. In fact, let $\underset{\sim}{B} = 1 \left(\underset{\sim}{A} \right)$ and put

$$Q = \{ f \in F \mid f \text{ is sufficient with respect to } \alpha \}.$$

Obviously, $r(\alpha) = \bigwedge Q$ and $r(\alpha)$ is sufficient with respect to α if and only if $r(\alpha) \in Q$, i.e., $(\exists f \in F)(r(\alpha) = f)$, (we shall call it the accessibility condition). Notice that

$$\left(\uparrow^1_{r(\alpha)} \left(\downarrow^1_{r(\alpha)} \underset{\sim}{B} \right) \right)(p, q) = \left(\downarrow^1_{r(\alpha)} \underset{\sim}{B} \right)(p) = \bigvee_{s \in X(1-r(\alpha))} \underset{\sim}{B}(p, s) \geq \underset{\sim}{B}(p, q)$$

where $(p, q) \in X(1) = X(r(\alpha)) \times X(1 - r(\alpha)) = X(r(\alpha)) \times X\left((r(\alpha))^c \right)$.
For any $f \in Q$, we have

$$\uparrow^1_{r(\alpha)} \left(\downarrow^1_{r(\alpha)} \underset{\sim}{B} \right) = \uparrow^1_f \left(\uparrow^f_{r(\alpha)} \left(\downarrow^1_f \left(\downarrow^f_{r(\alpha)} \underset{\sim}{B} \right) \right) \right).$$

Therefore, for any $(x, y, z) \in X(1) = X(r(\alpha)) \times X(f - r(\alpha)) \times X(f^c)$, we also have

$$\left(\uparrow^1_f \left(\uparrow^f_{r(\alpha)} \left(\downarrow^1_f \left(\downarrow^f_{r(\alpha)} \underset{\sim}{B} \right) \right) \right) \right)(x, y, z) = \left(\uparrow^f_{r(\alpha)} \left(\downarrow^1_f \left(\downarrow^f_{r(\alpha)} \underset{\sim}{B} \right) \right) \right)(x, y)$$

$$= \left(\downarrow^1_f \left(\downarrow^f_{r(\alpha)} \underset{\sim}{B} \right) \right)(x) = \bigvee_{z \in X(f^c)} \left(\downarrow^f_{r(\alpha)} \underset{\sim}{B} \right)(x, z) = \bigvee_{z \in X(f^c)} \left(\bigvee_{y \in X(f-r(\alpha))} \underset{\sim}{B}(x, y, z) \right).$$

If the following condition is satisfied:

$$(\forall (x, y, z) \in X(1)) \left(\bigvee_{t \in X(f-r(\alpha))} \underset{\sim}{B}(x, t, z) = \underset{\sim}{B}(x, y, z) \right),$$

then, we can simplify

$$\bigvee_{z \in X(f^c)} \left(\bigvee_{y \in X(f-r(\alpha))} \underset{\sim}{B}(x, y, z) \right) = \bigvee_{s \in X(f^c)} \underset{\sim}{B}(x, y, s) = \underset{\sim}{B}(x, y, z).$$

By proposition 15, the above condition is always satisfied, hence we have

THEOREM 12
The rank of the concept α, $r(\alpha)$ itself is sufficient with respect to α.

PROPOSITION 16

Let $(U, C, F]$ be a description frame, and $\underset{\sim}{A}$ be the extension of $\alpha \in C$. Set
$\underset{\sim}{B} = 1\left(\underset{\sim}{A}\right)$. *Then, for any $\alpha \in F$, we have the following:*

1) if f is sufficient with respect to α, then for any $(x, y) \in X(1) = X(f) \times X(f^c)$,

$$\underset{\sim}{B}(x, y) = \left(\downarrow_f^1 \underset{\sim}{B}\right)(x, y) \qquad (2.29)$$

2) if f is a surplus with respect to α, then for any $(x, y) \in X(1) = X(f \times X(f^c))$,

$$\left(\downarrow_f^1 \underset{\sim}{B}\right)(x) \equiv constant \qquad (2.30)$$

that is, $\downarrow_f^1 \underset{\sim}{B}$ is irrelevant with x.

PROOF

1) From proposition 15,

$$\underset{\sim}{B}(x, y) = \left(\uparrow_f^1 \left(\downarrow_f^1 \underset{\sim}{B}\right)\right)(x, y) = \left(\downarrow_f^1 \underset{\sim}{B}\right)(x).$$

2) Since f is a surplus, there exists a sufficient factor $f \in F$ such that $f \wedge g = \mathbf{0}$. Also,

$$1 = (f \vee g) \vee (f \vee g)^c = (f \vee g) \vee \left(f^c \wedge g^c\right),$$

and

$$X(1) = X(f) \times X(g) \times X\left(f^c \wedge g^c\right).$$

Because $f^c = g \vee (f \vee g)^c$, so for any $(x, y, z) \in X(1)$, by (2.27) and (2.29), we obtain

$$\left(\downarrow_f^1 \underset{\sim}{B}\right)(x) = \bigvee_{(y,z) \in X(f^c)} \underset{\sim}{B}(x, y, z) = \bigvee_{y \in X(g)} \left(\downarrow_g^1 \underset{\sim}{B}\right)(y),$$

which means that $\downarrow_f^1 \underset{\sim}{B}$ is irrelevant with x. ∎

COROLLARY 4

Let (U, C, F) be a description frame, and $\underset{\sim}{A}$ be the extension of $\alpha \in C$. Set $\underset{\sim}{B} = 1\left(\underset{\sim}{A}\right)$. Then, for any $f \in F$, f is sufficient with respect to α if and only if for any $(x_1, y_1), (x_2, y_2) \in X(f) \times X(f^c)$, and $x_1 = x_2 \Longrightarrow \underset{\sim}{B}(x_1, y_1) = \underset{\sim}{B}(x_2, y_2)$.

When a factor space F is an atomic lattice, we call F an atomic set of factors and $\{X(f)\}_{(f \in F)}$ an atomic factor space.

Let π be the family of all atomic factors in F. Then F is the same as $\mathcal{P}(\pi)$, i.e., $F = \mathcal{P}(\pi)$.

PROPOSITION 17

Let $(U, \mathcal{C}, F]$ be a description frame, $F = \mathcal{P}(\pi)$ be an atomic set of factors, and $\alpha \in \mathcal{C}$. If $\pi_1 = \pi - \pi_2$ where $\pi_2 = \{f \in \pi \mid f \text{ is a surplus with respect to } \alpha\}$, then

$$r(\alpha) = \bigvee \{f \mid f \in \pi_1\} = \pi_1 \qquad (2.31)$$

PROOF From the properties of atomic lattices, for any $f \in F$,

$$f = \bigvee \{g \in \pi \mid f \geq g \quad (i.e., \; g \in f)\}$$

Take an atomic factor $e \in \pi_1$ that is not a surplus. Then for an arbitrary sufficient factor f (with respect to α), $e \wedge f \neq \mathbf{0}$. This also implies that $e \leq f$. Thus,

$$e \leq r(\alpha) = \{f \in F \mid f \text{ is sufficient with respect to } \alpha\}$$

Therefore, $\pi_1 = \bigvee \{f \mid f \in \pi_1\} \leq r(\alpha)$.

We now prove that $\pi_1 = r(\alpha)$. If this is not the case, then there exists $h \in \pi_2$ such that $h \leq r(\alpha)$. That is, for an arbitrary sufficient factor f (with respect to α), $h \leq r(\alpha) \leq f$, which is contradictory to $h \in \pi_2$. So $\pi_1 = r(\alpha)$. ∎

The proposition means that when F is an atomic set of factors, the rank of a concept is formed by all of the non-surplus atomic factors. Under the same conditions of the proposition, we have the following:

COROLLARY 5

1) For any $f \in F$, f is sufficient with respect to α if and only if $f \geq r(\alpha)$;
2) For any $f \in F$, f is a surplus with respect to α if and only if $f \wedge r(\alpha) = \mathbf{0}$.

References

[1] Kandel, A., Peng, X.T., Cao, Z. Q., and Wang, P.-Z., Representation of concepts by factor spaces. *Cybernetics and Systems*, 21, 1990.

[2] Li, H.-X., *Fuzzy Mathematics Methods in Engineering and Its Applications*, Tianjin Scientific and Technical Press, Tianjin, 1993.

[3] Li, H.-X. and Yen, V. C., Factor Spaces and Fuzzy Decision Making, *Journal of Beijing Normal University*, 30(1), 1994, 41–46.

[4] Li, H.-X. and Wang, P.-Z., Falling shadow representation of fuzzy concepts on factor spaces. *Journal of Yantai University*, No. 2, 1994, 15–21.

[5] Li, H.-X. and Wang, P.-Z., *Fuzzy Mathematics*. National Defense Press, Beijing, 1994.

[6] Luo, C.-Z., *Mathematical Description of Factor Spaces Canes. Proceedings of First Asian Fuzzy Systems Symposium*, Singapore, 1993, 478–483.

[7] Wang, P.-Z., Stochastic differential equations. In *Advances in Statistical Physics*, Buo-Ling Hao and Lu Yu (Eds.), Science Press, Beijing, 1981.

[8] Wang, P.-Z. and Sugeno, M., The factor fields and background structure for fuzzy subsets. *Fuzzy Mathematics*, 2(2), 1982, 45–54.

[9] Wang, P.-Z., A factor space approach to knowledge representation. *Fuzzy Sets and Systems*, 36, 1990, 113–124.

[10] Wang, P.-Z. and Li, H.-X., *Mathematical Theory on Knowledge Representation*. Tinjing Scientific and Technical Press, Tianjin, 1994.

[11] Wang, P.-Z., *Fuzzy Engineering—Principles and Methods*. China Productivity Center, Taipei, 1993.

[12] Wang, P.-Z., *Factor Spaces and Fuzzy Tables. Proceedings of Fifth IFSA World Congress, Korea*, 1993, 683–686.

3

The Basics of Fuzzy Decision Making

3.1 Feedback Extension and its Applications

Let $(U, C, F]$ be a description frame and $A \in \mathcal{F}$ be the extension of $\alpha \in C$. According to Definition 2 of Chapter 2, for any factor $f \in F$, the representation extension $f\left(A_{\sim}\right) \in \mathcal{F}(X(f))$ of α in the representation universe $X(f)$ can be determined by $A_{\sim}$. Conversely, suppose the extension $A_{\sim}$ is unknown, but the representation extension $B_{\sim}(f)$ of α in $X(f)$ is known. How can the extension $A_{\sim}$ of α be determined in the universe U? To answer this question, we need to introduce a new tool.

DEFINITION 8   Let $(U, C, F]$ be a description frame $\alpha \in C$ and $f \in F$. Assume $B_{\sim}(f)$ to be the known representation extension of the concept α in the representation universe $X(f)$. Define

$$f^{-1}\left(B_{\sim}(f)\right) : U \longrightarrow [0, 1]$$

$$u \longmapsto f^{-1}\left(B_{\sim}(f)\right)(u) = B_{\sim}(f)(f(u))$$

*Then $f^{-1}\left(B_{\sim}(f)\right)$ is a fuzzy subset of the universe U. We call it the **feedback extension** of α with respect to f.*

Two questions of interest deserve attention. They arise from the following observations.

1) Let $A \in \mathcal{F}(U)$ be the given extension of the concept α. From definition 3, the representation extension of $\underset{\sim}{A}$ is $f\left(\underset{\sim}{A}\right) \in \mathcal{F}(X(f))$. Then we have the feedback extension $f^{-1}\left(f\left(\underset{\sim}{A}\right)\right)$ with respect to f, according to definition 8. Naturally, we would like to ask: Is $f^{-1}\left(f\left(\underset{\sim}{A}\right)\right)$ coincident with (equal to) $\underset{\sim}{A}$?

2) Let $\underset{\sim}{B}(f)$ be the known representation extension of the concept α in $X(f)$. From definition 8 we get its feedback extension $f^{-1}\left(\underset{\sim}{B}(f)\right)$ with respect to f. Then, according to the definition 3, we have its representation extension $f\left(f^{-1}\left(\underset{\sim}{B}(f)\right)\right)$. Naturally, we ask: Is $f\left(f^{-1}\left(\underset{\sim}{B}(f)\right)\right)$ coincident with (equal to) $\underset{\sim}{B}(f)$?

Answers to these questions are contained in

PROPOSITION 18

1) If the extension of a concept α is known to be $\underset{\sim}{A}$, then for any factor $f \in F$, we have

$$f^{-1}\left(f\left(\underset{\sim}{A}\right)\right) \supset \underset{\sim}{A} \tag{3.1}$$

It becomes an equality when f is an injection.

2) For any $f \in F$, if the representation extension of a concept $\alpha \in X(f)$ is known, then

$$f\left(f^{-1}\left(\underset{\sim}{B}(f)\right)\right) \subset \underset{\sim}{B}(f) \tag{3.2}$$

It becomes an equality when f is a surjection.

PROOF

1) For any $u \in U$, we have

$$f^{-1}\left(\underset{\sim}{A}(f)\right)(u) = f\left(\underset{\sim}{A}\right)(f(u)) = \bigvee_{f(u')=f(u)} \underset{\sim}{A}(u') \geq \underset{\sim}{A}(u).$$

When f is an injection, i.e., $f(u') = f(u) \implies u' = u$, then the preceding inequality becomes an equality.

2) For any $x \in X\,(f)$, we have

$$f\left(f^{-1}\left(\underset{\sim}{B}\,(f)\right)\right)(x) = \bigvee_{f(u)=x} f^{-1}\left(\underset{\sim}{B}\,(f)\right)(u) = \bigvee_{f(u)=x} \underset{\sim}{B}\,(f)\,(f\,(u))$$

$$= \begin{cases} \underset{\sim}{B}\,(f)\,(x) & ,\ (\exists u \in U)\,(f\,(u) = x) \\ 0 \leq \underset{\sim}{B}\,(f)\,(x) & ,\ (\forall u \in U)\,(f\,(u) \neq x), \end{cases}$$

where we stipulate that $\vee \Phi = 0$. Clearly, if f is a surjection, the inequality becomes an equality. ∎

Note: Expression (3.2) means that $f^{-1}\left(f\left(\underset{\sim}{A}\right)\right)$, obtained from $f\left(\underset{\sim}{A}\right)$, which is in turn formed from the extension $\underset{\sim}{A}$, is generally greater than $\underset{\sim}{A}$; it is equal to $\underset{\sim}{A}$ only when f is an injection. The injection condition, however, is too stringent to be satisfied by many factors. In fact, in a given description frame $(U, C, F]$, the universe U could be sensitive to factors in F that have different states on different objects, and U could be insensitive to factors that have the same state on different objects. The most insensitive factor is the zero factor $\mathbf{0}$, i.e., $\forall u \in U,\ \mathbf{0}\,(u) = \theta$.

THEOREM 13

Let $(U, C, F]$ be a description frame and $\underset{\sim}{A}$ be the extension of concept $\alpha \in C$.
Then

1) $\mathbf{1}^{-1}\left(\mathbf{1}\left(\underset{\sim}{A}\right)\right) = \underset{\sim}{A}$;

2) $\mathbf{0}^{-1}\left(\mathbf{0}\left(\underset{\sim}{A}\right)\right)(u) \equiv hgt\left(\underset{\sim}{A}\right)$, *where* $hgt\left(\underset{\sim}{A}\right) = \bigvee_{u \in U} \underset{\sim}{A}\,(u)$, *the height of* $\underset{\sim}{A}$;

3) $(\forall f, g \in F)\left(f \geq g \Longrightarrow f^{-1}\left(f\left(\underset{\sim}{A}\right)\right) \subset g^{-1}\left(g\left(\underset{\sim}{A}\right)\right)\right)$.

PROOF

1) This is a direct corollary from theorem 10 and proposition 18.
2) For any $u \in U$, we have

$$\mathbf{0}^{-1}\left(\mathbf{0}\left(\underset{\sim}{A}\right)\right)(u) = \mathbf{0}\left(\underset{\sim}{A}\right)(\mathbf{0}\,(u)) = \bigvee_{\mathbf{0}(u')=\mathbf{0}(u)} \underset{\sim}{A}\,(u')$$

$$= \bigvee_{u' \in U} A_{\sim} (u') = hgt \left(A_{\sim} \right)$$

3) For any $u \in U$, we have

$$f^{-1} \left(f \left(A_{\sim} \right) \right) (u) = f \left(A_{\sim} \right) (f (u)) = \bigvee_{f(u')=f(u)} A_{\sim} (u') ,$$

and

$$g^{-1} \left(g \left(A_{\sim} \right) \right) (u) = g \left(A_{\sim} \right) (g (u)) = \bigvee_{g(u')=g(u)} A_{\sim} (u') .$$

Since $f \geq g$, this implies that

$$\left(\forall u' \in U \right) \left(f \left(u' \right) = f (u) \Longrightarrow g \left(u' \right) = g (u) \right)$$

$$\Longrightarrow \left\{ u' \in U \mid f \left(u' \right) = f (u) \right\} \subset \left\{ u' \in U \mid g \left(u' \right) = g (u) \right\}$$

$$\Longrightarrow \bigvee_{f(u')=f(u)} A_{\sim} (u') \leq \bigvee_{g(u')=g(u)} A_{\sim} (u') .$$

From this we can conclude that $f^{-1} \left(f \left(A_{\sim} \right) \right) \subset g^{-1} \left(g \left(A_{\sim} \right) \right)$ is valid.   ∎

The theorem explains that 1) the feedback extension concerning the complete factor is completely coincident with the extension; and 2) the feedback extension concerning the zero factor coincides with $A_{\sim}$ if the extension $A_{\sim}$ satisfies the following accessibility condition:

$$(\exists u \in U) \left(A_{\sim} (u) = hgt \left(A_{\sim} \right) \right) .$$

3) The "greater" (or more "complicated") the factor, the closer it is between the feedback extension of that factor and the extension.

Figure 3.1 illustrates these three points.

The significance of the notion of feedback extension is that it offers a theoretical foundation and an operational method for the representation of concepts. In fact, for every concept α there is a description frame $(U, C, F]$ such that $\alpha \in C$. Generally speaking, its extension $A_{\sim}$ $(\in \mathcal{F} (U))$ is unknown. If we can obtain the representation extension $B_{\sim} (1) \in \mathcal{F} (X (1))$ of α in the complete representation universe $X (1)$, then from the results discussed above we immediately get $A_{\sim} = 1^{-1} \left(B_{\sim} (1) \right)$. Unfortunately, the complete factor 1 is often too complicated to

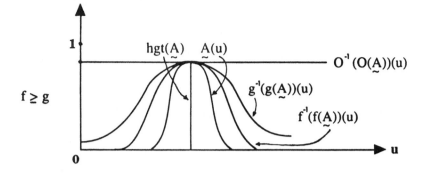

FIGURE 3.1
Approximate the extension by feedback extensions.

find directly. This leads us to consider: 1) decomposing a complicated factor into a set of simpler factors, 2) the representation extension of these simpler factors with respect to the concept α, and 3) the relationship of the representation extension of the complicated factor and the representation extension of its simpler factors. The following proposition points out this relationship.

PROPOSITION 19

Let $(U, C, F]$ be a description frame and $\underset{\sim}{A}$ be the extension of concept $\alpha \in C$. For any $f, g \in F$; if $f \geq g$, then

$$\uparrow_g^f \, g \left(\underset{\sim}{A} \right) \supset f \left(\underset{\sim}{A} \right) \tag{3.3}$$

PROOF   For any $(x, y) \in X(f) = X(g) \times X(f - g)$, we have

$$\left(\uparrow_g^f \, g \left(\underset{\sim}{A} \right) \right) (x, y) = g \left(\underset{\sim}{A} \right) (x) = \bigvee_{g(u)=x} \underset{\sim}{A} (u)$$

$$f \left(\underset{\sim}{A} \right) (x, y) = \bigvee_{f(u)=(x,y)} \underset{\sim}{A} (u)$$

Notice that $f(u) = (x, y) = g(u) = x$. Hence (3.3) is valid.   ∎

Note 1. In (3.3), let $f = 1$ and $g = f$; then

$$\uparrow_f^1 \, f \left(\underset{\sim}{A} \right) \supset 1 \left(\underset{\sim}{A} \right). \tag{3.4}$$

Note 2. Expression (3.3) indicates that, by means of cylindrical extension, we can get, from the representation extension $g\left(\underset{\sim}{A}\right)$ of α with respect to a simpler factor g, a "rough" representation extension $\uparrow_g^f \, g\left(\underset{\sim}{A}\right)$ of α with respect to a more complicated factor f than g. Thus we have a "rough" feedback extension

$$f^{-1}\left(\uparrow_g^f \, g\left(\underset{\sim}{A}\right)\right) \supset f^{-1}\left(f\left(\underset{\sim}{A}\right)\right) \tag{3.5}$$

Equation (3.4) results in

$$f^{-1}\left(\uparrow_f^1 \, f\left(\underset{\sim}{A}\right)\right) \supset 1^{-1}\left(1\left(\underset{\sim}{A}\right)\right) \tag{3.6}$$

The word "rough" used here means that the approximation of the feedback extension of a complicated factor f by the feedback extension formed by the representation extension of a simpler factor g is not precise enough. How to increase the precision of the above approximation is our next vital issue.

It is clear that the solution to this problem will be dependent upon the "collective power" of simpler factors; namely, the representation extension of complicated factors can be constructed through the use of representation extensions of a few, but important, simpler factors.

THEOREM 14
Let $(U, C, F]$ be a description frame, and $\underset{\sim}{A}$ be the extension of concept $\alpha \in C$. For any $f, g \in F$; if $f \wedge g = 0$, then

$$f^{-1}\left(f\left(\underset{\sim}{A}\right)\right) \cap g^{-1}\left(g\left(\underset{\sim}{A}\right)\right) =$$

$$(f \vee g)^{-1}\left(\left(\uparrow_f^{f\vee g} \, f\left(\underset{\sim}{A}\right)\right) \cap \left(\uparrow_g^{f\vee g} \, g\left(\underset{\sim}{A}\right)\right)\right)$$

PROOF   Since $f \wedge g = 0$ and $X(f \vee g) = X(f) \times X(g)$, then for any $u \in U$, we have

$$(f \vee g)(u) = (f(u), g(u)) \in X(f) \times X(g),$$

which means that $f \vee g$ is a vector-valued function. Therefore,

$$\left[f^{-1}\left(f\left(\underset{\sim}{A}\right)\right) \cap g^{-1}\left(g\left(\underset{\sim}{A}\right)\right)\right](u)$$

$$= f^{-1}\left(f\left(\underset{\sim}{A}\right)\right)(u) \wedge g^{-1}\left(g\left(\underset{\sim}{A}\right)\right)(u)$$

$$= f\left(\underset{\sim}{A}\right)\left(f(u) \wedge g\left(\underset{\sim}{A}\right)g(u)\right)$$

$$= \left(\uparrow_f^{f\vee g} f\left(\underset{\sim}{A}\right)\right)((f \vee g)(u)) \wedge \left(\uparrow_g^{f\vee g} g\left(\underset{\sim}{A}\right)\right)((f \vee g)(u))$$

$$= (f \vee g)^{-1}\left(\left(\uparrow_f^{f\vee g} f\left(\underset{\sim}{A}\right)\right) \cap \left(\uparrow_g^{f\vee g} g\left(\underset{\sim}{A}\right)\right)\right)(u).$$

This completes the proof. ∎

Note: The result can be generalized to the "infinite" case. For any subset $G \subset F$, set $\bigvee G = \bigvee\limits_{f\in G} f$. If the factors in G are mutually independent, then

$$\bigcap_{f\in G} f^{-1}\left(f\left(\underset{\sim}{A}\right)\right) = \left(\bigvee G\right)^{-1}\left(\bigcap_{f\in G}\left(\uparrow_f^{\vee G} f\left(\underset{\sim}{A}\right)\right)\right). \qquad (3.7)$$

COROLLARY 6

Under the same conditions of the above theorem, if F is an atomic set of factors, we have

$$\bigcap_{f\in\pi} f^{-1}\left(f\left(\underset{\sim}{A}\right)\right) = 1^{-1}\left(\bigcap_{f\in\pi}\left(\uparrow_f^1 f\left(\underset{\sim}{A}\right)\right)\right). \qquad (3.8)$$

Figure 3.2 illustrates theorem 14.

DEFINITION 9   *Let $(U, C, F]$ be a description frame and $\underset{\sim}{A}$ be the extension of concept $\alpha \in C$. Assume $G \subset F$ and elements of G are mutually independent. Write*

$$\underset{\sim}{A}[G] = \bigcap_{f\in G} f^{-1}\left(f\left(\underset{\sim}{A}\right)\right). \qquad (3.9)$$

$\underset{\sim}{A}[G]$ *is called the* **envelope of G-feedback extension** *of $\underset{\sim}{A}$, or simply,* **G-envelope** *of $\underset{\sim}{A}$.*

When f is an atomic set of factors, $\underset{\sim}{A}[\pi]$ is called the **closure of atomic feedback extensions,** *or simply, π-closure.*

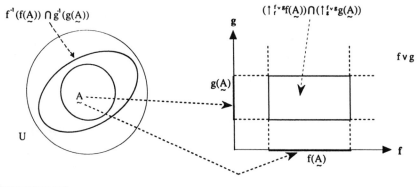

FIGURE 3.2
Illustration of theorem 14.

Figure 3.3 illustrates the *G*-envelope and π-closure.

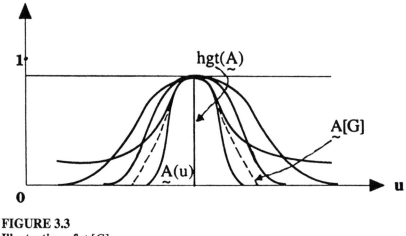

FIGURE 3.3
Illustration of $A[G]$.

The *G*-envelope (or π-closure) of A is an approximation of the extension of A by the concept of "collective power" described previously. This approach is similar to the approximation of a circle by using a polygon from the exterior of a circle.

3.2   Feedback Ranks and Degrees of Coincidence

Let $(U, C, F]$ be a description frame and $\underset{\sim}{A}$ ($\in \mathcal{F}(U)$) be the extension of concept $\alpha \in C$. For any factor $f \in F$, the feedback extension $f^{-1}\left(f\left(\underset{\sim}{A}\right)\right)$ is, in fact, the composition of two mappings: f and $f\left(\underset{\sim}{A}\right)$, i.e.,

$$f^{-1}\left(f\left(\underset{\sim}{A}\right)\right) = f\left(\underset{\sim}{A}\right) \circ f. \tag{3.10}$$

PROPOSITION 20
Let $(U, C, F]$ be a description frame and $\underset{\sim}{A}$ be the extension of concept $\alpha \in C$. For $f, g \in F$, if $f \geq g$, then

$$g\left(\underset{\sim}{A}\right) \circ g = \underset{\sim}{A} \Longrightarrow f\left(\underset{\sim}{A}\right) \circ f = \underset{\sim}{A}. \tag{3.11}$$

PROOF   According to 3) of theorem 13, we have

$$\underset{\sim}{A} \subset f\left(\underset{\sim}{A}\right) \circ f \subset g\left(\underset{\sim}{A}\right) \circ g = \underset{\sim}{A}.$$

Therefore, $f\left(\underset{\sim}{A}\right) \circ f = \underset{\sim}{A}.$ ∎

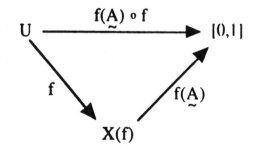

FIGURE 3.4
Equation 3.11.

This result inspired us to give the following

DEFINITION 10   *Let* $(U, C, F]$ *be a description frame and* $\underset{\sim}{A}$ *be the extension of concept* $\alpha \in C$. *Write*

$$P = \left\{ f \in F \mid f \left(\underset{\sim}{A} \right) \circ f = \underset{\sim}{A} \right\}.$$

Clearly $P \neq \Phi$ *(for* $\mathbf{1} \in P$*). For any* $f \in F$, f *is called* **coincident** *with respect to* α *if* $f \in P$. *We define*

$$\tau(\alpha) = \tau \left(\underset{\sim}{A} \right) = \bigwedge P = \bigwedge_{f \in P} f \qquad (3.12)$$

to be the **feedback rank** *of* α.

By using the feedback rank of a concept α, we can divide F into four parts as shown in Figure 3.5.

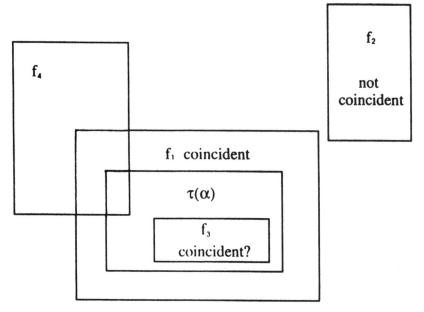

FIGURE 3.5
Classification of factors by the degree of coincidence.

When $f \geq \tau(\alpha)$, f is coincident with α; otherwise, it is not. We now look at subfactors of $\tau(\alpha)$. These subfactors have low dimensions. When they are used for the approximation of $\underset{\sim}{A}$, the difference is rather small (although they are not completely coincident with A). Our next question is: "What about the degree of coincidence of such subfactors?"

DEFINITION 11   *Given a description frame $(U, C, F]$, the mapping*

$$C : F \times \mathcal{F}(U) \longrightarrow [0, 1] \qquad \text{defined by}$$

$$\left(f, \underset{\sim}{A} \right) \longmapsto C \left(f, \underset{\sim}{A} \right) = \sup \left\{ 1 - f \left(\underset{\sim}{A} \right) (f(u)) + \underset{\sim}{A}(u) \mid u \in U \right\}$$

is called the **measure of coincidence.** *(See Figure 3.6.)*

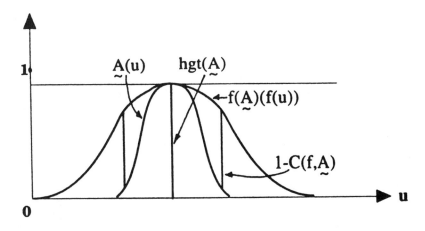

FIGURE 3.6
The degree of coincidence.

LEMMA 1
Given a mapping $f : X \longrightarrow Y$, and fuzzy subsets $\underset{\sim}{A}, \underset{\sim}{B} \in \mathcal{F}(X)$, the following expressions hold.

1) $\underset{\sim}{A} \subset \underset{\sim}{B} \Longrightarrow f^{-1} \left(f \left(\underset{\sim}{A} \right) \right) \subset f^{-1} \left(f \left(\underset{\sim}{B} \right) \right)$;

2) $f^{-1} \left(f \left(\underset{\sim}{A} \cup \underset{\sim}{B} \right) \right) = f^{-1} \left(f \left(\underset{\sim}{A} \right) \right) \cup f^{-1} \left(f \left(\underset{\sim}{B} \right) \right)$;

3) $f^{-1} \left(f \left(\underset{\sim}{A} \cap \underset{\sim}{B} \right) \right) \subset f^{-1} \left(f \left(\underset{\sim}{A} \right) \right) \cap f^{-1} \left(f \left(\underset{\sim}{B} \right) \right)$.

PROOF   We will prove 3) because 1) and 2) are straightforward.

For any $x \in X$, x satisfies

$$f^{-1}\left(f\left(\underset{\sim}{A} \cap \underset{\sim}{B}\right)\right)(x) = f\left(\underset{\sim}{A} \cap \underset{\sim}{B}\right)(f(x)) = \bigvee_{f(x')=f(x)}\left(\underset{\sim}{A} \cap \underset{\sim}{B}\right)(x')$$

$$= \bigvee_{f(x')=f(x)}\left(\underset{\sim}{A} \cap \underset{\sim}{B}\right)(x') = \bigvee_{f(x')=f(x)}\left(\underset{\sim}{A}(x') \wedge \underset{\sim}{B}(x')\right)$$

$$\leq \left(\bigvee_{f(x')=f(x)}\underset{\sim}{A}(x')\right)\bigwedge\left(\bigvee_{f(x')=f(x)}\underset{\sim}{B}(x')\right)$$

$$= f\left(\underset{\sim}{A}\right)(f(x)) \wedge f\left(\underset{\sim}{B}\right)(f(x))$$

$$= f^{-1}\left(f\left(\underset{\sim}{A}\right)\right)(x) \wedge f^{-1}\left(f\left(\underset{\sim}{B}\right)\right)(x).$$

Thus 3) is proved.   ∎

THEOREM 15
Let $(U, C, F]$ be a description frame and $\underset{\sim}{A}$ and $\underset{\sim}{B}$ be the extensions of the concept α and β in C, respectively. For any $f \in F$, if f is coincident with α and β, respectively, then f is also coincident with the conjunction and disjunction concept of α and β, i.e.,

$$f\left(\underset{\sim}{A} \cup \underset{\sim}{B}\right) \circ f = \underset{\sim}{A} \cup \underset{\sim}{B}, \quad and \quad f\left(\underset{\sim}{A} \cap \underset{\sim}{B}\right) \circ f = \underset{\sim}{A} \cap \underset{\sim}{B}. \qquad (3.13)$$

PROOF   By lemma 1,

$$f\left(\underset{\sim}{A} \cup \underset{\sim}{B}\right) \circ f = \left(f\left(\underset{\sim}{A}\right) \circ f\right) \cup \left(f\left(\underset{\sim}{B}\right) \circ f\right) = \underset{\sim}{A} \cup \underset{\sim}{B}$$

and,

$$\underset{\sim}{A} \cap \underset{\sim}{B} \subset f\left(\underset{\sim}{A} \cap \underset{\sim}{B}\right) \circ f \subset \left(f\left(\underset{\sim}{A}\right) \circ f\right) \cap \left(f\left(\underset{\sim}{B}\right) \circ f\right) = \underset{\sim}{A} \cap \underset{\sim}{B}.$$

Therefore (3.13) is valid. ∎

Note. Let $(U, C, F]$ be a description frame and $f \in F$. Put

$$\mathcal{F}_f(U) = \left\{ \underset{\sim}{A} \in \mathcal{F}(U) \mid f\left(\underset{\sim}{A}\right) \circ f = \underset{\sim}{A} \right\} \tag{3.14}$$

It is not difficult to show that the algebraic system $(\mathcal{F}_f(U), \cup, \cap)$ is a complete sublattice of $\mathcal{F}(U)$ and $U, \Phi \in \mathcal{F}_f(U)$. Moreover, by proposition 20, for any $f, g \in F$, we have

$$f \geq g \Longrightarrow \mathcal{F}_f(U) \supset \mathcal{F}_g(U),$$

and

$$\mathcal{F}_1(U) = \mathcal{F}(U), \quad \mathcal{F}_0(U) = \Phi.$$

THEOREM 16
Let $(U, C, F]$ be a description frame, C be a measure of coincidence in the frame, and $\underset{\sim}{A}$ and $\underset{\sim}{B}$ $(\in \mathcal{F}(U))$ be the extensions of concepts α, $\beta \in C$, respectively. Then for $f, g \in F$, they satisfy

1) $f \geq g \Longrightarrow C\left(f, \underset{\sim}{A}\right) \geq C\left(g, \underset{\sim}{A}\right)$,

2) $C\left(f, \underset{\sim}{A} \cup \underset{\sim}{B}\right) \leq C\left(f, \underset{\sim}{A}\right) \vee C\left(f, \underset{\sim}{B}\right)$, and

3) $C\left(f, \underset{\sim}{A} \cap \underset{\sim}{B}\right) \geq C\left(f, \underset{\sim}{A}\right) \wedge C\left(f, \underset{\sim}{B}\right)$.

PROOF
1) Since

$$f \geq g \Longrightarrow f\left(\underset{\sim}{A}\right) \circ f \subset g\left(\underset{\sim}{A}\right) \circ g$$

then,

$$C\left(f, \underset{\sim}{A}\right) = \sup\left\{1 - f\left(\underset{\sim}{A}\right)\left(f(u) + \underset{\sim}{A}(u) \mid u \in U\right)\right\}$$

$$\leq \sup\left\{1 - g\left(\underset{\sim}{A}\right)\left(g(u) + \underset{\sim}{A}(u) \mid u \in U\right)\right\} = C\left(g, \underset{\sim}{A}\right).$$

2) $\qquad C\left(f, \underset{\sim}{A} \cup \underset{\sim}{B}\right)$

$$= \sup\left\{1 - f\left(\underset{\sim}{A} \cup \underset{\sim}{B}\right)(f(u)) + \left(\underset{\sim}{A} \cup \underset{\sim}{B}\right)(u) \mid u \in U\right\}$$

$$= \sup \left\{ 1 - \left(f\left(\underset{\sim}{A}\right) f(u) \vee f\left(\underset{\sim}{B}\right) f(u) \right) + \left(\underset{\sim}{A}(u) \vee \underset{\sim}{B}(u) \right) \mid u \in U \right\}$$

Case 1. $f\left(\underset{\sim}{A}\right)(f(u)) \leq f\left(\underset{\sim}{B}\right)(f(u))$ and $\underset{\sim}{A}(u) \leq \underset{\sim}{B}(u)$.

$$C\left(f, \underset{\sim}{A} \cup \underset{\sim}{B}\right) = \sup \left\{ 1 - f\left(\underset{\sim}{B}\right)(f(u)) + \underset{\sim}{B}(u) \mid u \in U \right\}$$

$$= C\left(f, \underset{\sim}{B}\right) \leq C\left(f, \underset{\sim}{A}\right) \vee C\left(f, \underset{\sim}{B}\right)$$

Case 2. $f\left(\underset{\sim}{A}\right)(f(u)) \leq f\left(\underset{\sim}{B}\right)(f(u))$ and $\underset{\sim}{A}(u) > \underset{\sim}{B}(u)$.

$$C\left(f, \underset{\sim}{A} \cup \underset{\sim}{B}\right) = \sup \left\{ 1 - f\left(\underset{\sim}{A}\right)(f(u)) + \underset{\sim}{B}(u) \mid u \in U \right\}$$

$$\leq \sup \left\{ 1 - f\left(\underset{\sim}{A}\right)(f(u)) + \underset{\sim}{A}(u) \mid u \in U \right\}$$

$$= C\left(f, \underset{\sim}{A}\right) \leq C\left(f, \underset{\sim}{A}\right) \vee C\left(f, \underset{\sim}{B}\right)$$

Case 3. $f\left(\underset{\sim}{A}\right)(f(u)) > f\left(\underset{\sim}{B}\right)(f(u))$ and $\underset{\sim}{A}(u) \leq \underset{\sim}{B}(u)$.

$$C\left(f, \underset{\sim}{A} \cup \underset{\sim}{B}\right) = \sup \left\{ 1 - f\left(\underset{\sim}{A}\right)(f(u)) + \underset{\sim}{B}(u) \mid u \in U \right\}$$

$$\leq \sup \left\{ 1 - f\left(\underset{\sim}{B}\right)(f(u)) + \underset{\sim}{B}(u) \mid u \in U \right\}$$

$$= C\left(f, \underset{\sim}{B}\right) \leq C\left(f, \underset{\sim}{A}\right) \vee C\left(f, \underset{\sim}{B}\right)$$

Case 4. $f\left(\underset{\sim}{A}\right)(f(u)) > f\left(\underset{\sim}{B}\right)(f(u))$ and $\underset{\sim}{A}(u) > \underset{\sim}{B}(u)$.

$$C\left(f, \underset{\sim}{A} \cup \underset{\sim}{B}\right) = \sup \left\{ 1 - f\left(\underset{\sim}{A}\right)(f(u)) + \underset{\sim}{A}(u) \mid u \in U \right\}$$

$$= C\left(f, \underset{\sim}{B}\right) \leq C\left(f, \underset{\sim}{A}\right) \vee C\left(f, \underset{\sim}{B}\right)$$

3) The proof is similar to 2).   ∎

3.3 Equivalence Between Sufficient Factors and Coincident Factors

Are there any relationships between sufficient factors and coincident ones? An answer is in the following:

PROPOSITION 21

Let $(U, C, F]$ be a description frame and $\underset{\sim}{A}$ be the extension of concept $\alpha \in C$. For any $f \in F$, f satisfies

$$f^{-1}\left(f\left(\underset{\sim}{A}\right)\right) = \underset{\sim}{A} \Longleftrightarrow \uparrow_f^1 \left(\downarrow_f^1 1\left(\underset{\sim}{A}\right)\right) = 1\left(\underset{\sim}{A}\right) \qquad (3.15)$$

which means that f is sufficient if and only if f is coincident, with respect to α.

PROOF

$$\uparrow_f^1\left(\downarrow_f^1 1\left(\underset{\sim}{A}\right)\right) = 1\left(\underset{\sim}{A}\right) \Longleftrightarrow \underset{\sim}{A} = 1^{-1}\left(\uparrow_f^1\left(\downarrow_f^1 1\left(\underset{\sim}{A}\right)\right)\right)$$

$$\Longleftrightarrow \text{For any } u \in U,$$

$$\underset{\sim}{A}(u) = \left(\uparrow_f^1\left(\downarrow_f^1 1\left(\underset{\sim}{A}\right)\right)\right)(1(u))$$

$$= \left(\downarrow_f^1\left(\downarrow_f^1 1\left(\underset{\sim}{A}\right)\right)\right)(f(u), f^c(u))$$

$$= \left(\downarrow_f^1 1\left(\underset{\sim}{A}\right)\right)(f(u)) = \bigvee_{y \in X(f^c)} 1\left(\underset{\sim}{A}\right)(f(u), y)$$

$$= \bigvee_{y \in X(f^c)}\left(\bigvee\left\{\underset{\sim}{A}(u'') \mid 1(u'') = (f(u), y)\right\}\right)$$

$$= \bigvee_{y \in X(f^c)}\left(\bigvee\left\{\underset{\sim}{A}(u'') \mid (f(u''), f^c(u'')) = (f(u), y)\right\}\right)$$

Since the complete factor **1** is a surjection (see note 1 of theorem 10), the preceding simplifies to

$$= \bigvee \left\{ \underset{\sim}{A} \left(u' \right) \mid f \left(u' \right) = f \left(u \right) \right\}$$

$$= f \left(\underset{\sim}{A} \right) (f (u)) = f^{-1} \left(f \left(\underset{\sim}{A} \right) \right) (u)$$

This finishes the proof.   ∎

COROLLARY 7

Under the same conditions of the theorem, then

$$\tau (\alpha) = r (\alpha) \tag{3.16}$$

That means the rank of a concept is just the feedback rank of that concept.

Note: In applications, $\tau (\alpha)$ is simpler than $r (\alpha)$.

3.4   How to Improve the Precision of Feedback Extension

3.4.1   The Problem

Let $(U, C, F]$ be a description frame and $\underset{\sim}{A}$ be the extension of concept $\alpha \in C$. Assume $G (\subset F)$ is a family of mutually independent factors. From (3.9) we can get $G-$envelope $\underset{\sim}{A}[G]$ of $\underset{\sim}{A}$. For convenience, G is assumed to be a finite set, e.g., $G = \{f_1, f_2, ..., f_n\}$. Then

$$\underset{\sim}{A} [G] = \bigcap_{i=1}^{n} f_i^{-1} \left(f_i \left(\underset{\sim}{A} \right) \right).$$

If we put $f = \bigvee G = \bigvee_{i=1}^{n} f_i$, then $X (f) = \prod_{i=1}^{n} X (f_i)$. Since $u \in U$ and $\underset{\sim}{A} \subset \underset{\sim}{A} [G]$, then

$$\underset{\sim}{A} (u) \leq \underset{\sim}{A} [G] (u) = \bigwedge_{i=1}^{n} f_i \left(\underset{\sim}{A} \right) (f_i (u))$$

$$= \left(\prod_{i=1}^{n} f_i \left(\underset{\sim}{A} \right) \right) (f_1(u), f_2(u), ..., f_n(u)) \qquad (3.17)$$

This expression may be simplified to the following if we put $\underset{\sim}{B}(f_i) = f_i\left(\underset{\sim}{A}\right)$ and $x_i = f_i(u)$ for $1 \le i \le n$:

$$\underset{\sim}{A}(u) \le \underset{\sim}{A}[G](u) = \bigwedge_{i=1}^{n} \underset{\sim}{B}(f_i)(x_i) = \left(\prod_{i=1}^{n} \underset{\sim}{B}(f_i) \right)(x_1, x_2, ..., x_n) \qquad (3.18)$$

In practical applications, the extension $\underset{\sim}{A}$ is often unknown, and hence $f\left(\underset{\sim}{A}\right)$ is also unknown. A method that we consider to be the most convenient is to form representation extensions $\underset{\sim}{B}(f_i)$ of the concept α on the representation universe $X(f_i)$. (For methods on membership functions, see Chapter 4 and Chapter 8 in this book.) Next, we construct cylindrical extensions $\uparrow_{f_i}^{f} \underset{\sim}{B}(f_i)$. The intersection of cylindrical extensions is an approximate representation extension of α on representation universe $X(f)$. In mathematical terms,

$$\bigcap_{i=1}^{n} \left(\uparrow_{f_i}^{f} \underset{\sim}{B}(f_i) \right) \supset \uparrow_{f_i}^{f} \underset{\sim}{B}(f) \qquad (3.19)$$

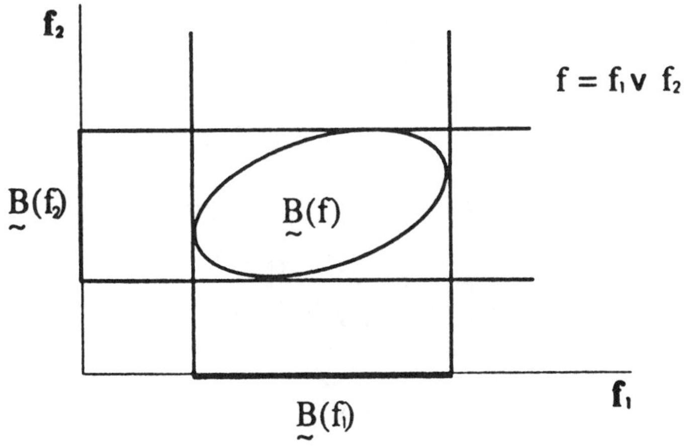

FIGURE 3.7
An approximation of the representation extension.

Figure 3.7 illustrates that the approximation method is quite rough. It is like "containing a potato with a box". How to improve the precision of the approximation method mentioned above is a key problem for our investigation. The following two approaches are good candidates in this direction:

1) "Trimming" the edges and corners of the box as close to the potato as possible (Figure 3.8)

2) "Subdividing" the box into a sufficient number of small boxes to better fit the entire potato (Figure 3.9).

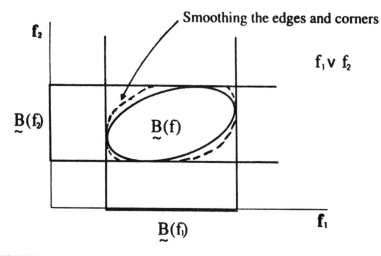

FIGURE 3.8
Trimming the edges and corners.

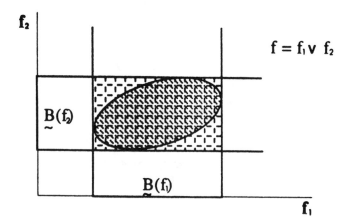

FIGURE 3.9
Subdivision. (Shaded areas are reserved.)

3.4.2 Operations of Fuzzy Sets on Different Universes

Let X and Y be two nonempty universes and $A \in \mathcal{F}(X)$ and $B \in \mathcal{F}(Y)$. It is well known that we cannot perform the operations of intersection and union between A and B because X and Y are different universes. However, in certain cases we do need to perform such operations. For example, let α, β, and γ be three concepts and let A, B, and C be the extensions of these concepts, respectively. Furthermore, assume that A, B, and C can be described on the universes X, Y, and $X \times Y$, respectively, i.e.;

$$A \in \mathcal{F}(X), \quad B \in \mathcal{F}(Y), \quad \text{and} \quad C \in \mathcal{F}(X \times Y).$$

If concept γ is determined by the concepts α and β, (e.g., $\gamma = \alpha$ and β, or $\gamma = \alpha$ or β), then it is necessary to perform the intersection and union operations on A and B . For this reason, we now expand the universes X and Y to $X \times Y$ by the method of **cylindrical extension**:

$$\uparrow A = \uparrow_X^{X \times Y} A \quad and \quad \uparrow B = \uparrow_X^{X \times Y} B . \tag{3.20}$$

Where $\forall (x, y) \in X \times Y$,

$$\uparrow A (x, y) = A (x) \quad and \quad \uparrow B (x, y) = B (y) . \tag{3.21}$$

Thus we can perform the intersection and union operations on A and B because now they are on the same universe $X \times Y$. These operations are defined below:

$$\left(A \cap B \right) (x, y) = \left(\left(\uparrow A \right) \cap \left(\uparrow B \right) \right) (x, y) = A (x) \wedge B (y) \tag{3.22}$$

$$\left(A \cup B \right) (x, y) = \left(\left(\uparrow A \right) \cup \left(\uparrow B \right) \right) (x, y) = A (x) \vee B (y) \tag{3.23}$$

Recall the definition of the direct product of fuzzy sets given in Chapter 1. We can state

$$A \cap B = A \times B . \tag{3.24}$$

Figure 3.10 illustrates the meaning of $A \cap B$.

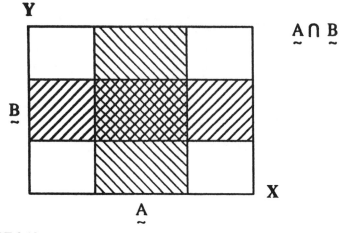

FIGURE 3.10

$A \cap B = A \times B$.
$\underset{\sim}{A} \cap \underset{\sim}{B} = \underset{\sim}{A} \times \underset{\sim}{B}$.

3.4.3   A Tool to Trim Edges and Corners — The Triangular Norm

From (3.18), (3.19), and (3.24), we can write

$$\underset{\sim}{A}[G] = \left(\bigcap_{i=1}^{n} \underset{\sim}{B}(f_i) \right) \circ f = \left(\bigcap_{i=1}^{n} f_i \left(\underset{\sim}{A} \right) \right) \circ f \qquad (3.25)$$

which means that $\underset{\sim}{A}[G]$, in fact, is the intersection of representation extensions $\underset{\sim}{B}(f_i)$. For the purpose of improving the ability of approximating $\underset{\sim}{A}$ by $\underset{\sim}{A}[G]$, it is necessary for us to modify the definition of fuzzy "and" and the operator "$\wedge$". Naturally, we are led to the triangular norm. In reality, "$\wedge$" is the greatest triangular norm; in other words, it is the roughest triangular norm. This suggests that there are triangular norms that can be more effective in trimming edges and corners of the box.

DEFINITION 12   *A mapping $T : [0, 1] \times [0, 1] \longrightarrow [0, 1]$ is called a* **quasi-triangular norm** *if it satisfies the following conditions:*

t.1) $T(0, 0) = 0,\ T(1, 1) = 1$;
t.2) $T(x, y) = T(y, x)$;
t.3) $(x \leq x',\ y \leq y') \Longrightarrow T(x, y) \leq T(x', y')$; and
t.4) $T(T(x, y)z) = T(x, T(y, z))$.

A quasi-triangular norm T is called a **triangular norm** if it satisfies
       t.1') $T(x, 1) = x$,
and T is called a **complementary triangular norm** if it satisfies

t.1") $T(x, 0) = x$.

Note that either t.1') or t.1") will imply t.1).

When a quasi-triangular (triangular, or complementary) norm is a continuous function, we call it a continuous quasi-triangular (triangular, or complementary) norm.

DEFINITION 13   *Let T be a triangular norm and T^* be a complementary triangular norm. Then T and T^* are called* **correlated** *if they satisfy*

t.5) $T(x, y) + T^*(1 - x, 1 - y) = 1$.

PROPOSITION 22

For any triangular norm T, there exists a unique complementary triangular norm T^* that correlates with T; if T is continuous, so is T^*. Conversely, for any complementary triangular norm T^*, there exists a unique triangular norm T that correlates with T^*; if T^* is continuous, so is T.

PROOF   We will prove the "existence" since the "uniqueness" and the "continuity" are trivial.

From the condition t.5), for any triangular norm T we can set

$$T^*(x, y) = 1 - T(1 - x, 1 - y).$$

Clearly, this is a mapping from $[0, 1] \times [0, 1]$ to $[0, 1]$.

We now prove T^* satisfies t.1"), t.2), t.3), and t.4).

t.1"): $T^*(0, x) = 1 - T(1 - 0, 1 - x) = 1 - (1 - x) = x$.

t.2): $T^*(x, y) = 1 - T(1 - x, 1 - y) = 1 - T(1 - y, 1 - x) = T^*(y, x)$.

t.3): If $x \le x'$ and $y \le y'$ then

$$T^*(x, y) = 1 - T(1 - x, 1 - y) \le 1 - T\left(1 - x', 1 - y'\right) = T^*(y, x).$$

t.4):

$$T^*\left(T^*(x, y), z\right) = 1 - T(1 - T(x, y), 1 - z)$$

$$= 1 - T(T(1 - x, 1 - y), 1 - z)$$

$$= 1 - T(1 - x, T(1 - y, 1 - z))$$

$$= 1 - T\left(1 - x, 1 - T^*(y, z)\right)$$

$$= T^*\left(x, T^*(y, z)\right).$$

So T^* is a complementary triangular norm and it correlates with T. The other half of the proof is similar and hence omitted.   ∎

Example 14
Following are examples of triangular norms from $[0, 1]$ to $[0, 1]$.

$\bigwedge : (x, y) \longmapsto \bigwedge (x, y) = x \wedge y = \min \{x, y\}$

$\bullet : (x, y) \longmapsto (x, y) = x \bullet y = xy$

$\Delta : (x, y) \longmapsto \Delta (x, y) = x \Delta y = \begin{cases} y, & x = 1 \\ x, & y = 1 \\ 0, & x \neq 1, \; and \; y \neq 1 \end{cases}$

$\odot : (x, y) \longmapsto \odot (x, y) = x \odot y = \max \{x + y - 1, 0\}$ ▯

Example 15
Following are examples of complementary triangular norms from $[0, 1]$ to $[0, 1]$.

$\bigvee : (x, y) \longmapsto \bigvee (x, y) = x \vee y = \max \{x, y\}$

$\overset{\bullet}{+} : (x, y) \longmapsto \overset{\bullet}{+} (x, y) = x \overset{\bullet}{+} y = x + y - xy$

$\nabla : (x, y) \longmapsto \nabla (x, y) = x \nabla y = \begin{cases} y, & x = 0 \\ x, & y = 0 \\ 0, & xy \neq 0 \end{cases}$

$\oplus : (x, y) \longmapsto \oplus (x, y) = x \oplus y = \min \{x + y, 1\}$ ▯

Applying these examples, we can show the following:

$$\bigwedge{}^* = \bigvee, \quad \bullet^* = \overset{\bullet}{+}, \quad \Delta^* = \nabla, \quad and \quad \odot^* = \oplus.$$

Let $\mathcal{T} (2) = \{T \mid T \text{ is a triangular norm}\}$ and $\mathcal{T}^* (2) = \{T^* \mid T^* \text{ is a comple-}$ mentary triangle$\}$. We define an ordered relation in $\mathcal{T} (2)$ and $\mathcal{T}^* (2)$ as follows:

$$T_1 \geq T_2 \iff (\forall x, y \in [0, 1]) (T_1 (x, y) \geq T_2 (x, y));$$

$$T_1^* \geq T_2^* \iff (\forall x, y \in [0, 1]) \left(T_1^* (x, y) \geq T_2^* (x, y)\right).$$

Then we can easily verify the validity of

$$(\forall T \in \mathcal{T} (2)) \left(\Delta \leq T \leq \bigwedge\right)$$

and

$$(\forall T^* \in \mathcal{T}^* (2)) \left(\bigvee \leq T^* \leq \nabla\right).$$

We note that proper selection of a suitable triangular norm can improve the approximation precision of $A[G]$ to A. The question, then, is how to select a good norm.

3.4.4 Multidimensional Triangular Norms

For purposes of operations of multiple fuzzy sets, it is useful to define the notion of multidimensional triangular norms. Let $[0, 1]^m$ be an m-dimensional cube and $X = (x_1, x_2, ..., x_m)$, and $Y = (y_1, y_2, ..., y_m) \in [0, 1]^m$. We define $X \leq Y$ if and only if $(\forall j)\,(x_j \leq y_j)$. Then "$\leq$" is a partial relation on the cube. Now we define three transformations on the cube:

$$p_i, q_i, \sigma_{ij}: [0, 1]^m \longrightarrow [0, 1]^m.$$

Explicitly,

$$p_i\,(X) = (1, ..., 1, x_i, 1, ..., 1)$$

$$q_i\,(X) = (0, ..., 0, x_i, 0, ..., 0)$$

$$\sigma_{ij}\,(X) = \sigma_{ij}\left(x_1, ..., x_i, ..., x_j, ..., x_m\right)$$

$$= \left(x_1, ..., x_{i-1}, x_j, x_{i+1}, ..., x_{j-1}, x_i, x_{j+1}, ..., x_m\right)$$

DEFINITION 14   *A mapping* $T_m : [0, 1]^m \longrightarrow [0, 1]$ *is called an* **m-dimensional quasi-triangular norm** *if it satisfies the following conditions:*

T.1) $T_m\,(0, ..., 0) = 0$ *and* $T_m\,(1, ..., 1) = 1$,
T.2) $T_m\left(\sigma_{ij}\,(X)\right) = T_m\,(X)$,
T.3) $X \leq Y \Longrightarrow T_m\,(X) \leq T_m\,(Y)$, *and,*
T.4) For any $X = (x_1, x_2, ..., x_m)$ *and* $Y = (x_m, ..., x_{2m-1})$,

$$T_m\,(T_m\,(X), x_{m+1}, ..., x_{2m-1}) = T_m\,(x_1, ..., x_{m-1}, T_m\,(Y)).$$

Obviously, T_2 is a (two-dimensional) quasi-triangular norm.

An m-dimensional quasi-triangular norm T_m is called an m-dimensional triangular norm if it satisfies

T.1') $T_m\,(P_i\,(X)) = x_i$.

Similarly, an m-dimensional quasi-triangular norm T_m is called an m-dimensional complementary triangular norm if it satisfies

T.1") $T_m\,(q_i\,(X)) = x_i$.

Let T_m be an m-dimensional triangular norm. Then T_m is called a reducible **m-dimensional triangular norm** if there exists triangular norms T_2, T_r, and T_{m-r}, where $r < m$, and $m \geq 2$, such that T_m satisfies

T.5) $T_m\,(X) = T_2\,(T_r\,(x_1, ..., x_r), T_{m-r}\,(x_{r+1}, ..., x_m))$

An m-dimensional triangular norm T_m is called a **completely reducible** m-dimensional triangular norm if there exists a triangular norm T_2 such that

$$T_m(X) = T_2(T_2(...T_2(T_2(x_1, x_2), x_3)..., x_{m-1}), x_m).$$

When the norm of an m-dimensional quasi-triangular (or triangular, or complementary triangular) is a continuous function, we call it a continuous m-dimensional quasi-triangular (or triangular, or complementary triangular) norm.

Let T_m be an m-dimensional triangular norm and T^* be an m-dimensional complementary triangular norm. We call T_m and T^* are correlated if they satisfy

T.7) $T_m(X) + T_m^*(X)(1 - x_1, ..., 1 - x_m) = 1$.

Similar to the proof of proposition 22, we can derive the following:

PROPOSITION 23

For any m-dimensional triangular norm T_m, there exists a unique m-dimensional complementary triangular norm T_m^* that correlates with T_m. If T_m is continuous, so does T_m^*. Conversely, for any m-dimensional complementary triangular norm T_m^*, there exists a unique m-dimensional triangular norm T_m that correlates with T_m^*. If T_m^* is continuous, so is T_m.

We can easily verify that T.1') or T.1") $\Longrightarrow$ T.1).

Example 16

Here are four examples of m-dimensional triangular norms from $[0, 1]^m$ to $[0, 1]$.

1. $\bigwedge : X \longmapsto \bigwedge(X) = \bigwedge\limits_{j=1}^{m} x_j.$

2. $\prod : X \longmapsto \prod(X) = \prod\limits_{j=1}^{m} x_j.$

3. $\triangle : X \longmapsto \triangle(X) = \begin{cases} x_i, & x_j = 1, \ j \neq i, 1 \leq j \leq m \\ 0, & x_j \neq 1, \ 1 \leq j \leq m \end{cases}$

4. $\odot : X \longmapsto \odot(X) = \max\left\{ \sum\limits_{j=1}^{m} x_j - m + 1, 0 \right\}$ ☐

Example 17

Here are four examples of m-dimensional complementary triangular norms from $[0, 1]^m$ to $[0, 1]$.

1. $\bigvee : X \longmapsto \bigvee(X) = \bigvee\limits_{j=1}^{m} x_j.$

2. $\prod' : X \longmapsto \prod'(X) = 1 - \prod\limits_{j=1}^{m} (1 - x_j).$

3. $\nabla : X \longmapsto \nabla(X) = \begin{cases} x_i, & x_j = 0, \ j \neq i, 1 \leq j \leq m \\ 1, & x_j \neq 0, \ 1 \leq j \leq m \end{cases}$

4. $\oplus : X \longmapsto \oplus(X) = \min\left\{ \sum\limits_{j=1}^{m} x_j, 1 \right\}$ 　□

From the last two examples, we see that $\bigwedge^* = \bigvee$, $\prod^* = \prod'$, $\triangle^* = \nabla$ and $\odot^* = \oplus$ hold.

Let $\mathcal{T}(m) = \{T_m \mid T_m \text{ is an m-dimensional triangular norm}\}$ and
$\mathcal{T}^*(m) = \{T_m^* \mid T_m^* \text{ is an m-dimensional complementary triangular norm}\}$.
Now we define an ordered relation in $\mathcal{T}(m)$ and $\mathcal{T}^*(m)$ as follows:

$$T_m^{(1)} \geq T_m^{(2)} \Longleftrightarrow (\forall X)\left(T_m^{(1)}(X) \geq T_m^{(2)}(X)\right)$$

$$T_m^{*1} \geq T_m^{*2} \Longleftrightarrow (\forall X)\left(T_m^{*1}(X) \geq T_m^{*2}(X)\right)$$

We can readily verify

$$(\forall T_m \in \mathcal{T}(m))\left(\triangle \leq T_m \leq \bigwedge\right)$$

and,

$$(\forall T_m^* \in \mathcal{T}^*(m))\left(\bigvee \leq T_m^* \leq \nabla\right).$$

3.5 Representation of the Intension of a Concept

3.5.1 ε-Essential Factors

Now we come to the point of attacking one of the most difficult questions in mathematics: How can the intension of a concept be represented mathematically? Factor space theory offers an answer to this question. First, we explain what is meant by ε-essential factors.

DEFINITION 15 *Let $(U, \mathcal{C}, F]$ be a description frame, $A \in \mathcal{F}(U)$ be the extension of $\alpha \in \mathcal{C}$, and C be the measure of coincidence in the frame. For any $f \in F$, f is called an ε-**essential factor** with respect to α if for any $\varepsilon \in [0, 1]$; then*

$$C\left(f, \underset{\sim}{A}\right) \geq 1 - \varepsilon. \tag{3.26}$$

3.5.2 Rough Representations of the Intension of a Concept

Let $(U, C, F]$ be a description frame and $\underset{\sim}{A} \in \mathcal{F}(U)$ be the extension of $\alpha \in C$. Define

$$G = \{f_i \mid f_i \in F, \ 1 \leq i \leq n\}$$

to be a family of mutually independent factors in F and each f_i to be an ε-essential factor. Put $f = \bigwedge_{i=1}^{n} f_i$. From (3.18) we have

$$\underset{\sim}{A}(u) \leq_{\underset{\sim}{A}} [G](u) = \bigwedge_{i=1}^{n} f_i \left(\underset{\sim}{A} \right) (f_i(u)).$$

If we take the G-envelope of α, $\underset{\sim}{A}[G]$, as an approximation of $\underset{\sim}{A}$, then the formula just described is a subdivision of the extension $\underset{\sim}{A}$ in its state spaces (/representation universes). Thus, we obtain this group of propositions:

$$f_1(u) \ is \ f_1 \left(\underset{\sim}{A} \right) \ and \ f_2(u) \ is \ f_2 \left(\underset{\sim}{A} \right) \ and \ ... \ and \ f_n(u) \ is \ f_n \left(\underset{\sim}{A} \right). \quad (3.27)$$

Let C be a measure of coincidence in the frame. Set $\varepsilon = 1 - C \left(f, \underset{\sim}{A} \right)$. Then the group of propositions is called the ε-**intension** of the concept α; it is a kind of (rough) representation of the intension of a concept, and ε is a real number measuring the precision of the approximation.

In practice, it is not easy to find ε, but with the conditions stated above, we can show

PROPOSITION 24

$$\varepsilon \leq \bigwedge_{i=1}^{n} \varepsilon_i.$$

PROOF

$$1 - \varepsilon = C \left(f, \underset{\sim}{A} \right) = C \left(\bigvee_{i=1}^{n} f_i, \underset{\sim}{A} \right) \geq \bigvee_{i=1}^{n} C \left(f_i, \underset{\sim}{A} \right)$$

$$\geq \bigvee_{i=1}^{n} (1 - \varepsilon_i) = 1 - \bigwedge_{i=1}^{n} \varepsilon_i \Longrightarrow \varepsilon \leq \bigwedge_{i=1}^{n} \varepsilon_i.$$

∎

The proposition provides a way for estimating ε. The smaller the ε is, the higher the degree of coincidence of the intension is. Also, the subdivision of the intension becomes more reasonable as ε gets smaller.

The group of propositions (3.27) says that the intension of α can be determined by the extension of α. Conversely, if we knew the intension of α, then we could obtain an approximate extension of α, $\underset{\sim}{A}$ [G], by (3.27) and (3.18).

The theory of factor spaces can describe the real world more realistically, more generally, and more figuratively, and it is a vital means for unifying both the intension and the extension of a concept.

3.5.3 More Precise Representations of the Intension

We now develop ways for increasing the precision of representation of the intension by means of refining the subdivisions.

Let $(U, \mathcal{C}, F]$ be a description frame and $\underset{\sim}{A} \in \mathcal{F}(U)$ be the extension of $\alpha \in \mathcal{C}$. Define

$$G = \{f_i \mid f_i \in F, \ 1 \leq i \leq n\}$$

to be a family of mutually independent factors in F, so $G \subset F$. Put $f = \bigvee_{i=1}^{n} f_i$. Referring to Figure 3.9, the representation extension $\underset{\sim}{B} = f\left(\underset{\sim}{A}\right)$ is divided into m rectangular parts. Let each of them be denoted by $\underset{\sim ij}{B}$. Then

$$\underset{\sim}{B} \approx \bigcup_{j=1}^{m} \left(\prod_{i=1}^{n} \underset{\sim ij}{B} \right) \tag{3.28}$$

Now we can state a formula of approximation for any $u \in U$:

$$\underset{\sim}{A}(u) \approx f\left(\underset{\sim}{A}\right)(f(u)) \approx \bigvee_{j=1}^{m} \left(\bigwedge_{i=1}^{n} \underset{\sim ij}{B}(f_i(u)) \right). \tag{3.29}$$

We can state the above expression in logical statements as follows:

$$
\begin{Bmatrix}
\left(f_1(u) \text{ is } B_{\sim 11} \right) \text{ and } \left(f_2(u) \text{ is } B_{\sim 21} \right) \text{ and } \dots \text{ and } \left(f_n(u) \text{ is } B_{\sim n1} \right) \\
\text{or} \\
\left(f_1(u) \text{ is } B_{\sim 12} \right) \text{ and } \left(f_2(u) \text{ is } B_{\sim 22} \right) \text{ and } \dots \text{ and } \left(f_n(u) \text{ is } B_{\sim n2} \right) \\
\text{or} \\
\vdots \\
\vdots \\
\text{or} \\
\left(f_1(u) \text{ is } B_{\sim 1m} \right) \text{ and } \left(f_2(u) \text{ is } B_{\sim 2m} \right) \text{ and } \dots \text{ and } \left(f_n(u) \text{ is } B_{\sim nm} \right)
\end{Bmatrix}
$$
$$\tag{3.30}$$

Define $\varepsilon = 1 - C\left(f, \underset{\sim}{A} \right)$. Then the above logical statements are called an ε-intension of the concept α.

Expression (3.30) is important in that it not only gives us a means for constructing a more precise representation of the intension of a concept, but also a means to constructing a more precise representation of the (representation) extension.

3.6   Basic Forms of Fuzzy Decision Making

3.6.1   Principles of the Maximum Membership

The First Principle of the Maximum Membership

Let $(U, \mathcal{C}, F]$ be a description frame and $\underset{\sim}{A}_1, \underset{\sim}{A}_2, \dots, \underset{\sim}{A}_n \in \mathcal{F}(U)$ be the extensions of concepts $\alpha_1, \alpha_2, \dots, \alpha_n \in \mathcal{C}$, respectively. For a given object $u_0 \in U$, if there exists an index $i \in \{1, 2, \dots, n\}$ such that $\underset{\sim}{A}_i$ satisfies

$$
\underset{\sim}{A}_i(u_0) = \max\left\{ \underset{\sim}{A}_1(u_0), \underset{\sim}{A}_2(u_0), \dots, \underset{\sim}{A}_n(u_0) \right\}
\tag{3.31}
$$

then u_0 is said to belong to $\underset{\sim}{A}_i$ according to the **first maximum membership principle**.

The Second Principle of the Maximum Membership

Let $(U, \mathcal{C}, F]$ be a description frame and $\underset{\sim}{A} \in \mathcal{F}(U)$ be the extension of $\alpha \in \mathcal{C}$. For n objects $u_1, u_2, \dots, u_n \in U$, if there exists an index $i \in \{1, 2, \dots, n\}$ such that

u_i satisfies

$$A_{\sim}(u_i) = \max\left\{A_{\sim}(u_1), A_{\sim}(u_2), ..., A_{\sim}(u_n)\right\} \qquad (3.32)$$

then u_i is said to belong to $A_{\sim}$ according to the **second maximum membership principle**.

3.6.2   DFE Decisions and Its Types

Let's consider a more concrete setting under the description frame $(U, C, F]$ by defining:

U—a group of tactics, called tactics set

C—a group of concepts upon tactics in U, for example, "good tactics", "fair tactics", and "bad tactics", etc.

F—the factor set with respect to these tactics.

If the extensions of concepts in C are known, then decision making will be simple because one can use principles of the highest membership. However, decisions must be made when the extensions of concepts are unknown. An approach to decision making under such circumstances is to find the extensions of concepts in C. These extensions could be found if we could obtain their feedback extensions (which, in turn, could be realized by G-envelopes). Decision making through this process is called **decision making based on feedback extensions**, or simply, **DFE**.

There are three types of **DFE**s.

Type 1. Orderable

In this case, $C = \{\alpha\}$ is a singleton, for instance, $\alpha =$ "good tactics". If we can find the G-envelope, $A_{\sim}[G]$, then $A_{\sim}[G] : U \longrightarrow [0, 1]$, (or $A_{\sim}[\pi] : U \longrightarrow [0, 1]$) will order tactics of U in $[0, 1]$. The first in the ordered list is the best tactic.

Type 2. Competitive

In this case $U = \{u\}$ is a singleton and C contains at least two concepts. Let $C = \{\alpha_1, \alpha_2, ..., \alpha_k\}$ and $A_{\sim i}$ be the extension of α_i $1 \leq i \leq k$. If we can get $A_{\sim i}[G]$ for each i, $1 \leq i \leq k$ $\left(\text{or } \pi\text{-closures } A_{\sim i}[\pi]\right)$, then we will be able to determine the concept (or $A_{\sim i}$) to which u belongs.

Type 3. Competitive/Orderable

In this case, both U and C are not singletons. Let $U = \{u_1, u_2, ..., u_n\}$ and $C = \{\alpha_1, \alpha_2, ..., \alpha_n\}$. First we classify U by the competition. For example, if u_{i1}, $u_{i2}, ..., u_{ip}$, $p \leq n$ belong to α_q, some q $(\leq k)$, we can order $u_{i1}, u_{i2}, ..., u_{ip}$ via $A_{\sim q}[G]$ (or $A_{\sim q}[\pi]$); the first on the ordered list is the best tactic. Likewise, we can obtain a best tactic for each α_j, $1 \leq j \leq k$. We can adopt one or more of these best tactics if the condition dictates to do so.

3.6.3 An Implementation Procedure for DFE

We outline our DFE implementation procedure in the following steps. The illustration is tailored to the type 1 DFE previously defined.

Step 1. Define a tactics set $U = \{u_1, u_2, ..., u_n\}$, which is a group of tactics or strategies.

Step 2. Determine the concept α in $C = \{\alpha\}$ and name that concept, e.g., "good tactic". U is the universe of the concept α.

Step 3. Determine the set of atomic factors $\pi = \{f_1, f_2, ..., f_m\}$ of U and its factor spaces

$$\{X(f_j)\}_{(1 \leq j \leq m)}.$$

Step 4. Set $F = \mathcal{P}(\pi)$, $\bigvee = U$, $\bigwedge = \cap$, $- = \backslash$, $\mathbf{1} = \pi$, and $\mathbf{0} = \Phi$. Then $(F, \bigvee, \bigwedge, c, \mathbf{1}, \mathbf{0})$ is a Boolean algebra, and therefore, $(U, C, F]$ is a description frame.

Step 5. Construct $\underset{\sim}{B}(f_i)$, $1 \leq i \leq m$, the representation extensions of α, on the representation universes $X(f_j)$, $1 \leq j \leq m$, using methods discussed later.

Step 6. Take an appropriate m-dimensional triangular norm T_m and form the representation extension $\underset{\sim}{B}(\mathbf{1})$ in $X(\mathbf{1})$ from T_m and $\underset{\sim}{B}(f_i)$ as in

$$\underset{\sim}{B}(\mathbf{1})(x_1, x_2, ..., x_m) = T_m\left(\underset{\sim}{B}(f_1)(x_1), \underset{\sim}{B}(f_2)(x_2), ..., \underset{\sim}{B}(f_m)(x_m)\right).$$

Step 7. Determine $f_j(u_i)$, the state of the tactic i on the atomic factor j, where $i = 1, 2, ..., n$ and $j = 1, 2, ..., m$. Then, we can obtain the state of the complete factor $\mathbf{1}$ on each tactic as in

$$\mathbf{1}(u_i) = (f_1(u_i), f_2(u_i), ..., f_m(u_i)), \qquad i = 1, 2, ..., n.$$

Step 8. Construct $\mathbf{1}^{-1}\left(\underset{\sim}{B}(\mathbf{1})\right)$, the feedback extension of α, which is regarded as the approximation of $\underset{\sim}{A}$. For any $u_i \in U$, then

$$\underset{\sim}{A}(u_i) \approx \left(\mathbf{1}^{-1}\left(\underset{\sim}{B}(\mathbf{1})\right)\right)(u_i) = \underset{\sim}{B}(\mathbf{1})(\mathbf{1}(u_i))$$

$$= \underset{\sim}{B}(\mathbf{1})(f_1(u_i), f_2(u_i), ..., f_m(u_i))$$

$$= T_m\left(\underset{\sim}{B}(f_1)(f_1(u_i)), \underset{\sim}{B}(f_2)(f_2(u_i)), ..., \underset{\sim}{B}(f_m)(f_m(u_i))\right).$$

Now we can proceed to pick the best tactic u_i^* by the principles of the maximum membership.

Example 18

The Problem of Selecting the Best Student.

Let us consider the problem of how to select an excellent student among three candidates: Henry, Lucy, and John. Following the procedure just described, we have

Step 1. Let $u_1 =$ Henry, $u_2 =$ Lucy, and $u_3 =$ John, so $U = \{u_1, u_2, u_3\}$;

Step 2. Define $\alpha =$ "excellent student"; then $C=\{\alpha\} =$ {excellent student} ;

Step 3. Let $f_1 =$ mathematics, $f_2 =$ physics, $f_3 =$ chemistry, and $f_4 =$ foreign language. Set

$$\pi = \{f_1, f_2, f_3, f_4\} \quad and \quad X(f_j) = [0, 100], \; j = 1, 2, 3, 4;$$

Step 4. Let $F = \mathcal{P}(\pi)$. Then (U, C, F) is a description frame.

Step 5. Define

$$\underset{\sim}{B}(f_j)(x) = \begin{cases} 1 & , \; 90 \le x \le 100 \\ \frac{x-80}{10} & , \; 80 \le x < 90 \\ 0 & , \; 0 \le x < 80 \end{cases}$$

Step 6. Construct $T_m \in \mathcal{T}(4)$, a four-dimensional triangular norm, as

$$T_4(x_1, x_2, x_3, x_4) = \prod_{j=1}^{4} x_j = x_1 \cdot x_2 \cdot x_3 \cdot x_4.$$

Hence, $\underset{\sim}{B}(1)(x_1, x_2, x_3, x_4)$

$$= T_4\left(\underset{\sim}{B}(f_1)(x_1), \underset{\sim}{B}(f_2)(x_2), \underset{\sim}{B}(f_3)(x_3), \underset{\sim}{B}(f_4)(x_4)\right)$$

$$= \underset{\sim}{B}(f_1)(x_1) \cdot \underset{\sim}{B}(f_2)(x_2) \cdot \underset{\sim}{B}(f_3)(x_3) \cdot \underset{\sim}{B}(f_4)(x_4).$$

Step 7. The scores of each subject area (f_j) by each student (u_i) is given in the following:

$u \backslash f$	mathematics	physics	chemistry	foreign language
Henry	86	91	95	93
Lucy	98	89	93	90
John	90	92	85	96

Its corresponding membership function values $\underset{\sim}{B}$ (f_i) $(f(u_i))$ are given as follows:

$u \backslash f$	f_1	f_2	f_3	f_4
u_1	0.6	1	1	1
u_2	1	0.9	1	1
u_3	1	1	0.5	1

Step 8. Calculate $\underset{\sim}{A}$ (u_i) for $i = 1, 2, 3$.

$$\underset{\sim}{A}(u_1) \approx \underset{\sim}{B}(\mathbf{1})(\mathbf{1}(u_1)) = \underset{\sim}{B}(\mathbf{1})(f_1(u_1), f_2(u_1), f_3(u_1), f_4(u_1))$$

$$= T_4\left(\underset{\sim}{B}(f_1)(f_1(u_1)), \underset{\sim}{B}(f_2)(f_2(u_1)), \underset{\sim}{B}(f_3)(f_3(u_1)), \underset{\sim}{B}(f_4)(f_4(u_1))\right)$$

$$= \underset{\sim}{B}(f_1)(f_1(u_1)) \cdot \underset{\sim}{B}(f_2)(f_2(u_1)) \cdot \underset{\sim}{B}(f_3)(f_3(u_1)) \cdot \underset{\sim}{B}(f_4)(f_4(u_1))$$

$$= 0.6 \times 1 \times 1 \times 1 = 0.6$$

Similarly, we get $\underset{\sim}{A}$ $(u_2) \approx 0.9$ and $\underset{\sim}{A}$ $(u_3) \approx 0.5$. So Lucy (u_2) is the best student of the three.   ▯

3.7   Limitations of the Weighted Average Formula

Let $(U, C, F]$ be a description frame, $G = \{f_j \mid 1 \le j \le m\}$ be a family of pairwise independent factors in $\mathcal{F}$, and let $f = \overset{m}{\underset{j=1}{\vee}} f_j$. Assume α is a concept in C and $A \in \mathcal{F}(U)$ is its extension. A very important problem is how to form $\underset{\sim}{B}(f)$, the representation extension of α, in the representation universe $X(f)$ by using $\left\{\underset{\sim}{B}(f_j)\right\}_{(1 \le j \le m)}$

We know that $\underset{\sim}{B}(f)$ has an upper bound, i.e.,

$$\bigcap_{j=1}^{m} \underset{\sim}{B}(f_j) = \prod_{j=1}^{m} \underset{\sim}{B}(f_j) \supset \underset{\sim}{B}(f) \tag{3.33}$$

which means that if $(x_1, x_2, ..., x_m) \in \prod_{j=1}^{m} X(f_j)$, then

$$\underset{\sim}{B}(f)(x_1, x_2, ..., x_m) \leq \bigwedge_{j=1}^{m} \underset{\sim}{B}(f_j)(x_j). \tag{3.34}$$

However, the common practice in setting up $\underset{\sim}{B}(f)$ is to employ the weighted average formula as

$$\underset{\sim}{B}(f)(x_1, x_2, ..., x_m) \approx \sum_{j=1}^{m} a_j \underset{\sim}{B}(f_j)(x_j) \ or \ \sum_{j=1}^{m} a_j(x_j) \underset{\sim}{B}(f_j)(x_j),$$

where $a_j, a_j(x_j) \in [0, 1]$, and $\sum_{j=1}^{m} a_j = \sum_{j=1}^{m} a_j(x_j) = 1$.

Unfortunately, the weighted average approach is not reasonable because it exceeds the upper bound of $\underset{\sim}{B}(f)$. That is,

$$\bigwedge_{j=1}^{m} \underset{\sim}{B}(f_j)(x_j) \leq \sum_{j=1}^{m} a_j \underset{\sim}{B}(f_j)(x_j) \quad or \quad \sum_{j=1}^{m} a_j(x_j) \underset{\sim}{B}(f_j)(x_j). \tag{3.35}$$

Figure 3.11 graphically illustrates this viewpoint.

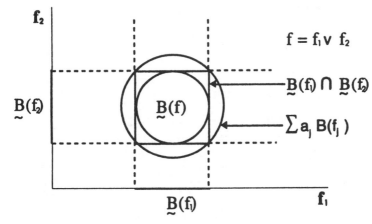

FIGURE 3.11
Unreasonableness of the weighted average approach.

Note. The composition of the states and the composition of the degree of membership of representation extensions are different. The unreasonableness in this case happens to the composition of the degree of membership.

References

[1] Duan, Q.-Z. and Li, H.-X., N-dimensional t-norm. *Journal of Tianjin College of Textile Engineering*, 7(2), 1988, 9–16.

[2] Li, H.-X., *Interesting Talks on Fuzzy Mathematics*. Sichuan Education Press, Sichuan, 1987. (In Chinese.)

[3] Li, H.-X., Multifactorial functions in fuzzy set theory. *Fuzzy Sets and Systems*, 35(1), 1990, 69–84.

[4] Li, H.-X., Luo, C.-Z., and Wang, P.-Z., The cardinality of fuzzy sets and the continuum hypothesis, *Fuzzy Sets and Systems*, 55(1), 1993, 61–77.

[5] Li, H.-X., *Fuzzy Mathematics Methods in Engineering and Their Applications*. Tianjin Scientific and Technical Press, Tianjin, 1993. (In Chinese.)

[6] Li, H.-X. and Yen, V. C., Factor spaces and fuzzy decision making, *Journal of Beijing Normal University*, 30(1), 1994, 41–46.

[7] Li, H.-X. and Wang, P.-Z., Falling shadow representation of fuzzy concepts on factor spaces, *Journal of Yantai University*, No. 2, 1994, 15–21.

[8] Li, H.-X. and Wang, P.-Z., *Fuzzy Mathematics*. National Defense Press, Beijing, 1994. (In Chinese.)

[9] Wang, P.-Z., *Fuzzy Set Theory and Its Applications*. Shanghai Science Press, Shanghai, 1983. (In Chinese.)

[10] Wang, P.-Z., A factor space approach to knowledge representation, *Fuzzy Sets and Systems*, 36, 1990, 113–124.

[11] Wang, P.-Z. and Li, H.-X., *A Mathematical Theory on Knowledge Representation*. Tianjin Scientific and Technical Press, Tianjin, 1994. (In Chinese.)

4

Determination of Membership Functions

In real world applications of fuzzy sets, an important task is to determine membership functions of the fuzzy sets in question. Like the estimation of probabilities in the probability theory, we can only obtain an approximate membership function of a fuzzy set because of our cognitive limitations. In this chapter we discuss how to determine a membership function of a fuzzy set.

4.1 A General Method for Determining Membership Functions

In our natural world and daily lives, we experience all kinds of phenomena; broadly speaking, we can divide them into two types: phenomena of certainty and phenomena of uncertainty.

The class of uncertain phenomena can further be subdivided into random (stochastic) phenomena and fuzzy phenomena. Therefore, we have three categories of phenomena and their associated mathematical models:

1. Deterministic mathematical models—This is a class of models where the relationships between objects are fixed or known with certainty.

2. Random (stochastic) mathematical models—This is a class of models where the relationships between objects are uncertain or random in nature.

3. Fuzzy mathematical models—This is a class of models where objects and relationships between objects are fuzzy.

The main distinction between random phenomena and fuzzy phenomena is that random events themselves have clear and well-defined meaning, whereas a fuzzy concept does not have a precise extension because it is hard to judge if an object belongs to the concept. We may say that randomness is a deficiency of the law of causality and that fuzziness is a deficiency of the law of the excluded middle. Probability theory applies the random concept to generalized laws of causality— laws of probability. Fuzzy set theory applies the fuzzy property to the generalized law of the excluded middle—the law of membership from fuzziness.

Probability reflects the internal relations and interactions of events under certain conditions. It could be very objective if a stable frequency is available from repeated experiments. Similarly, a stable frequency results from fuzzy statistical tests (discussed later) and can serve as the degree of membership in the objective sense. In many cases, the degree of membership can be determined by fuzzy statistical methods.

Before entering into fuzzy statistics, we first outline some basic notions of probability and statistics.

A random experiment has four basic requirements:

1. A sample space Ω that is a high-dimensional direct product space formed by all related factors;

2. An event A that is a fixed and crisp subset of Ω;

3. A variable ω that is in Ω; once ω is determined, so are all the factors on their state spaces;

4. A condition S that sets forth the restrictions on variable ω.

The basic reason for the existence of randomness is that the condition S is too weak to restrict ω to a fixed point. Moreover, if $S \cap A \neq \Phi$ and $S \cap A^c \neq \Phi$, then $\omega \in S \cap A$ signifies that the event A has occurred; otherwise it has not. That means A is a random event under the condition S. On random experiments we have the following observations:

1. The purpose of a random experiment is to study the uncertainty through the use of certain or deterministic procedures.

2. A fundamental requirement of a random experiment is to unambiguously tell whether an event A has occurred or not.

3. A special characteristic of a random experiment is that A is fixed, while ω is not (see Figure 4.1a).

4. After n times of repeated trials (experiments), we compute the frequency of A by

$$\text{Frequency of A} = \frac{\text{The number of trials when } \omega \in A}{n}.$$

It is well known that as n becomes very large, the above frequency tends to stabilize or converge to a fixed number. This number is called the probability of A under S.

A **fuzzy statistical experiment** also has four basic requirements:

1. A universe U;

2. A fixed element $u_0 \in U$;

3. An alterable crisp set A_* in U that is related to a fuzzy set $\underset{\sim}{A}$ (the extension of some fuzzy concept α). Every fixed instance of A_* is a partition of the concept α; it also represents an approximate extension of α.

4. A condition S that relates to all objective and psychological factors during the process of partitioning of the concept α, and limits the range of change that A_* may have.

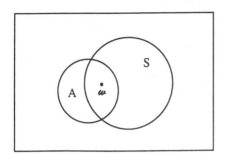 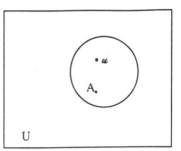

FIGURE 4.1
(a) A Random Experiment: A is fixed, but w varies. (b) A Fuzzy Statistical Experiment: u_0 is fixed, but A_* varies.

On the properties of fuzzy statistical experiments we have the following observations:

1. The purpose of fuzzy statistical experiments is to study such uncertainties with certain or definite procedures.

2. A fundamental requirement of a fuzzy statistical experiment is to unambiguously tell whether $u_0 \in A_*$ or not.

3. A special characteristic of a fuzzy statistical experiment is that u_0 is fixed while X_* varies.

4. After collecting n sample observations from an experiment, we compute the frequency of u_0 in A_* by

$$\text{Frequency of } u_0 \text{ in } A_* = \frac{\text{The number of observations of } u_0 \in A_*}{n}.$$

As n increases, the frequency tends to stabilize or converge to a fixed number; this number is called the **degree of membership** of u_0 in A_*.

Example 19
Let $U = [0, 100]$ be the "age" universe and $A \in \mathcal{F}(U)$ be the extension of the fuzzy concept α : "a young man". Choose a fixed age, say 27, i.e., $u_0 = 27$; we wish to determine its degree of membership in A. Zhang [5] conducted a fuzzy statistical experiment at Wuhan Institute of Building Materials. He picked 129 suitable people from the institute for his experiment. He asked them to seriously consider what is the acceptable range of age for the class "young men"? Results of the 129 responses are given in Table 1. Table 2 shows the frequency of membership $u_0 (= 27)$ in these age ranges. ☐

Table 2 demonstrates that the normalized frequency of membership for age 27 stabilizes at 0.78 as the sample size increases. (The sum of the relative frequencies

Table 1   The Age Ranges for "Young Men" Specified by 129 Respondents.

18–25	17–30	17–28	18–25	16–35	14–25	18–30	18–35	18–35	16–25
15–30	18–35	17–30	18–25	10–25	18–35	20–30	18–30	16–30	20–35
18–30	18–30	15–25	18–30	15–25	16–28	16–30	18–30	16–30	18–35
18–25	18–25	16–28	18–30	16–30	16–28	18–35	18–35	17–27	16–28
15–28	16–30	19–28	15–30	15–26	17–25	15–36	18–30	17–30	18–35
16–35	15–25	15–25	18–28	16–30	15–28	18–35	18–30	17–28	18–35
15–28	18–30	15–25	15–25	18–30	16–24	15–25	16–32	15–27	18–35
16–25	18–28	16–28	18–30	18–35	18–30	18–30	17–30	18–30	18–35
16–30	18–35	17–25	15–30	18–25	17–30	14–25	18–26	18–29	18–35
18–28	18–30	18–25	16–35	17–29	18–25	17–30	16–28	18–30	16–28
15–30	15–35	18–30	20–30	20–30	16–25	17–30	15–30	18–30	16–30
18–28	18–35	16–30	15–30	18–35	18–35	18–30	17–30	18–35	17–30
15–25	18–35	15–30	15–25	15–30	18–30	17–25	18–29	18–28	—

Table 2   Cumulative Frequency of Membership for Age 27

(Continued from Table 1)

n	Count	Frequency
10	6	0.60
20	14	0.70
30	23	0.77
40	31	0.78
50	39	0.78
60	47	0.78
70	53	0.76
80	62	0.78
90	68	0.76
100	76	0.76
110	85	0.75
120	95	0.79
129	101	0.78

column in Table 3 is 13.6589.) We may now define

$$A\,(u_0) = A\,(27) = 0.78.$$

To find the membership function for the "young man" that is denoted by A, we partition the universe U into unit length intervals with integers as the midpoint of the intervals. Table 3 contains the normalized frequencies of each interval. We can draw a histogram based on the values of Table 3 (Figure 4.2). This way we obtain an empirical membership curve for $A\,(u)$.

Table 3 Frequency of Membership

Order	Grouping	Frequency	Relative Frequency
1	13.5–14.5	2	0.0155
2	14.5–15.5	27	0.2093
3	15.5–16.5	51	0.0155
4	16.5–17.5	67	0.2093
5	17.5–18.5	124	0.9612
6	18.5–19.5	125	0.9690
7	19.5–20.5	129	1.0000
8	20.5–21.5	129	1.0000
9	21.5–22.5	129	1.0000
10	22.5–23.5	129	1.0000
11	23.5–24.5	129	1.0000
12	24.5–25.5	128	0.9922
13	25.5–26.5	103	0.7984
14	26.5–27.5	101	0.7829
15	27.5–28.5	99	0.9922
16	28.5–29.5	80	0.6202
17	29.5–30.5	77	0.5969
18	30.5–31.5	27	0.2093
19	31.5–32.5	27	0.2093
20	32.5–33.5	26	0.2016
21	33.5–34.5	26	0.2016
22	34.5–35.5	26	0.2016
23	35.5–36.5	1	0.0078

4.2 The Three-Phase Method

The **three-phase method** is another fuzzy experimental procedure that uses random intervals. For example, suppose we want to establish a membership function for each type of man called: short, medium, and tall. Let the universe be $U = [0, 3]$ (in meters), $A_{\sim 1}$ be the short type, $A_{\sim 2}$ be the medium type, and $A_{\sim 3}$ then be the tall type. Every fuzzy statistical experiment determines a pair of numbers ζ and η, where ζ is a demarcation point of "short man" and "medium man", and η a demarcation point of "medium man" and "tall man". We can view (ζ, η) as a two-dimensional random variable. Then through sampling (Figure 4.3) we obtain its marginal probability distributions $p_\zeta (u)$ and $p_\eta (u)$. The membership function for each type of man, therefore, is

$$A_{\sim 1} (u) = \int_u^{+\infty} p_\zeta (u)\, du$$

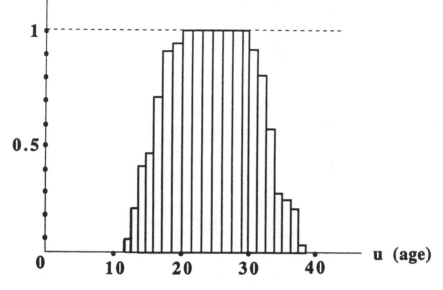

FIGURE 4.2
Histogram of the membership function for the "young men".

$$A_{\sim 2}(u) = \int_{-\infty}^{u} p_\eta(u)\, du$$

and

$$A_{\sim 3}(u) = 1 - A_{\sim 1}(u) - A_{\sim 2}(u)$$

respectively.

In general, ζ and η follow a normal distribution. Assume

$$\zeta \sim N(\mu_1, \sigma_1) \qquad \text{and} \qquad \eta \sim N(\mu_2, \sigma_2)$$

then

$$A_{\sim 1}(u) = 1 - \varphi\left(\frac{u - \mu_1}{\sigma_1}\right)$$

$$A_{\sim 2}(u) = \varphi\left(\frac{u - \mu_2}{\sigma_2}\right)$$

and

$$A_{\sim 3}(u) = \varphi\left(\frac{u - \mu_1}{\sigma_1}\right) - \varphi\left(\frac{u - \mu_2}{\sigma_2}\right),$$

where

$$\varphi(u) = \int_{-\infty}^{u} \frac{1}{\sqrt{2\pi}} e^{-\frac{x^2}{2}}\, dx.$$

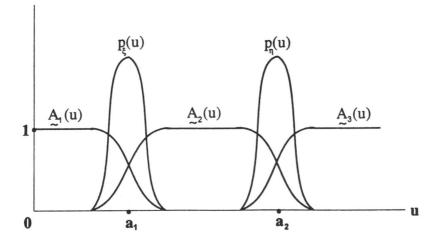

FIGURE 4.3
The three-phase method.

4.3 The Incremental Method

We explain, through an example, how to apply the incremental method for calibrating membership functions. Let A be the extension of the fuzzy concept "old man" and $A \in \mathcal{F}([0, 100])$. For simplicity, we define $\mu(u) = A(u)$, $u \in [0, 100]$.

Given an arbitrary increment Δu on u, there will be a corresponding incremental change $\Delta \mu$ on μ. For simplicity, we assume that $\Delta \mu$ is directly proportional to Δu. Also, for the same increment Δu, the bigger the value of u is, the larger the $\Delta \mu$ will be. Since μ is bounded by 1, $\Delta \mu$ should become smaller as μ is getting close to 1. That is,

$$\Delta \mu = k \cdot \Delta u \cdot u (1 - \mu) \tag{4.1}$$

where k is a constant of proportionality. Dividing both sides by Δu, we obtain

$$\frac{\Delta \mu}{\Delta u} = k \cdot u (1 - \mu).$$

When $\Delta u \longrightarrow 0$, we get a differential equation:

$$\frac{d\mu}{du} = k \cdot u (1 - \mu) \tag{4.2}$$

whose solution is

$$\mu(u) = 1 - ce^{-\frac{kx^2}{2}} \tag{4.3}$$

where c is an integral constant. If we properly choose k and c, then $\mu(u)$ will be completely determined, and so will $\underset{\sim}{A}(u)$.

4.4 The Multiphase Fuzzy Statistical Method

Strictly speaking, the two fuzzy statistical methods mentioned above belong to the two-phase method. Let's analyze the way we establish the degree of membership for age 27 ($=u_0$) in the concept of "young man". The steps taken are as follows:

1. Select a set $P = \{p_1, p_2, \cdots, p_n\}$ of n subjects for sampling.
2. Collect a response of p_1, in terms of a subset of U on the concept of "young man". For example, to p_1, a young man means any man whose age is in the range of $[18, 29]$. Let's denote it as

$$\underset{\sim}{A}(u_0, p_1) = 1, \quad u_0 \in [18, 29].$$

Similarly, for p_2 we may have

$$\underset{\sim}{A}(u_0, p_2) = 1, \quad u_0 \in [16, 25].$$

Thus, we collect n such responses. Each of them can affirmatively say yes or no to the question of whether a twenty-seven-year-old man is "young" or "not". The "young" and "not young" are what we mean by phases; in this case we have two.

3. Compute the degree of membership by

$$\underset{\sim}{A}(u_0) = \frac{1}{n}\sum_{i=1}^{n}\underset{\sim}{A}(u_0, p_i).$$

The three-phase method discussed earlier is a three-phase fuzzy statistical method.

In many cases, it is necessary to consider more than two fuzzy sets simultaneously. Therefore, we need to generalize the two-phase fuzzy statistical method to a multiphase fuzzy statistical method.

Let $\underset{\sim}{A}_1, \underset{\sim}{A}_2, \cdots, \underset{\sim}{A}_m \in \mathcal{F}(U)$. To see if $u \in U$ belongs to some $\underset{\sim}{A}_i$, $1 \le i \le m$, compute $\underset{\sim}{A}_i(u)$. Let $P = \{p_1, p_2, \cdots, p_n\}$ as defined earlier. We assume that for any $p_j \in P$, it satisfies

1) $A_{\sim i}(u, p_j) = \begin{cases} 1, & p_j \text{ says } u \text{ belongs to } A_{\sim i} \\ 0, & p_j \text{ says } u \text{ does not belong to } A_{\sim i} \end{cases}$

2) $\sum_{i=1}^{m} A_{\sim i}(u, p_j) = 1$, that is u belongs to one and only one of the $A_{\sim}'$ s.

Then we can compute $A_{\sim i}(u)$ from the following formula:

$$A_{\sim i}(u) = \frac{1}{n} \sum_{j=1}^{n} A_{\sim i}(u, p_j), \quad i = 1, 2, \cdots, m.$$

Example 20

Find the degree of membership of John's height (u) in fuzzy sets of $A_{\sim 1}$ (short men), $A_{\sim 2}$ (medium size men), and $A_{\sim 3}$ (tall men).

We apply the three-phase fuzzy statistical method to this problem. Let $P = \{p_1, p_2, \cdots, p_{10}\}$ be a set of ten subjects in this experiment. The responses of them from this experiment is in Table 4. ☐

Table 4 Degree of Membership by Respondents

$A_{\sim i}$ \ p	p_1	p_2	p_3	p_4	p_5	p_6	p_7	p_8	p_9	p_{10}
$A_{\sim 1}$	0	0	1	1	1	0	0	0	1	0
$A_{\sim 2}$	1	1	0	0	0	1	1	0	1	1
$A_{\sim 3}$	0	0	0	0	0	0	0	1	0	0

From the table, we compute

$$A_{\sim 1}(u) = \frac{1}{10} \sum_{j=1}^{10} A_{\sim 1}(u, p_j) = \frac{4}{10} = 0.4.$$

Likewise, we find

$$A_{\sim 2}(u) = 0.5 \quad and \quad A_{\sim 3}(u) = 0.1.$$

Notice that

$$A_{\sim 1}(u) + A_{\sim 2}(u) + A_{\sim 3}(u) = 0.4 + 0.5 + 0.1 = 1.$$

In general, the multiphased fuzzy statistical method has the following two properties:

Property 1. $\sum\limits_{i=1}^{m} A_{\sim i}(u) = 1.$

PROOF

$$\sum_{i=1}^{m} A_{\sim i}(u) = \sum_{i=1}^{m}\left(\frac{1}{n}\sum_{j=1}^{n} A_{\sim i}(u, p_j)\right)$$

$$= \frac{1}{n}\sum_{i=1}^{m}\sum_{j=1}^{n} A_{\sim i}(u, p_j)$$

$$= \frac{1}{n}\sum_{j=1}^{n}\left(\sum_{i=1}^{m} A_{\sim i}(u, p_j)\right)$$

$$= \frac{1}{n}\sum_{j=1}^{n} 1 = 1.$$

∎

Property 2. Let $U = \{u_1, u_2, \cdots, u_k\}$ be a universe with k elements. Then,

$$\sum_{i=1}^{m}\sum_{j=1}^{k} A_{\sim i}(u_j) = k.$$

PROOF

$$\sum_{i=1}^{m}\sum_{j=1}^{k} A_{\sim i}(u_j) = \sum_{j=1}^{k}\left(\sum_{i=1}^{m} A_{\sim i}(u_j)\right) = \sum_{j=1}^{k} 1 = k.$$

∎

4.5   The Method of Comparisons

4.5.1   Binary Comparisons

Very often in a multiphase fuzzy statistical experiment, participants have difficulty declaring the highest degree of membership of objects being evaluated. In practice, pairwise comparisons have been used to solve this problem. For example, "George is more enthusiastic than Martin". If we let the extension of the fuzzy concept "enthusiastic" be denoted by $\underset{\sim}{A}$, then

$$\underset{\sim}{A} \, (George) \geq \underset{\sim}{A} \, (Martin).$$

The comparison made between George and Martin on the basis of the degree of membership in the "enthusiastic" set is called the **binary comparison**.

In the process of learning and recognition, binary comparison is used routinely by people. In simple cases, a binary comparison can establish an order relation ($\geq$), and from it we can roughly determine a membership function. Unfortunately, the order relation generated by the binary comparison does not satisfy the transitivity property. For instance, if George is more enthusiastic than Martin, and Martin is more enthusiastic than Peter, we may not conclude that George is more enthusiastic than Peter. It could be that Peter is more enthusiastic than George—a feature of fuzzy concepts. Therefore, to overcome this problem, we need to modify the binary comparison method.

4.5.2 Preferred Comparisons

Let $P = \{p_1, p_2, \cdots, p_n\}$ be the set of subjects or participants in the fuzzy statistical experiment, U be the universe, and $\underset{\sim 1}{A}, \underset{\sim 2}{A}, \cdots, \underset{\sim m}{A} \in \mathcal{F}(U)$ be m fuzzy sets. Our problem is this: for a given $u \in U$, find its degree of membership in each $\underset{\sim i}{A}$, i.e., $\underset{\sim i}{A}\,(u)$, for $i = 1, 2, \cdots, m$.

For every pair of fuzzy sets $\left(\underset{\sim s}{A}, \underset{\sim k}{A} \right)$, $1 \leq s \leq k \leq m$, and any $p_j \in P$, we stipulate that

$$\underset{\sim i}{A}\,(u, p_j) = \begin{cases} 1, & p_j \text{ says } u \text{ belongs to } \underset{\sim i}{A} \\ 0, & p_j \text{ says } u \text{ does not belong to } \underset{\sim i}{A} \end{cases}$$

and

$$\underset{\sim s}{A}\,(u, p_j) + \underset{\sim k}{A}\,(u, p_j) = 1.$$

Thus, the comparison made by p_k between $\underset{\sim s}{A}$ and $\underset{\sim k}{A}$ if $\underset{\sim k}{A}\,(u) = 1$ (so $\underset{\sim s}{A}\,(u) = 0$) is determined. Then we can write

$$f_{\underset{\sim s}{A}} \left(\underset{\sim k}{A}, p_j \right) = 1, \text{ and } f_{\underset{\sim k}{A}} \left(\underset{\sim s}{A}, p_j \right) = 0.$$

We sum up all comparisons made by p_j in Table 5.

Table 5 $f_{A_{\sim k}}\left(A_{\sim s}, p_j\right)$ from p_j by Binary Comparisons

$A_{\sim s}\backslash A_{\sim k}$	$A_{\sim 1}$	$A_{\sim 2}$	$A_{\sim 3}$	$\cdots$	$A_{\sim m}$
$A_{\sim 1}$	$-$	0	1	$\cdots$	0
$A_{\sim 2}$	1	$-$	0	$\cdots$	0
$A_{\sim 3}$	0	1	$-$	$\cdots$	1
$\cdots$	$\cdots$	$\cdots$	$\cdots$	$\cdots$	$\cdots$
$A_{\sim m}$	1	1	0	$\cdots$	$-$

We present the results of the binary comparisons made by n participants in Table 6.

When $s \neq k$, we can state the following properties:

1) $\sum_{j=1}^{n} f_{A_{\sim s}}\left(A_{\sim k}, p_j\right) + \sum_{j=1}^{n} f_{A_{\sim k}}\left(A_{\sim s}, p_j\right) = \sum_{j=1}^{n}\left(f_{A_{\sim s}}\left(A_{\sim k}, p_j\right) + f_{A_{\sim k}}\left(A_{\sim s}, p_j\right)\right) = \sum_{j=1}^{n} 1 = n$, and,

2) $\sum_{k=1}^{m} \sum_{s=1}^{m}\left(\sum_{j=1}^{n} f_{A_{\sim k}}\left(A_{\sim s}, p_j\right)\right) = \frac{n(m^2-m)}{2} = \frac{nm(m-1)}{2}$.

Finally, the degree of membership $A_{\sim i}(u)$, $i = 1, 2, .., m$ can be computed by

$$A_{\sim i}(u) = \frac{\sum_{k=1}^{m}\left(\sum_{j=1}^{n} f_{A_{\sim k}}\left(A_{\sim i}, p_j\right)\right)}{\frac{1}{2}nm(m-1)}.$$

Obviously, the above $A_{\sim i}(u)'s$ satisfies

$$\sum_{i=1}^{m} A_{\sim i}(u) = 1.$$

4.5.3 A Special Case of Preferred Comparisons

Let $U = \{u_1, u_2, \cdots, u_q\}$ be a finite universe and $A_{\sim}$ be a fuzzy set on U. Find the membership function $A_{\sim}(u_i)$ for each i, $i = 1, 2, \cdots, q$. Let $P = \{p_1, p_2, \cdots, p_n\}$ be the set of subjects or participants in the fuzzy statistical experiment. For every

Table 6 Binary Comparisons Made by n Participants

$A_s \backslash A_k$	A_1	A_2	A_3	$\ldots$	A_m	Σ
A_1	—	$\sum_{j=1}^{n} f_{A_2}\left(A_1, P_j\right)$	$\sum_{j=1}^{n} f_{A_3}\left(A_1, P_j\right)$	$\ldots$	$\sum_{j=1}^{n} f_{A_m}\left(A_1, P_j\right)$	$\cdot$
A_2	$\sum_{j=1}^{n} f_{A_1}\left(A_2, P_j\right)$	—	$\sum_{j=1}^{n} f_{A_3}\left(A_2, P_j\right)$	$\ldots$	$\sum_{j=1}^{n} f_{A_m}\left(A_2, P_j\right)$	$\cdot$
A_3	$\sum_{j=1}^{n} f_{A_1}\left(A_3, P_j\right)$	$\sum_{j=1}^{n} f_{A_2}\left(A_3, P_j\right)$	—	$\ldots$	$\sum_{j=1}^{n} f_{A_m}\left(A_3, P_j\right)$	$\cdot$
$\vdots$	$\vdots$	$\vdots$	$\vdots$	$\vdots$	$\vdots$	$\cdot$
A_m	$\sum_{j=1}^{n} f_{A_1}\left(A_m, P_j\right)$	$\sum_{j=1}^{n} f_{A_2}\left(A_m, P_j\right)$	$\sum_{j=1}^{n} f_{A_3}\left(A_m, P_j\right)$	$\ldots$	—	$\cdot$

pair (u_s, u_k), where $1 \leq s \leq k \leq m$, and any $p_j \in P$, we stipulate that

$$\underset{\sim}{A} \left(u_i, p_j\right) = \begin{cases} 1, & p_j \text{ says } u_i \text{ belongs to } \underset{\sim}{A} \\ 0, & p_j \text{ says } u_i \text{ does not belong to } \underset{\sim}{A} \end{cases}$$

and

$$\underset{\sim}{A} \left(u_s, p_j\right) + \underset{\sim}{A} \left(u_k, p_j\right) = 1.$$

When p_j compares u_s to u_k, if $\underset{\sim}{A} \left(u_k\right) = 1$ (so that $\underset{\sim}{A} \left(u_s\right) = 0$) is determined, then we can write

$$f_{u_s} \left(u_k, p_j\right) = 1 \text{ and } f_{u_k} \left(u_s, p_j\right) = 0.$$

This is summed up in Table 7.

Table 7 $f_{u_k} \left(u_s, p_j\right)$ from p_j by Binary Comparisons

$u_s \setminus u_k$	u_1	u_2	u_3	$\cdots$	u_q
u_1	$-$	0	1	$\cdots$	0
u_2	0	$-$	1	$\cdots$	1
u_3	1	0	$-$	$\cdots$	0
$\cdots$	$\cdots$	$\cdots$	$\cdots$	$\cdots$	$\cdots$
u_q	1	0	1	$\cdots$	$-$

The results of binary comparisons by n participants are in Table 8.
When $s \neq k$, the following properties hold:

1) $\sum\limits_{j=1}^{n} \left(f_{u_k} \left(u_s, p_j\right) + f_{u_s} \left(u_k, p_j\right)\right) = n;$ and

2) $\sum\limits_{k=1}^{q} \sum\limits_{s=1}^{q} \left(\sum\limits_{j=1}^{n} f_{u_k} \left(u_s, p_j\right)\right) = \frac{1}{2}nq \left(q - 1\right).$

The degree of membership of $\underset{\sim}{A} \left(u_i\right)$, $i = 1, 2, \cdots, q$, may be calculated from

$$\underset{\sim}{A} \left(u_i\right) = \frac{\sum\limits_{k=1}^{q} \left(\sum\limits_{j=1}^{n} f_{u_k} \left(u_s, p_j\right)\right)}{\frac{1}{2}nq \left(q - 1\right)}.$$

Clearly, these $\underset{\sim}{A} \left(u_i\right)'s$ satisfy

$$\sum\limits_{k=1}^{q} \underset{\sim}{A} \left(u_i\right) = 1.$$

Table 8   Binary Comparisons Made by n Participants

$u_s \backslash u_k$	u_1	u_2	u_3	$\cdots$	u_q	$\sum$
u_1	—	$\sum_{j=1}^{n} f_{u_2}(u_1, p_j)$	$\sum_{j=1}^{n} f_{u_3}(u_1, p_j)$	$\cdots$	$\sum_{j=1}^{n} f_{u_q}(u_1, p_j)$	$\cdot$
u_2	$\sum_{j=1}^{n} f_{u_1}(u_2, p_j)$	—	$\sum_{j=1}^{n} f_{\underset{\sim}{A}_3}\left(\underset{\sim}{A}_2, p_j\right)$	$\cdots$	$\sum_{j=1}^{n} f_{u_q}(u_2, p_j)$	$\cdot$
u_3	$\sum_{j=1}^{n} f_{u_1}(u_3, p_j)$	$\sum_{j=1}^{n} f_{u_2}(u_3, p_j)$	—	$\cdots$	$\sum_{j=1}^{n} f_{u_q}(u_3, p_j)$	$\cdot$
$\cdots$	$\cdots$	$\cdots$	$\cdots$	$\cdots$	$\cdots$	$\cdot$
u_q	$\sum_{j=1}^{n} f_{u_1}(u_q, p_j)$	$\sum_{j=1}^{n} f_{u_2}(u_q, p_j)$	$\sum_{j=1}^{n} f_{u_3}(u_q, p_j)$	$\cdots$	—	$\cdot$

108

Fuzzy Sets and Fuzzy Decision-Making

4.5.4 An Example

In the production of ping-pong paddles, we would like to know which color is the most preferred by the players? Let the universe of colors be

$$U = \{\text{red, orange, yellow, green, blue}\}$$

We now randomly select 500 players. Each player is asked to make two comparisons, and each comparison proceeds according to the order as shown in Table 9. The player then selects his or her most preferred color. The results are given in Table 10.

Table 9 Order of Comparison

Color	Red	Orange	Yellow	Green	Blue
Red	—	—	—	—	—
Orange	1	—	—	—	—
Yellow	5	2	—	—	—
Green	8	6	3	—	—
Blue	10	9	7	4	—

Table 10 Frequency

$u_i \backslash u_j$	Red	Orange	Yellow	Green	Blue	$\sum$
Red	—	517	525	545	661	2248
Orange	483	—	841	477	576	2237
Yellow	475	159	—	534	614	1782
Green	455	523	466	—	643	2087
Blue	339	524	386	357	—	1506

Let α be the concept "good color" and $\underset{\sim}{A}$ is its extension. Then

$$\underset{\sim}{A} (\text{Red}) = \frac{2248}{1000 \times 5 \times 4 \times 0.5} = 0.2248,$$

$$\underset{\sim}{A} (\text{Orange}) = 0.2377, \quad \underset{\sim}{A} (\text{Yellow}) = 0.1782,$$

$$\underset{\sim}{A} (\text{Green}) = 0.2087, \quad \underset{\sim}{A} (\text{Blue}) = 0.1506.$$

4.6 The Absolute Comparison Method

The pairwise comparison used in the last section must satisfy

$$
\begin{cases}
A_{\sim i}(u, p_j) = 1 \ or \ 0, \quad and \\
A_{\sim s}(u) + A_{\sim k}(u) = 1, \ 1 \le s \le k \le 1.
\end{cases}
$$

Now we modify this condition. We allow the values of $A_{\sim s}(u)$ and $A_{\sim k}(u)$ from participants/subjects of an experiment to be any number in $[0, 1]$. Especially, in certain problems, we can use a more convenient approach called the absolute comparison method now described.

Let $A_{\sim 1}, A_{\sim 2}, \cdots, A_{\sim m} \in \mathcal{F}(U)$ be m fuzzy sets. For any $u \in U$, we want to determine the degree of membership of u in $A_{\sim i}$, i.e., $A_{\sim i}(u)$, $i = 1, 2, \cdots, m$.

Suppose there exists an index $r \in \{1, 2, \cdots, m\}$ such that u obviously belongs to $A_{\sim r}$ than others, i.e.,

$$
A_{\sim r}(u) = \max \left\{ A_{\sim i}(u) \mid 1 \le i \le m \right\}.
$$

Then we do not need to perform a complete set of pairwise comparisons. Instead, we need only to perform pairwise comparisons with respect to $A_{\sim r}$ (a partial set of pairwise comparisons). That is to find

$$
f_{A_{\sim r}}\left(A_{\sim i}, p_j \right), \quad i = 1, 2, \cdots, m,
$$

where $f_{A_{\sim r}}\left(A_{\sim r}, p_j \right)$ acts as a standard reference value.

Assume $P = \{p_1, p_2, \cdots, p_m\}$ to be the set of subjects in our experiment. Let

$$
a_i = \frac{1}{n} \sum_{j=1}^{n} f_{A_{\sim r}}\left(A_{\sim i}, p_j \right). \tag{4.4}
$$

Then we may define the degree of membership of u in $A_{\sim i}$ as

$$
A_{\sim i}(u) = a_i \left(\sum_{k=1}^{m} a_k \right)^{-1} \tag{4.5}
$$

It can be readily verified that $A_{\sim i}(u)$ satisfies this normalized condition:

$$\sum_{i=1}^{m} A_{\sim i}(u) = \sum_{i=1}^{m}\left(a_i\left(\sum_{k=1}^{m}a_k\right)^{-1}\right) = \left(\sum_{k=1}^{m}a_k\right)^{-1}\left(\sum_{i=1}^{m}a_i\right) = 1.$$

Now suppose $U = \{u_1, u_2, \cdots, u_k\}$ to be a finite universe and $A_{\sim}$ to be a fuzzy set on U. The problem is to find $A_{\sim}(u_i)$ for all $i \in \{1, 2, \cdots, k\}$. We may proceed as follows:

Step 1. Determine an index r such that

$$A_{\sim}(u_r) = \max\left\{A_{\sim}(u_1), A_{\sim}(u_2), \cdots, A_{\sim}(u_k)\right\},$$

i.e., u_r is perceived as best fit in $A_{\sim}$ than other u's.

Step 2. Find

$$f_{u_r}(u_i, p_j), \quad i = 1, 2, \cdots, k$$

by each p_j, $j = 1, 2, \cdots, n$.

Step 3. Compute a_i that sums up the results of binary comparisons from n participants as in

$$a_i = \frac{1}{n}\sum_{j=1}^{n} f_{u_r}(u_i, p_j), \quad i = 1, 2, \cdots, k.$$

Step 4. Calculate the degree of membership according to

$$A_{\sim}(u_i) = a_i\left(\sum_{j=1}^{k}a_j\right), \quad i = 1, 2, \cdots, k.$$

Example 21

In an engineering project evaluation, assume there are four basic (atomic) factors in a factor set V. Let $V = \{v_1, v_2, v_3, v_4\}$, where

v_1—technology feasibility
v_2—facility investment
v_3—fixed operating costs, and
v_4—cost of labor and material

Find a weight vector for V. Stated in other words, find a fuzzy set $A_{\sim}$ on V, where

$$A_{\sim} = \left(A_{\sim}(v_1), A_{\sim}(v_2), A_{\sim}(v_3), A_{\sim}(v_4)\right) \in \mathcal{F}(V).$$

Choose a group $P = \{p_1, p_2, \cdots, p_{10}\}$ of ten evaluators. They all agree that v_4 is the primary factor concerning economic benefits. This is recorded as $f_{\underset{\sim}{A}}(v_4)$, and a score of 10 is assigned to it. Moreover, we have

$$
\begin{aligned}
&f_{v_4}(v_1, p_1) = 4, \quad f_{v_4}(v_2, p_1) = 9, \quad f_{v_4}(v_3, p_1) = 6 \\
&f_{v_4}(v_1, p_2) = 4, \quad f_{v_4}(v_2, p_2) = 8, \quad f_{v_4}(v_3, p_2) = 7 \\
&f_{v_4}(v_1, p_3) = 4, \quad f_{v_4}(v_2, p_3) = 8, \quad f_{v_4}(v_3, p_3) = 7 \\
&f_{v_4}(v_1, p_4) = 5, \quad f_{v_4}(v_2, p_4) = 8, \quad f_{v_4}(v_3, p_4) = 5 \\
&f_{v_4}(v_1, p_5) = 5, \quad f_{v_4}(v_2, p_5) = 8, \quad f_{v_4}(v_3, p_5) = 5 \\
&f_{v_4}(v_1, p_6) = 4, \quad f_{v_4}(v_2, p_6) = 8, \quad f_{v_4}(v_3, p_6) = 5 \\
&f_{v_4}(v_1, p_7) = 5, \quad f_{v_4}(v_2, p_7) = 9, \quad f_{v_4}(v_3, p_7) = 5 \\
&f_{v_4}(v_1, p_8) = 4, \quad f_{v_4}(v_2, p_8) = 9, \quad f_{v_4}(v_3, p_8) = 5 \\
&f_{v_4}(v_1, p_9) = 4, \quad f_{v_4}(v_2, p_9) = 9, \quad f_{v_4}(v_3, p_9) = 6 \\
&f_{v_4}(v_1, p_{10}) = 4, \quad f_{v_4}(v_2, p_{10}) = 9, \quad f_{v_4}(v_3, p_{10}) = 6
\end{aligned}
$$

The a_i's are found by computing the averages:

$$
a_1 = \frac{1}{10} \sum_{j=1}^{10} f_{v_4}(v_1, p_j) = 4.3
$$

$$
a_2 = \frac{1}{10} \sum_{j=1}^{10} f_{v_4}(v_2, p_j) = 8.5
$$

$$
a_3 = \frac{1}{10} \sum_{j=1}^{10} f_{v_4}(v_3, p_j) = 5.7.
$$

For a_4, due to the initial agreement, we have

$$
a_4 = \frac{1}{10} \sum_{j=1}^{10} f_{v_4}(v_4, p_j) = \frac{1}{10} \sum_{j=1}^{10} 10 = 10.
$$

Normalizing a_1, a_2, a_3, a_4, we obtain

$$
\underset{\sim}{A}(v_1) = a_1 \left(\sum_{j=1}^{10} a_j \right)^{-1} = \frac{4.3}{4.3 + 8.5 + 5.7 + 10} \approx 0.35
$$

Similarly, $\underset{\sim}{A}(v_2) \approx 0.30$, $\underset{\sim}{A}(v_3) \approx 0.20$, $\underset{\sim}{A}(v_4) \approx 0.15$. Hence,

$$
\underset{\sim}{A} = (0.15, 0.30, 0.20, 0.35). \quad \square
$$

4.7 The Set-Valued Statistical Iteration Method

4.7.1 Statement of the Problem

Let $U = \{u_1, u_2, \cdots, u_k\}$ be a finite universe, $\underset{\sim}{A}$ be a fuzzy set of interest in $\mathcal{F}(U)$, and $P = \{p_1, p_2, \cdots, p_m\}$ be the set of subjects in our experiment. The problem is to find the degree of membership $\underset{\sim}{A}(u_i)$ for $i = 1, 2, \cdots, k$.

When k is large, it is hard to determine the values of $f_{u_r}(u_i, p_j)$ via pairwise comparisons. The following method can overcome this difficulty.

4.7.2 Basic Steps of Set-Valued Statistical Method

First we choose an initial number q such that $1 \leq q \ll k$, and then a p_j in P so that we can carry out the statistical experiment according to the following steps:

(1) Select $r_1 = q$ elements from U such that they are the first group of elements best fit to $\underset{\sim}{A}$ by p_j. This generates a subset of U, and it is referred to as set-valued statistics denoted by

$$U_1^{(j)} = \left\{ u_{i_1}^{(j)}, u_{i_2}^{(j)}, \cdots, u_{i_q}^{(j)} \right\} \subset U.$$

(2) Select $r_2 = 2q$ elements from U (which includes the q elements already selected in step (1)) in such a way that all $2q$ elements are considered better fit to $\underset{\sim}{A}$ than other elements of U by p_j. This generates another subset of U:

$$U_2^{(j)} = \left\{ u_{i_1}^{(j)}, u_{i_2}^{(j)}, \cdots, u_{i_q}^{(j)}, u_{i_{q+1}}^{(j)}, u_{i_{2q}}^{(j)} \right\} \supset U_1^{(j)}.$$

The reason that the earlier q elements must be a part of $2q$ elements is that the first q elements are considered better fit to $\underset{\sim}{A}$ than the next q elements. So when selecting a total of $2q$ elements from U that are considered as best fit to $\underset{\sim}{A}$ we must include the q elements already chosen.

(3) In a similar manner, the s-th subset of U is established. This subset consists of $r_s = s \cdot q$ elements of U. That is,

$$U_s^{(j)} = \left\{ u_{i_1}^{(j)}, u_{i_2}^{(j)}, \cdots, u_{i_{sq}}^{(j)} \right\} \supset U_{s-1}^{(j)}.$$

If t is a natural number that satisfies $k = t \cdot q + v$, where $1 \leq v \leq q$, then the iterative process stops at step $(t + 1)$, setting

$$U_{t+1}^{(j)} = U.$$

Next, we calculate $m(u_i)$, the average frequency of u_i, using

$$m(u_i) = \frac{1}{n(t+1)} \sum_{s=1}^{t+1} \sum_{j=1}^{n} \chi_{U_s^{(j)}}(u_i), \quad i = 1, 2, \cdots, k, \qquad (4.6)$$

where $\chi_{U_s^{(j)}}$ is the characteristic function of the set $U_s^{(j)}$.

We obtain the degree of membership of u_i in $\underset{\sim}{A}$ by normalizing the values of $m(u_i)$, for each $i = 1, 2, \cdots, k$. Therefore,

$$\underset{\sim}{A}(u_i) = m(u_i) \left(\sum_{j=1}^{k} m(u_j) \right)^{-1}, \quad i = 1, 2, \cdots, k. \qquad (4.7)$$

Example 22
Let $U = \{u_1, u_2, u_3, u_4\}$, $\underset{\sim}{A}$, and $P = \{p_1, p_2, \cdots, p_5\}$ be the same as in the last section.

Take $q = 1$. Each participant's selection process can be presented in a triangular form:

$p_1 : r_1 = 1 \qquad u_1$
$ r_2 = 2 \qquad u_2 \qquad u_1$
$ r_3 = 3 \qquad u_2 \qquad u_1 \qquad u_4$
$ r_4 = 4 \qquad u_2 \qquad u_1 \qquad u_4 \qquad u_3$

The presentation may be simplified as

$p_1 :$	u_2	u_1	u_4	u_3
	4	3	2	1

Likewise, the results of other participants are given below.

$p_2 :$	u_2	u_4	u_1	u_3
	4	3	2	1

$p_3 :$	u_1	u_2	u_4	u_3
	4	3	2	1

$p_4 :$	u_2	u_1	u_3	u_4
	4	3	2	1

$$p_5: \qquad u_2 \qquad u_3 \qquad u_1 \qquad u_4$$

$$4 \qquad 3 \qquad 2 \qquad 1$$

The average frequency counts of u_i's are

$$m(u_1) = \frac{14}{4 \times 5} = \frac{7}{10}, \quad m(u_2) = \frac{19}{20},$$

$$m(u_3) = \frac{8}{20} = \frac{2}{5}, \qquad m(u_4) = \frac{9}{20}.$$

After normalization, we obtain

$$\underset{\sim}{A}(u_1) = \frac{7}{25} \approx 0.28, \quad \underset{\sim}{A}(u_2) = \frac{19}{50} \approx 0.38,$$

$$\underset{\sim}{A}(u_3) = \frac{4}{25} \approx 0.16, \quad \underset{\sim}{A}(u_4) = \frac{9}{50} \approx 0.18.$$

Therefore, $\underset{\sim}{A} = (0.28, 0.38, 0.16, 0.18)$. ☐

4.8   Ordering by Precedence Relations

Among n objects $u_1, u_2, \cdots, u_n$, we wish to determine an order by a precedence criterion. Very often a precedence criterion is a fuzzy concept whose extension $\underset{\sim}{A}$ is a fuzzy set on $U = \{u_1, u_2, \cdots, u_n\}$. If we have an "order" relationship, then we can use it to determine the membership function $\underset{\sim}{A}(u)$.

4.8.1   Precedence Relations

First we establish a precedence relation among n objects. Let $C = (c_{ij})_{n \times n}$ be a matrix where c_{ij} is a measure of precedence of u_i over u_j, and satisfies
1) $c_{ii} = 0, i = 1, 2, \cdots, n,$
2) $0 \leq c_{ii} \leq 1, i \neq j, i, j = 1, 2, \cdots, n,$ and,
3) $c_{ij} + c_{ji} = 1, i \neq j, i, j = 1, 2, \cdots, n.$
Condition 1) says that the precedence measure is 0 when compared to the object itself. Condition 3) says that the sum of the precedence measure of u_i over u_j and the precedence measure of u_j over u_i is 1. When the precedence of u_i over u_j and the precedence of u_j over u_i are indistinguishable, we set $c_{ij} = c_{ji} = 0.5$. If u_i overwhelmingly precedes u_j, then c_{ij} closes to 1 and c_{ji} closes to 0.

The matrix $C = \left(c_{ij}\right)_{n \times n}$ is called the precedence relation matrix. It is a fuzzy set or a fuzzy matrix on U^2, in other words, $C \in \mathcal{F}\left(U \times U\right)$.

4.8.2 Creating Order

Take a "threshold" $\lambda \in [0, 1]$ and form a cut matrix:

$$
C_\lambda = \begin{bmatrix}
c_{11}^{(\lambda)} & c_{12}^{(\lambda)} & \cdot & \cdot & \cdot & c_{1n}^{(\lambda)} \\
c_{21}^{(\lambda)} & c_{22}^{(\lambda)} & \cdot & \cdot & \cdot & c_{2n}^{(\lambda)} \\
& & \cdot & \cdot & \cdot & \\
& & \cdot & \cdot & \cdot & \\
& & \cdot & \cdot & \cdot & \\
c_{n1}^{(\lambda)} & c_{n2}^{(\lambda)} & \cdot & \cdot & \cdot & c_{nn}^{(\lambda)}
\end{bmatrix},
$$

where

$$
c_{ij}^{(\lambda)} = \begin{cases} 1, & c_{ij} \geq \lambda \\ 0, & c_{ij} < \lambda. \end{cases}
$$

When λ decreases from 1 to 0, and if λ_1 is the threshold where for the first time all of the entries except the diagonal one in the $i_1 - th$ row of C_{λ_1} are one, then u_{i_1} is taken as an element in the first batch of the precedence set (it may not be unique). We take away the first batch of elements from U and work out another batch in the same way from the remaining elements of U. Repeating this procedure, we can create a precedence order for all the elements of U.

4.8.3 An Example

Let $U = \{u_1, u_2, u_3\}$ and $\underset{\sim}{A} \in \mathcal{F}\left(U\right)$, a fuzzy set of interest. Suppose we know the precedence matrix, say

$$
C = \begin{bmatrix} 0 & 0.9 & 0.2 \\ 0.1 & 0 & 0.7 \\ 0.8 & 0.3 & 0 \end{bmatrix}.
$$

When λ decreases from 1 to 0, we have the corresponding cut matrices:

$$
C_{0.9} = \begin{bmatrix} 0 & 1 & 0 \\ 0 & 0 & 0 \\ 0 & 0 & 0 \end{bmatrix}, \quad C_{0.8} = \begin{bmatrix} 0 & 1 & 0 \\ 0 & 0 & 0 \\ 1 & 0 & 0 \end{bmatrix},
$$

$$
C_{0.7} = \begin{bmatrix} 0 & 1 & 0 \\ 0 & 0 & 1 \\ 0 & 0 & 0 \end{bmatrix}, \quad C_{0.3} = \begin{bmatrix} 0 & 1 & 0 \\ 0 & 0 & 1 \\ 1 & 1 & 0 \end{bmatrix}.
$$

When $\lambda = 0.3$, we find for the first time that there is a row, namely the third row in $C_{0.3}$, that has 1's in every entry except the diagonal one. This means that the precedence measure of u_3 over the other two is definitely greater than 0.3. So u_3 is an element of the first batch of the precedence set.

After deleting u_3, we obtain a new precedence matrix of u_1 and u_2 as follows:

$$C^{(1)} = \begin{bmatrix} 0 & 0.9 \\ 0.1 & 0 \end{bmatrix}.$$

Since

$$C^{(1)}_{0.9} = \begin{bmatrix} 0 & 1 \\ 1 & 0 \end{bmatrix}$$

we see that the elements in the first row has the aforementioned "property", so u_1 is an element of the second batch of the precedence set. In conclusion, u_3 has the highest precedence; next is u_1, and the last is u_2. Applying the set-valued statistical iteration method, we have

$$\underset{\sim}{A}(u_3) = \frac{3}{3} = 1, \quad \underset{\sim}{A}(u_1) = \frac{2}{3} \approx 1, \quad \underset{\sim}{A}(u_2) = \frac{1}{3} \approx 0.33.$$

4.8.4 Generalizations

We now generalize the method for establishing the degree of membership to a more general case.

Let $U_j = \left\{ u_{i_1}, u_{i_2}, \cdots, u_{i_{k_j}} \right\}$ be the j-th batch of the precedence set, where $j = 1, 2, \cdots, s$, and $k_1 + k_2 + \cdots + k_s = n$. The degree of membership can be obtained by the following formula:

$$\underset{\sim}{A}(u) = \left(n - \sum_{p=1}^{j-1} k_p \right) n^{-1}, \tag{4.8}$$

where $u \in U_j, \quad j = 1, 2, \cdots, s, \quad$ *and* $\quad$ define $\sum_{p=1}^{0} k_p = 0$.

4.9 The Relative Comparison Method and the Mean Pairwise Comparison Method

4.9.1 The Relative Comparison Method

Let $\underset{\sim}{A}_i \in \mathcal{F}(U)$, $i = 1, 2, \cdots, m$, be m fuzzy sets of interest. We want to determine the degree of membership $\underset{\sim}{A}_i(u)$ of $u \in U$ for $i = 1, 2, \cdots, m$. Let the set $P = \{p_1, p_2, \cdots, p_n\}$ be interpreted as before, and let $f_A\left(\underset{\sim}{A}_k, p_j\right)$ be a value assigned by p_j for $\underset{\sim}{A}_k$ that is a result of the comparison of $\underset{\sim}{A}_k$ relative to $\underset{\sim}{A}_s$. See Table 11.

Table 11 Pairwise Comparisons by p_j.

$\underset{\sim}{A}_k \backslash \underset{\sim}{A}_s$	$\underset{\sim}{A}_1$	$\underset{\sim}{A}_2$	$\underset{\sim}{A}_3$	$\cdots$	$\underset{\sim}{A}_m$
$\underset{\sim}{A}_1$	$-$	$f_{A_2}\left(\underset{\sim}{A}_1, p_j\right)$	$f_{A_3}\left(\underset{\sim}{A}_1, p_j\right)$	$\cdots$	$f_{A_m}\left(\underset{\sim}{A}_1, p_j\right)$
$\underset{\sim}{A}_2$	$f_{A_1}\left(\underset{\sim}{A}_2, p_j\right)$	$-$	$f_{A_3}\left(\underset{\sim}{A}_2, p_j\right)$	$\cdots$	$f_{A_m}\left(\underset{\sim}{A}_2, p_j\right)$
$\underset{\sim}{A}_3$	$f_{A_1}\left(\underset{\sim}{A}_3, p_j\right)$	$f_{A_2}\left(\underset{\sim}{A}_3, p_j\right)$	$-$	$\cdots$	$f_{A_m}\left(\underset{\sim}{A}_3, p_j\right)$
$\vdots$	$\vdots$	$\vdots$	$\vdots$	$\vdots$	$\vdots$
$\underset{\sim}{A}_m$	$f_{A_1}\left(\underset{\sim}{A}_m, p_j\right)$	$f_{A_2}\left(\underset{\sim}{A}_m, p_j\right)$	$f_{A_3}\left(\underset{\sim}{A}_m, p_j\right)$	$\cdots$	$-$

In the above terms, we agree that

$$0 \le f_A\left(\underset{\sim}{A}_k, p_j\right) \le 1 \quad and \quad f_A\left(\underset{\sim}{A}_s, p_j\right) = 1$$

but they may not need to satisfy

$$f_A\left(\underset{\sim}{A}_k, p_j\right) + f_A\left(\underset{\sim}{A}_s, p_j\right) = 1.$$

Define

$$f_A\left(\underset{\sim}{A}_k\right) = \frac{1}{n}\sum_{j=1}^{n} f_A\left(\underset{\sim}{A}_k, p_j\right).$$

Table 12   Values of $f_{A_{\sim s}}\left(A_{\sim k}\right)$ from the n Participants

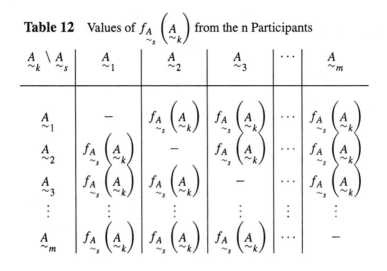

$A_{\sim k} \setminus A_{\sim s}$	$A_{\sim 1}$	$A_{\sim 2}$	$A_{\sim 3}$	$\cdots$	$A_{\sim m}$
$A_{\sim 1}$	$-$	$f_{A_{\sim s}}\left(A_{\sim k}\right)$	$f_{A_{\sim s}}\left(A_{\sim k}\right)$	$\cdots$	$f_{A_{\sim s}}\left(A_{\sim k}\right)$
$A_{\sim 2}$	$f_{A_{\sim s}}\left(A_{\sim k}\right)$	$-$	$f_{A_{\sim s}}\left(A_{\sim k}\right)$	$\cdots$	$f_{A_{\sim s}}\left(A_{\sim k}\right)$
$A_{\sim 3}$	$f_{A_{\sim s}}\left(A_{\sim k}\right)$	$f_{A_{\sim s}}\left(A_{\sim k}\right)$	$-$	$\cdots$	$f_{A_{\sim s}}\left(A_{\sim k}\right)$
$\vdots$	$\vdots$	$\vdots$	$\vdots$	$\vdots$	$\vdots$
$A_{\sim m}$	$f_{A_{\sim s}}\left(A_{\sim k}\right)$	$f_{A_{\sim s}}\left(A_{\sim k}\right)$	$f_{A_{\sim s}}\left(A_{\sim k}\right)$	$\cdots$	$-$

Then we obtain results from the n participants as in Table 12.

By setting

$$f\left(A_{\sim s} \,|\, A_{\sim k}\right) = \frac{f_{A_{\sim k}}\left(A_{\sim s}\right)}{\max\left\{f_{A_{\sim s}}\left(A_{\sim k}\right),\, f_{A_{\sim k}}\left(A_{\sim s}\right)\right\}}$$

we get a matrix as shown in Table 13.

Table 13   A Comparison Matrix

$A_{\sim k} \setminus A_{\sim s}$	$A_{\sim 1}$	$A_{\sim 2}$	$A_{\sim 3}$	$\cdots$	$A_{\sim m}$
$A_{\sim 1}$	$-$	$f\left(A_{\sim 1}\,|\,A_{\sim 2}\right)$	$f\left(A_{\sim 1}\,|\,A_{\sim 3}\right)$	$\cdots$	$f\left(A_{\sim 1}\,|\,A_{\sim m}\right)$
$A_{\sim 2}$	$f\left(A_{\sim 2}\,|\,A_{\sim 1}\right)$	$-$	$f\left(A_{\sim 2}\,|\,A_{\sim 3}\right)$	$\cdots$	$f\left(A_{\sim 2}\,|\,A_{\sim m}\right)$
$A_{\sim 3}$	$f\left(A_{\sim 3}\,|\,A_{\sim 1}\right)$	$f\left(A_{\sim 3}\,|\,A_{\sim 2}\right)$	$-$	$\cdots$	$f\left(A_{\sim 3}\,|\,A_{\sim m}\right)$
$\vdots$	$\vdots$	$\vdots$	$\vdots$	$\vdots$	$\vdots$
$A_{\sim m}$	$f\left(A_{\sim m}\,|\,A_{\sim 1}\right)$	$f\left(A_{\sim m}\,|\,A_{\sim 2}\right)$	$f\left(A_{\sim m}\,|\,A_{\sim 3}\right)$	$\cdots$	$-$

Clearly, we have

$$f\left(\underset{\sim s}{A} \mid \underset{\sim k}{A}\right) = \begin{cases} \dfrac{f_A\left(\underset{\sim k}{A}\right)}{f_A\left(\underset{\sim s}{A}\right)}, & f_A\left(\underset{\sim k}{A}\right) \leq f_A\left(\underset{\sim s}{A}\right) \\[4mm] 1, & f_A\left(\underset{\sim k}{A}\right) > f_A\left(\underset{\sim s}{A}\right) \text{ or } s = k \end{cases}$$

By synthesizing the values of $f\left(\underset{\sim s}{A} \mid \underset{\sim k}{A}\right)$ we can obtain a degree of membership for u in $\underset{\sim i}{A}$. For example,

$$\underset{\sim i}{A}(u) = \bigwedge_{s=1}^{m} f\left(\underset{\sim s}{A} \mid \underset{\sim k}{A}\right), \quad i = 1, 2, \cdots, m. \tag{4.9}$$

Note. In the next chapter we present a basic tool, a multifactorial function M_m, for "multifactorial analysis". It can be used for building membership functions. The way to do this is to determine an appropriate M_m from the context of the problem, and then compute

$$\underset{\sim i}{A}(u) = M_m\left(f\left(\underset{\sim 1}{A} \mid \underset{\sim i}{A}\right), f\left(\underset{\sim 2}{A} \mid \underset{\sim i}{A}\right), \cdots, \left(\underset{\sim m}{A} \mid \underset{\sim i}{A}\right)\right). \tag{4.10}$$

4.9.2 The Mean Pairwise Comparison Method

From Table 12 and with an appropriate M_m, we can assign the degree of membership of u by

$$\underset{\sim i}{A}(u) = M_m\left(f_{A_{\sim 1}}\left(\underset{\sim i}{A}\right), f_{A_{\sim 2}}\left(\underset{\sim i}{A}\right), \cdots, f_{A_{\sim m}}\left(\underset{\sim i}{A}\right)\right). \tag{4.11}$$

In particular, take M_m as the mean function. Then

$$\underset{\sim i}{A}(u) = \frac{1}{m}\sum_{j=1}^{m} f_{A_{\sim j}}\left(\underset{\sim i}{A}\right). \tag{4.12}$$

This is a familiar formula.

Note. When U is a finite universe, and there is only one fuzzy set $\underset{\sim}{A}$ $[\in \mathcal{F}(U)]$ of interest, then we can follow the method in previous sections by replacing $\underset{\sim s}{A}$ with u_s as the basis of comparison. To illustrate, we give two examples below:

Example 23

A father has three sons named u_1, u_2, and u_3. Let $U = \{u_1, u_2, u_3\}$ and $\underset{\sim}{A}$ be the fuzzy concept of "resemblance to their father". Suppose we obtained Table 13 by pairwise comparisons, and relative to the fuzzy set $\underset{\sim}{A}$ we have

$$f_{u_1}(u_2) = 0.5, \quad f_{u_2}(u_1) = 0.8, \quad f_{u_1}(u_3) = 0.3,$$

$$f_{u_3}(u_1) = 0.5, \quad f_{u_2}(u_3) = 0.7, \quad f_{u_3}(u_2) = 0.4.$$

Table 14   Resemblance by Pairwise Comparisons

$u_j \backslash u_i$	u_1	u_2	u_3
u_1	1	0.8	0.5
u_2	0.5	1	0.4
u_3	0.3	0.7	1

Next, we calculate the following values:

$$f(u_1 \mid u_2) = \frac{f_{u_2}(u_1)}{\max\{f_{u_1}(u_2), f_{u_2}(u_1)\}} = \frac{0.8}{\max\{0.5, 0.8\}} = 1$$

Similarly,

$$f(u_2 \mid u_1) \approx 0.62, \quad f(u_1 \mid u_3) = 1, \quad f(u_3 \mid u_1) = 0.6,$$

$$f(u_2 \mid u_3) \approx 0.57, \quad f(u_3 \mid u_2) = 1.$$

We summarize these values in Table 15.

Table 15   Values of $f(u_i \mid u_j)$

$u_j \backslash u_i$	u_1	u_2	u_3
u_1	1	1	1
u_2	0.62	1	0.57
u_3	0.6	1	1

We use the operator $\wedge$ on each column in Table 15 to derive

$$\underset{\sim}{A}(u_1) = 1 \wedge 0.62 \wedge 0.6 = 0.6,$$

Likewise, $\underset{\sim}{A}(u_2) = 1$ and $\underset{\sim}{A}(u_3) = 0.57$. That is, $\underset{\sim}{A} = (0.6, 1, 0.57)$. $\square$

Example 24

Let $U = \{u_1, u_2, u_3\}$ be a universe where u_1 represents an oriental cherry, u_2 represents a chrysanthemum, and u_3 represents a dandelion. Also, let $\underset{\sim}{A}$ be a fuzzy concept "beautiful" on U. Find the membership function $\underset{\sim}{A}(u_i)$, $i = 1, 2, 3$.

Let the results of pairwise comparisons be

$$f_{u_i}(u_i) = 1, \quad i = 1, 2, 3.$$

and

$$f_{u_2}(u_1) = 0.8, \quad f_{u_1}(u_2) = 0.7, \quad f_{u_3}(u_1) = 0.9,$$

$$f_{u_1}(u_3) = 0.5, \quad f_{u_2}(u_3) = 0.4, \quad f_{u_3}(u_2) = 0.8.$$

The mean value of each row is

$$\underset{\sim}{A}(u_1) = \frac{2.8}{3} \approx 0.93, \quad \underset{\sim}{A}(u_2) \approx 0.83, \quad and \quad \underset{\sim}{A}(u_3) \approx 0.63.$$

Hence, $\underset{\sim}{A} = (0.93, 0.83, 0.63)$. 　$\Box$

References

[1] Duan, Q.-Z. and Li, H.-X., N-dimensional t-norm. *Journal of Tianjin College of Textile Engineering*, 7(2), 1988, 9–16.

[2] Li, H.-X., *Interesting Talks on Fuzzy Mathematics*. Sichuan Education Press, Sichuan, 1987. (In Chinese.)

[3] Li, H.-X., Multifactorial functions in fuzzy sets theory. *Fuzzy Sets and Systems*, 35(1), 1990, 69–84.

[4] Li, H.-X., Luo, C.-Z., and Wang, P.-Z., The cardinality of fuzzy sets and the continuum hypothesis, *Fuzzy Sets and Systems*, 55(1), 1993, 61–77.

[5] Li, H.-X., *Fuzzy Mathematics Methods in Engineering and Their Applications*. Tianjin Scientific and Technical Press, Tianjin, 1993. (In Chinese.)

[6] Li, H.-X. and Yen, V. C., Factor spaces and fuzzy decision making, *Journal of Beijing Normal University*, 30(1), 1994, 41–46.

[7] Li, H.-X. and Wang, P.-Z., Falling shadow representation of fuzzy concepts on factor spaces, *Journal of Yantai University*, No. 2, 1994, 15–21.

[8] Li, H.-X. and Wang, P.-Z., *Fuzzy Mathematics*. National Defense Press, Beijing, 1994. (In Chinese.)

[9] Wang, P.-Z., *Fuzzy Set Theory and Its Applications*. Shanghai Science Press, Shanghai, 1983. (In Chinese.)

[10] Wang, P.-Z., A factor space approach to knowledge representation, *Fuzzy Sets and Systems*, 36, 1990, 113–124.

[11] Wang, P.-Z. and Li, H.-X., *A Mathematical Theory on Knowledge Representation*. Tianjin Scientific and Technical Press, Tianjin, 1994. (In Chinese.)

5

Multifactorial Analysis

5.1 Background of the Problem

Let $\left(U, \mathcal{C}, \{X(f)\}_{(f \in F)}\right]$ be a description frame. When the factor f is quite complex, i.e., high dimensions (f is a composite of many factors), then its state space $X(f)$ of f will be difficult to determine. Consequently, we often do not know the mapping $f : U \longrightarrow X(F)$. So our basic problem is "How do we determine the states of a complex factor?" The more complex the factors are, the more difficult the states will be. One of the approaches in dealing with the complexity of factors is by decomposition. When a complex factor is decomposed into a group of (independent) simple factors, their state spaces should be more easily identified. Building upon such state spaces of simple factors, we can determine the state space of the complex factor.

Let $\{f_t\}_{(t \in T)}$ be a family of mutually independent factors and define $f = \bigvee_{t \in T} f_t$. Then

$$
X(f) = \prod_{t \in T} X(f_t) = \left\{ w \mid w : T \longrightarrow \bigcup_{t \in T} X(f_t), \quad w(t) \in X(f_t) \right\}.
$$

In practice, the index set most likely is a finite set; we assume $T = \{1, 2, \cdots, m\}$. Then $f = \bigvee_{j=1}^{m} f_j$, and

$$
X(f) = \prod_{j=1}^{m} X(f_j) = \left\{ (x_1, x_2, \cdots, x_m) \mid x_j \in X(x_j), 1 \leq j \leq m \right\}.
$$

For any $u \in U$, if $f_j(u)$ is known for $j = 1, 2, \cdots, m$, then we have

$$
f(u) = (f_1(u), f_2(u), \cdots, f_m(u)). \tag{5.1}
$$

The expression does not give us more information than simply saying it is an m-dimensional point. How can we find an easier operational form without a loss of its informational content? An effective approach is to use a low-dimensional state space, say $X'(f)$, to approximate the high-dimensional state space $X(f) = \prod_{j=1}^{m} X(f_j)$. (See Figure 5.1.)

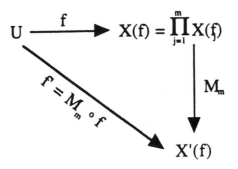

FIGURE 5.1
The functional relationships of U, $X'(f)$, and $X(f)$.

Notice that the increase and decrease of the dimensions are related. As mentioned previously, when the dimension of state spaces decreases, the dimension of factors increases. That is, the decrease in the dimension of state spaces depends upon the increase in the dimension of factors, and conversely, the increase in the dimension of factors depends upon the decrease in the dimension of state spaces. From Figure 5.1, we see that the dimension of $X(f)$ decreases to that of $X'(f)$, but the dimension of f increases to that of f'.

Thus, our problem is shifted to determine the mapping M_m that will decrease the dimension of state spaces. As shown in Figure 5.1, f' has a lower dimensional state space, and $X(f') = X'(f)$. This means that we can replace f with f', and therefore reduce the complexity from f — our basic idea.

5.2 Multifactorial Functions

The effect of the mapping M_m is to synthesize an m-dimensional vector $f(u) = (f_1(u), f_2(u), \cdots, f_m(u))$ into a one-dimensional scalar, functionally represented by

$$M_m(f(u)) = M_m(f_1(u), f_2(u), \cdots, f_m(u)).$$

Since M_m is a function of factors, we call it a **multifactorial function**.

On many occasions, it is possible to transform state spaces into closed unit intervals

$$M_m : [0, 1]^m \longrightarrow [0, 1], \quad (x_1, x_2, \cdots, x_m) \longmapsto M_m ((x_1, x_2, \cdots, x_m))$$

that we call **standard multifactorial functions**. For what follows, we will focus our discussion on standard multifactorial functions.

The standard multifactorial functions can be classified into two groups:

1. Additive standard multifactorial functions.

The functions in this class satisfy the condition: $\forall (x_1, x_2, \cdots, x_m) \in [0, 1]^m$,

$$\bigwedge_{j=1}^{m} x_j \leq M_m (x_1, x_2, \cdots, x_m) \leq \bigvee_{j=1}^{m} x_j, \tag{5.2}$$

which means that the synthesized value should not be greater than the largest of component states and should not be less than the smallest of the component states.

Example 25

Let the factor f be "the learning ability of students". We decompose f into four mutually independent factors represented by scores of four tests, f_1, f_2, f_3, and f_4 such that

$$f = f_1 \vee f_2 \vee f_3 \vee f_4,$$

where f_1=mathematics, f_2=physics, f_3=chemistry, and f_4=foreign language.

We can make a transformation from the usual range of scores between 0 and 100 to [0, 1]. Then

$$X (f) = \prod_{j=1}^{4} X (f_j) = [0, 1]^4.$$

Now suppose u (John) $\in U$ has the following scores: mathematics, 84; physics, 78; chemistry, 90; and foreign language, 66. After transformation, the new scores are: mathematics, 0.84; physics, 0.78; chemistry, 0.90; and foreign language, 0.66. Then the value of the multifactorial function for John is

$$M_4 (f (u)) = M_4 (f_1 (u), f_2 (u), f_3 (u), f_4 (u))$$

$$= M_4 (0.84, 0.78, 0.90, 0.66).$$

It should satisfy

$$0.66 \leq M_4 (0.84, 0.78, 0.90, 0.66) \leq 0.90.$$

For instance, we may choose M_4 as the mean (average) function. Then the above condition is satisfied. In this case,

$$M_4 (0.84, 0.78, 0.90, 0.66) = \frac{1}{4} (0.84 + 0.78 + 0.90 + 0.66) = 0.795.$$

▯

2. Non-additive standard multifactorial functions.

This class of functions does not satisfy condition (5.2). That is, the synthesized value can exceed the boundaries of condition (5.2).

For example, a department is led and managed by three people; each of them has a strong leading ability. But for some reason, they cannot work smoothly among themselves. Hence the collective leading ability (a multifactorial score) falls below the individual's, i.e.,

$$M_3 (x_1, x_2, x_3) \leq \bigwedge_{j=1}^{3} x_j,$$

where x_i is the leading ability of the individual, i, $i = 1, 2, 3$, and $M_3 (x_1, x_2, x_3)$ is the multifactorial leading ability indicator for the group of three.

On the other hand, it is possible for the three management people to work together exceedingly well. This implies that the combined leadership score can be higher than any one of the three individual's, i.e.,

$$M_3 (x_1, x_2, x_3) \geq \bigvee_{j=1}^{3} x_j.$$

It has the same meaning as in the Chinese old saying: "Three cobblers with their wits combined can exceed Chukeh Liang, the master minded".

Non-additive standard multifactorial functions can also be subdivided into two types:

(a) **Catastrophic standard multifactorial functions** — This type of functions can be described by elementary catastrophe models — an interesting problem in its own right.

(b) **Singular standard multifactorial functions** — This type of functions cannot be described by elementary catastrophe models.

However, in principle, they can be described by non-elementary catastrophe models. Since the non-elementary catastrophe theory is far from perfection at present, this type of multifactorial functions has not been dealt with by catastrophe theory — an open problem to all.

5.3 Axiomatic Definition of Additive Standard Multifactorial Functions

We begin by making use of five transformations: p_j, q_j, σ_{ij}, r_j, and k_j from $[0, 1]^m \longrightarrow [0, 1]$, p_j, q_j, and σ_{ij}. These have been defined in Section 3.4.4. The other two are defined below: For any $X = (x_1, x_2, \cdots, x_m) \in [0, 1]^m$,

$$r_j(X) = \left(x_1, \cdots, x_{j-1}, 0, x_{j+1}, \cdots, x_m\right)$$

and

$$k_j(X) = \left(x_1, \cdots, x_{j-1}, 1, x_{j+1}, \cdots, x_m\right).$$

DEFINITION 16 *A mapping $M_m : [0, 1]^m \longrightarrow [0, 1]$ is called an $m - ary$* **additive standard multifactorial function** *if it satisfies the following axioms:*

(m.1) $X \le Y \Longrightarrow M_m(X) \le M_m(Y)$;

(m.2) $\bigwedge\limits_{j=1}^{m} x_j \le M_m(X) \le \bigvee\limits_{j=1}^{m} x_j$; *and*

(m.3) $M_m(x_1, x_2, ..., x_m)$ *is a continuous function of each variable x_j.*

We call this kind of function an **ASM$_m$-func**, *and the set of all ASM$_m$-funcs is denoted by $\mathcal{M}_m$. An ASM$_1$-func is an identity mapping from $[0, 1]$ to $[0, 1]$.*

We now add the following additional conditions to ASM$_m$-funcs:

(m.4) $M_m\left(r_j(X)\right) = 0$;

(m.5) $M_m\left(p_j(X)\right) = x_j$;

(m.6) $M_m\left(\sigma_{ij}(X)\right) = M_m(X)$;

(m.7) $M_m\left(q_j(X)\right) = x_j$;

(m.8) $M_m\left(k_j(X)\right) = 1$;

(m.9) there exists $M_r \in \mathcal{M}_r$, $M_{m-r} \in \mathcal{M}_{m-r}$, $1 < r < m$, and $M_2 \in \mathcal{M}_2$ such that

$\forall X = (x_1, x_2, \cdots, x_m)$,

$M_m(X) = M_2(M_r(x_1, x_2, \cdots, x_m), M_{m-r}(x_1, x_2, \cdots, x_m))$;

(m.10) there exists an $M_2 \in \mathcal{M}_2$ such that $\forall X$,

$M_m(X) = M_2(M_2(\cdots M_2(M_2(x_1, x_2), x_3)\cdots), x_m)$;

(m.11) For every $X = (x_1, \cdots, x_m)$ and $Y = (x_{m+1}, \cdots, x_{2m-1})$,

$M_m(M_m(X), x_{m+1}, \cdots, x_{2m-1}) = M_m(x_1, \cdots, x_{m-1}, M_m(Y))$.

Example 26

The following are examples of ASM$_m$-funcs from $[0, 1]^m$ to $[0, 1]$.

(a)

$$\bigwedge : X \longrightarrow \bigwedge(X) = \bigwedge_{j=1}^{m} x_j. \tag{5.3}$$

(b)

$$\bigvee : X \longrightarrow \bigvee (X) = \bigvee_{j=1}^{m} x_j. \tag{5.4}$$

(c)

$$\sum : X \longrightarrow \sum (X) = \sum_{j=1}^{m} a_j x_j \tag{5.5}$$

where $a_j \in [0, 1]$, and $\sum\limits_{j=1}^{m} a_j = 1$.

(d)

$$M_m (X) = \sum_{j=1}^{m} a_j (x_j) x_j \tag{5.6}$$

where $a_j : [0, 1] \longrightarrow [0, 1]$, $x \longmapsto a_j (x_j)$ is a continuous function and satisfies $\sum\limits_{j=1}^{m} a_j (x_j) = 1$.

(e)

$$M_m (X) = \bigvee_{j=1}^{m} (a_j x_j) \tag{5.7}$$

where $a_j \in [0, 1]$, and $\bigvee\limits_{j=1}^{m} a_j = 1$.

(f)

$$M_m (X) = \bigvee_{j=1}^{m} (a_j \wedge x_j) \tag{5.8}$$

where $a_j \in [0, 1]$, and $\bigvee\limits_{j=1}^{m} a_j = 1$.

(g)

$$M_m (X) = \left(\prod_{j=1}^{m} x_j \right)^{\frac{1}{m}} \tag{5.9}$$

(h)

$$M_m (X) = \left(\frac{1}{m} \sum_{j=1}^{m} x_j^p \right)^{\frac{1}{p}}, \quad p > 0, \tag{5.10}$$

(i)

$$M_m (X) = \left(\sum_{j=1}^{m} a_j x_j^p \right)^{\frac{1}{p}}, \quad p > 0, \tag{5.11}$$

where $a_j \in [0, 1]$, and $\sum\limits_{j=1}^{m} a_j = 1$. ☐

We can easily verify the following claims on these ASM_m-funcs.

Function (a) satisfies conditions (m.i), $i = 4, 5, 6, 9, 10, 11$.

Function (b) satisfies conditions (m.i), $i = 6, 7, 8, 9, 10, 11$.

Function (c) and function (d) satisfy condition (m.9); they satisfy condition (m.7) when $a_j = 1$ and $a_j(x_j) = 1$.

Function (e) satisfies condition (m.9); it satisfies condition (m.7) when $a_j = 1$.

Function (f) satisfies condition (m.9); it satisfies condition (m.7) when $a_j \geq x_j$.

Function (g) satisfies conditions (m.4), (m.6), and (m.11); it satisfies condition (m.5) when $x_j = 1$.

Function (h) satisfies conditions (m.6).

Function (i) satisfies condition (m.7) when $a_j = 1$.

5.4   Properties of ASM_m-funcs

We introduce a partial ordering "$\leq$" to the set $\mathcal{M}_m$ as follows: For $\forall M_m, M'_m \in \mathcal{M}_m$, then

$$M_m \leq M'_m \iff (\forall X)\left(M_m(X) \leq M'_m(X)\right).$$

It is simple to prove.

PROPOSITION 25
The ordered set $(\mathcal{M}_m, \leq)$ is a compete distributive lattice; $\bigwedge$ is the least element (see Eq. 5.3) and $\bigvee$ is the greatest element in $\mathcal{M}_m$.

PROPOSITION 26
For any $M_m \in \mathcal{M}_m$, we have
1) $(\forall j)\left(x_j = a\right) \implies M_m(x_1, ..., x_m) = a$;
2) $M_m(1, ..., 1) = 1$, $M_m(0, ..., 0) = 0$.

PROOF   Since (m.2) $\implies$ 1) $\implies$ 2).   ∎

PROPOSITION 27
Let $I = (1, 1, ..., 1)$ and $I - X = (1 - x_1, 1 - x_2, ..., 1 - x_m)$. For any $M_m \in \mathcal{M}_m$, define

$$M_m^*(X) = 1 - M_m(I - X).$$

Then, $M_m^* \in \mathcal{M}_m$ and $\left(M_m^*\right)^* = M_m$.

The proof is omitted since it is straightforward.

From the proposition, we obtain $\bigwedge^* (X) = \bigvee (X)$ and $\bigvee^* (X) = \bigwedge (X)$.

Example 27
With proposition 27 and example 26, the following functions from $[0, 1]^m$ to $[0, 1]$
are all ASM_m funcs.
(a)

$$\Sigma^* (X) = 1 - \sum_{j=1}^{m} a_j \left(1 - x_j\right) \tag{5.12}$$

where $a_j \in [0, 1]$, and $\sum_{j=1}^{m} a_j = 1$.
(b)

$$M_m (X) = \bigwedge_{j=1}^{m} \left(1 - a_j \left(1 - x_j\right)\right) \tag{5.13}$$

where $a_j \in [0, 1]$, and $\bigvee_{j=1}^{m} a_j = 1$.
(c)

$$M_m (X) = \bigwedge_{j=1}^{m} \left(\left(1 - a_j\right) \vee x_j\right) \tag{5.14}$$

where $a_j \in [0, 1]$, and $\bigvee_{j=1}^{m} a_j = 1$.
(d)

$$M_m (X) = 1 - \left(\prod_{j=1}^{m} \left(1 - x_j\right)\right)^{\frac{1}{m}} \tag{5.15}$$

(e)

$$M_m (X) = 1 - \left(\frac{1}{m} \sum_{j=1}^{m} \left(1 - x_j\right)^p\right)^{\frac{1}{p}}, \quad p > 0. \tag{5.16}$$

(f)

$$M_m (X) = 1 - \left(\sum_{j=1}^{m} a_j \left(1 - x_j^p\right)\right) \tag{5.17}$$

where $p > 0$, $a_j \in [0, 1]$, and $\sum_{j=1}^{m} a_j = 1$. ∎

PROPOSITION 28

For any $M_m \in \mathcal{M}_m$, the following properties hold:

1) M_m satisfies (m.4) $\Longleftrightarrow$ M_m^* satisfies (m.8);

2) M_m satisfies (m.5) $\Longleftrightarrow$ M_m^* satisfies (m.7); and,

3) M_m satisfies (m.i) $\Longleftrightarrow$ M_m^* satisfies (m.i) for $i = 6, 9, 10,$ and 11.

PROOF

1) First we show the validity of "$\Longrightarrow$".

If $\forall X \in [0, 1]^m$, then

$$M_m^* \left(k_j \left(X \right) \right) = 1 - M_m \left(I - k_j \left(X \right) \right)$$

$$= 1 - M_m(p_j \left(I - X \right) = 1 - 0 = 1.$$

"$\Longleftarrow$" may be proved in the similar fashion.

2) Proof for "$\Longrightarrow$" : $\forall X \in [0, 1]^m$; X satisfies

$$M_m^* \left(q_j \left(X \right) \right) = 1 - M_m \left(I - q_j \left(X \right) \right)$$

$$= 1 - M_m(p_j \left(I - X \right)$$

$$= 1 - \left(1 - x_j \right) = x_j.$$

The proof of sufficiency is similar.

3) It is obvious when i=6. We prove for the case i=9.

Proof for "$\Longrightarrow$ " : $\forall X \in [0, 1]^m$; X satisfies

$M_m^* \left(X \right) = 1 - M_m \left(I - X \right)$

$\quad = 1 - M_2 \left(M_r \left(1 - x_1, \cdots, 1 - x_r \right), M_{m-r} \left(1 - x_{r+1}, \cdots, 1 - x_m \right) \right)$

$\quad = M_2^* \left(1 - M_r \left(1 - x_1, \cdots, 1 - x_r \right), 1 - M_{m-r} \left(1 - x_{r+1}, \cdots, 1 - x_m \right) \right)$

$\quad = M_2^* \left(M_r^* \left(x_1, \cdots, x_r \right), M_{m-r}^* \left(x_{r+1}, \cdots, x_m \right) \right)$

Similar proof for "$\Longleftarrow$".

The proof for i=10 is just like the previous proof.

We now prove for the case i=11.

Proof for "$\Longrightarrow$": Let $X = (x_1, \cdots, x_m)$ and $Y = (x_{m+1}, \cdots, x_{2m-1})$. Then

$M_m^* \left(M_m^* \left(X \right), x_{m+1}, \cdots, x_{2m-1} \right)$

$\quad = 1 - M_m \left(1 - M_m^* \left(X \right), 1 - x_{m+1}, \cdots, 1 - x_{2m-1} \right)$

$\quad = 1 - M_m \left(M_m \left(I - X \right), 1 - x_{m+1}, \cdots, 1 - x_{2m-1} \right)$

$\quad = 1 - M_m \left(1 - x_1, \cdots, 1 - x_m, M_m \left(I - Y \right) \right)$

$\quad = 1 - M_m \left(1 - x_1, \cdots, 1 - x_m, 1 - M_m^* \left(Y \right) \right)$

$\quad = M_m^* \left(x_1, \cdots, x_m, M_m^* \left(Y \right) \right)$

Sufficiency can be proved in the same manner. ∎

PROPOSITION 29

For any $M_2 \in \mathcal{M}_2$, set

$$M_m(X) = M_2(M_2(...M_2(M_2(x_1, x_2), x_3)...), x_m)$$

then $M_m \in \mathcal{M}_m$, and for $i = 4, 5, 6, 7$, and 8. If M_2 satisfies (m.i), then so does M_m.

The proof is omitted since it is simple.

PROPOSITION 30

Given an $M_m^0 \in \mathcal{M}_m$ and a $t \in [0, 1]$.
   1) Let $X \in [0, 1]^m$ and set

$$M_m(X) = \begin{cases} M_m^0(X), & M_m^0(X) \in [t, 1] \\ \bigwedge\limits_{j=1}^{m} x_j, & M_m^0(X) \in [0, t] \end{cases}$$

Then $M_m \in \mathcal{M}_m$, and $i = 4, 5, 6, 9, 10$, and 11. If M_m^0 satisfies (m.i), then so does M_m.
   2) Let $X \in [0, 1]^m$ and set

$$M_m(X) = \begin{cases} \bigvee\limits_{j=1}^{m} x_j, & M_m^0(X) \in [t, 1] \\ M_m^0(X), & M_m^0(X) \in [0, t] \end{cases}$$

Then $M_m \in \mathcal{M}_m$, and $i = 6, 7, 8, 9, 10$, and 11. If M_m^0 satisfies (m.i), then so does M_m.

The proof is simple and hence omitted.

PROPOSITION 31

Let $M_n \in \mathcal{M}_n$, and $M_m^{(k)} \in \mathcal{M}_m$ for k=1,2,...,n. For any $X \in [0, 1]^m$ and setting,

$$M_m(X) = M_n\left(M_m^{(1)}(X), M_m^{(2)}(X), ..., M_m^{(n)}(X)\right)$$

Then $M_m \in \mathcal{M}_m$; for $i = 4, 5, 6, 7, 8$, and 10, if $M_m^{(k)}$ satisfies (m.i) for $k = 1, 2, ..., n$, then so does M_n. For $i = 4$ and 8, if $M_m^{(k)}$ and M_n satisfy (m.i) then so does M_m.

We will not prove this because it is straightforward.

Example 28

Take $M_n = \bigwedge$ and $M_m^{(k)}(X) = \sum_{j=1}^{m} a_{kj} x_j$ for $k = 1, 2, ..., n$, where $a_{kj} \in [0, 1]$

and $\sum_{j=1}^{m} a_{kj} = 1$, for $k = 1, 2, ..., n$. Define

$$M_m(X) = \bigwedge_{k=1}^{n} \left(\sum_{j=1}^{m} a_{kj} x_j \right).$$

Then $M_m \in \mathcal{M}_m$. □

Note. Let $M_n \in \mathcal{M}_n$; $M_r^1, M_r^2, \cdots, M_r^n \in \mathcal{M}_r$; $M_m^{11}, M_m^{12}, \cdots, M_m^{1r}; M_m^{21}$, $M_m^{22}, \cdots, M_m^{2r}; \cdots; M_m^{n1}, M_m^{n2}, \cdots, M_m^{n1} \in \mathcal{M}_m$, and define

$$M_m(X) = M_n \left(M_r^1 \left(M_m^{11}(X), \cdots, M_m^{1r}(X) \right), \cdots, M_r^n \left(M_m^{n1}(X), \cdots, M_m^{n1}(X) \right) \right).$$

Then $M_m \in \mathcal{M}_m$.

Example 29

Take $M_n = \bigvee$, $M_r^k = \bigwedge$, $M_m^{ki}(X) = \sum_{j=1}^{m} a_{kij} x_j$, and set

$$M_m(X) = \bigvee_{k=1}^{n} \left(\bigwedge_{i=1}^{r} \left(\sum_{j=1}^{m} a_{kij} x_j \right) \right),$$

where $a_{kij} \in [0, 1]$ and $\sum_{j=1}^{m} a_{kij} = 1$. Then $M_m \in \mathcal{M}_m$. □

5.5 Generations of ASM$_m$-funcs

In this section, we study the problem of how to generate complicated ASM$_m$-funcs from some simple and well-known ASM$_m$-funcs.

Let $g : [0, 1] \longrightarrow [0, 1]$ be a continuous and strict monotonically increasing function with $g(0) = 0$ and $g(1) = 1$. So $G : [0, 1] \longrightarrow [0, 1]$, the inverse function of g, exists, and it is also a strict monotonically increasing function with $G(0) = 0$ and $G(1) = 1$. Note that both g and G belong to $\mathcal{M}_1$. We show that ASM_m-funcs can be generated by g's.

THEOREM 17
Let $M_m^0 \in \mathcal{M}_m$ and

$$M_m(X) = G\left(M_m^0\left(g(x_1), g(x_2), \cdots, g(x_m)\right)\right). \qquad (5.18)$$

Then $M_m \in \mathcal{M}_m$, and when M_m^0 satisfies (m.i), so does M_m, where i=4,...,11.

PROOF   We will prove (m.9), (m.10), and (m.11), since the rest of the cases are obvious.

Case (m.9): Because M_m^0 satisfies (m.9), there exists $M_r^0 \in \mathcal{M}_r$, $M_{m-r}^0 \in \mathcal{M}_{m-r}$ and $M_2^0 \in \mathcal{M}_2$
such that

$$M_m^0(X) = M_2^0\left(M_r^0\left(x_{1,} \cdots, x_r\right), M_{m-r}^0\left(x_{r+1}, \cdots, x_m\right)\right).$$

We now take

$$M_r\left(x_{1,} \cdots, x_r\right) = G\left(M_r^0\left(g(x_1), \cdots, g(x_r)\right)\right)$$

$$M_{m-r}(y_1, \cdots, y_{m-r}) = G\left(M_{m-r}^0\left(g(y_1), \cdots, g(y_{m-r})\right)\right)$$

and

$$M_2(z_1, z_2) = G\left(M_2^0\left(g(z_1, z_2)\right)\right).$$

Then,

$$\begin{aligned}
&M_2\left(M_r\left(x_{1,} \cdots, x_r\right), M_{m-r}(y_1, \cdots, y_{m-r})\right)\\
&= G\left(M_2^0\left(g\left(M_r\left(x_{1,} \cdots, x_r\right)\right), g\left(M_{m-r}(y_1, \cdots, y_{m-r})\right)\right)\right)\\
&= G\left(M_2^0\left(M_r^0\left(g(x_1), \cdots, g(x_r)\right), M_{m-r}^0\left(g(x_{r+1}), \cdots, g(x_m)\right)\right)\right)\\
&= G\left(M_m^0\left(g(x_1), \cdots, g(x_m)\right)\right)\\
&= M_m(X).
\end{aligned}$$

So, we have proved (m.9).
Case (m.10): Because M_m^0 satisfies (m.10), there exists $M_2^0 \in \mathcal{M}_2$ such that

$$M_m^0(X) = M_2^0\left(M_2^0\left(\cdots M_2^0\left(M_2^0(x_1, x_2), x_3\right)\cdots\right), x_m\right).$$

Take

$$M_2(y_1, y_2) = G\left(M_2^0\left(g\left(y_1\right), g\left(y_2\right)\right)\right).$$

Then,

$$M_2\left(M_2\left(\cdots M_2\left(M_2\left(x_1, x_2\right), x_3\right)\cdots\right), x_m\right)$$
$$= G\left(M_2^0\left(g\left(M_2\left(\cdots M_2\left(M_2\left(x_1, x_2\right), x_3\right)\cdots\right)\right), g\left(x_m\right)\right)\right)$$
$$= \cdots$$
$$= G\left(M_2^0\left(M_2^0\left(\cdots M_2^0\left(M_2^0\left(g\left(x_1\right), g\left(x_2\right)\right), g\left(x_3\right)\right)\cdots\right), g\left(x_m\right)\right)\right)$$
$$= G\left(M_m^0\left(g\left(x_1\right), \cdots, g\left(x_m\right)\right)\right)$$
$$= M_m(X).$$

So, we have proved (m.10).

Case (m.11): $\forall X = (x_1, \cdots, x_m)$ and $Y = (x_m, \cdots, x_{2m-1})$,

$$M_m\left(M_m(X), x_{m+1}, \cdots, x_{2m-1}\right)$$
$$= G\left(M_m^0\left(g\left(M_m(X)\right), g\left(x_{m+1}\right), \cdots, g\left(x_{2m-1}\right)\right)\right)$$
$$= G\left(M_m^0\left(M_m^0\left(g\left(x_1\right), \cdots, g\left(x_m\right)\right), g\left(x_{m+1}\right), \cdots, g\left(x_{2m-1}\right)\right)\right)$$
$$= G\left(M_m^0\left(g\left(x_1\right), \cdots, g\left(x_{m-1}\right), M_m^0\left(g\left(x_m\right), \cdots, g\left(x_{2m-1}\right)\right)\right)\right)$$
$$= G\left(M_m^0\left(g\left(x_1\right), \cdots, g\left(x_{m-1}\right), g\left(G\left(M_m^0\left(g\left(x_m\right), \cdots, g\left(x_{2m-1}\right)\right)\right)\right)\right)\right)$$
$$= M_m\left(x_1, \cdots, x_{m-1}, M_m(Y)\right).$$

This completes the proof. ∎

Example 30

Let $M_m^0 = \bigwedge$ and $g(x) = x$. Then, $G(x) = x$, and

$$M_m(X) = \bigwedge_{j=1}^{m} x_j.$$

☐

Example 31

Let $M_m^0 = \sum$ and $g(x) = x^p$, $p > 0$. Then, $G(x) = x^{\frac{1}{p}}$, and

$$M_m(X) = \left(\sum_{j=1}^{m} a_j x_j^p\right)^{\frac{1}{p}}.$$

☐

Example 32

Let $g(x) = \sin\left(\frac{\pi x}{2}\right)$. Then $G(x) = \frac{2}{\pi}\arcsin x$. The following functions are all ASM$_m$-funcs.

(a)

$$M_m\left(X\right) = \frac{2}{\pi}\arcsin\left(\bigwedge_{j=1}^{m}\sin\left(\frac{\pi}{2}\right)x_j\right).$$

(b)

$$M_m\left(X\right) = \frac{2}{\pi}\arcsin\left(\bigvee_{j=1}^{m}\sin\left(\frac{\pi}{2}\right)x_j\right).$$

(c)

$$M_m\left(X\right) = \frac{2}{\pi}\arcsin\left(\sum_{j=1}^{m}a_j\sin\left(\frac{\pi}{2}\right)x_j\right),$$

where $a_j \in [0, 1]$ and $\sum_{j=1}^{m}a_j = 1$.

(d)

$$M_m\left(X\right) = \frac{2}{\pi}\arcsin\left(\bigwedge_{j=1}^{m}\left(1 - a_j\left(1 - \sin\left(\frac{\pi}{2}\right)x_j\right)\right)\right),$$

where $a_j \in [0, 1]$ and $\sum_{j=1}^{m}a_j = 1$.

(e)

$$M_m\left(X\right) = \frac{2}{\pi}\arcsin\left(\bigwedge_{j=1}^{m}\left((1 - a_j)\vee\sin\left(\frac{\pi}{2}\right)x_j\right)\right),$$

where $a_j \in [0, 1]$ and $\sum_{j=1}^{m}a_j = 1$.

(f)

$$M_m\left(X\right) = \frac{2}{\pi}\arcsin\left(1 - \left(\prod_{j=1}^{m}\left(1 - \sin\left(\frac{\pi}{2}\right)x_j\right)^{\frac{1}{m}}\right)\right).$$

(g)

$$M_m\left(X\right) = \frac{2}{\pi}\arcsin\left(1 - \left(\frac{1}{m}\sum_{j=1}^{m}\left(1 - \sin\left(\frac{\pi}{2}\right)x_j\right)^{p}\right)^{\frac{1}{p}}\right), \quad p > 0.$$

(h)

$$M_m\left(X\right) = \frac{2}{\pi}\arcsin\left(1 - \left(\frac{1}{m}\sum_{j=1}^{m}a_j\left(1 - \left(\sin\left(\frac{\pi}{2}\right)x_j\right)^{p}\right)\right)^{\frac{1}{p}}\right),$$

where $p > 0$, $a_j \in [0, 1]$ and $\sum_{j=1}^{m}a_j = 1$. $\square$

Let $h : [0, +\infty] \longrightarrow [0, +\infty]$ be a continuous and strict monotonically decreasing function with $h(0) = +\infty$, $h(1) = 1$ and $h(+\infty) = 0$. The inverse function of h, $H : [0, +\infty] \longrightarrow [0, +\infty]$ exists and is also a continuous and strict monotonically decreasing function with $H(0) = +\infty$, $H(1) = 1$ and $H(+\infty) = 0$. ASM_m-funcs can likewise be generated by such functions as h.

THEOREM 18
Let $M_m^0 \in \mathcal{M}_m$ and

$$M_m(X) = H\left(\left(M_m^0\left(\frac{1}{h(x_1)}, \cdots, \frac{1}{h(x_m)}\right)\right)^{-1}\right).$$

Then $M_m \in \mathcal{M}_m$, and when M_m^0 satisfies (m.i), so does M_m for $i = 4, ..., 11$.

PROOF Let $g(x) = 1/h(x)$. Then the inverse of g is $G(x) = H(1/x)$. Since g satisfies the assumptions of the last theorem, so does $H(x) = G(1/x)$. Hence,

$$M_m(X) = H\left(\left(M_m^0\left(\frac{1}{h(x_1)}, \cdots, \frac{1}{h(x_m)}\right)\right)^{-1}\right)$$

$$= G\left(M_m^0(g(x_1), \cdots, g(x_m))\right).$$

By theorem 17, the proof is complete. ∎

Example 33
Let $h(x) = \frac{1}{2}\left(e - e^{-1}\right)\csc hx$. Then

$$H(x) = \frac{1}{2}\ln\frac{\left[1 + \left[4x^2/\left(e - e^{-1}\right)^2\right]\right]^{\frac{1}{2}} + 1}{\left[1 + \left[4x^2/\left(e - e^{-1}\right)^2\right]\right]^{\frac{1}{2}} - 1}.$$

Thus, the following functions are ASM_m-funcs:

$$M_m(X) = \frac{1}{2}\ln\frac{\left[1 + \left[4/\left[\bigwedge_{j=1}^{m}\left(e^{x_j} - e^{-x_j}\right)\right]^2\right]\right]^{\frac{1}{2}} + 1}{\left[1 + \left[4/\left[\bigwedge_{j=1}^{m}\left(e^{x_j} - e^{-x_j}\right)\right]^2\right]\right]^{\frac{1}{2}} - 1};$$

$$M_m(X) = \frac{1}{2} \ln \frac{\left[1 + \left[4 / \left[\bigvee_{j=1}^{m} \left(e^{x_j} - e^{-x_j}\right)\right]^2\right]\right]^{\frac{1}{2}} + 1}{\left[1 + \left[4 / \left[\bigvee_{j=1}^{m} \left(e^{x_j} - e^{-x_j}\right)\right]^2\right]\right]^{\frac{1}{2}} - 1};$$

$$M_m(X) = \frac{1}{2} \ln \frac{\left[1 + \left[4 / \left[\sum_{j=1}^{m} a_j \left(e^{x_j} - e^{-x_j}\right)\right]^2\right]\right]^{\frac{1}{2}} + 1}{\left[1 + \left[4 / \left[\sum_{j=1}^{m} a_j \left(e^{x_j} - e^{-x_j}\right)\right]^2\right]\right]^{\frac{1}{2}} - 1},$$

where $a_j \in [0, 1]$ and $\sum_{j=1}^{m} a_j = 1$. ☐

5.6 Applications of ASM$_m$-funcs in Fuzzy Decision Making

5.6.1 Fuzzy Decision Making with Several Criteria

Let $A = \{a_1, \cdots, a_n\}$ be a set of events, $B = \{b_1, \cdots, b_m\}$ be the set of policies, and $C = \{c_1, \cdots, c_p\}$ be the set of criteria. For every criterion, there exists a game matrix:

$$R^{(k)} = \begin{bmatrix} r_{11}^{(k)} & r_{12}^{(k)} & \cdots & r_{1m}^{(k)} \\ r_{21}^{(k)} & r_{22}^{(k)} & \cdots & r_{2m}^{(k)} \\ \vdots & \vdots & \vdots & \vdots \\ r_{n1}^{(k)} & r_{n2}^{(k)} & \cdots & r_{nm}^{(k)} \end{bmatrix}$$

where $r_{ij}^{(k)}$ is the degree of success using policy b_j on the event a_i under criterion c_k.

Choose an appropriate ASM$_m$-func $M_p \in \mathcal{M}_p$ and put

$$r_{ij}^* = M_p\left(r_{ij}^{(1)}, r_{ij}^{(2)}, \cdots, r_{ij}^{(p)}\right).$$

Then we have a multifactorial decision matrix:

$$R^* = \begin{bmatrix} r_{11}^* & r_{12}^* & \cdots & r_{1m}^* \\ r_{21}^* & r_{22}^* & \cdots & r_{2m}^* \\ \vdots & \vdots & \cdots & \vdots \\ r_{n1}^* & r_{n2}^* & \cdots & r_{nm}^* \end{bmatrix}.$$

For every $i \in \{1, 2, \cdots, n\}$, if there exists a j_0 such that

$$r_{ij}^* = \max \left\{ r_{i1}^*, \ r_{i2}^*, \ \cdots \ , r_{im}^* \right\}$$

then b_{j_0} is the optimal decision on the event a_i.

5.6.2 Multifactorial Estimation of Quality

Let $F = \{f_1, f_2, \cdots, f_n\}$ be a set of factors used for the measurement of the quality of product β, and $P = \{p_1, p_2, \cdots, p_r\}$ be a panel of evaluators.

On factor f_i, an evaluator p_j independently assigns three to five scores on the scale of 0 (poor) to 1 (excellent), as shown in Figure 5.2. The range of these scores is denoted by $\left[a_j, b_j\right]$ — a form of set-valued statistics.

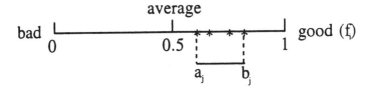

FIGURE 5.2
Evaluation of quality based on one factor.

For every index $i \in \{1, 2, \cdots, n\}$, we calculate

$$a_i^* = \frac{\sum\limits_{j=1}^{r} (b_j - a_j)\left(\frac{a_j + b_j}{2}\right)}{\sum\limits_{j=1}^{r} (b_j - a_j)} = \frac{\sum\limits_{j=1}^{r} \left(b_j^2 - a_j^2\right)}{2\sum\limits_{j=1}^{r} (b_j - a_j)}.$$

Let $A = \left(a_1^*, a_2^*, \cdots, a_n^*\right)$. Then A is a distribution of quality measures of product β on the n factors. Now take an appropriate ASM_m-func $M_m \in \mathcal{M}_n$ and define

$$a = M_n \left(a_1^*, a_2^*, \cdots, a_n^*\right).$$

Then a is an estimation of overall quality of product β.

5.6.3 Fuzzy Multifactorial Evaluation

Let $F = \{f_1, f_2, \cdots, f_n\}$ be a set of n factors and $E = \{e_1, e_2, \cdots, e_m\}$ be a set of m evaluations. First, we define a one-factor evaluation mapping φ from F to $\mathcal{F}(E)$ as follows:

$$f_i :\longmapsto \varphi(f_i) = R_i = (r_{i1}, r_{i2}, \cdots, r_{im}).$$

From these R_i we form a matrix and call it a one-factor evaluation matrix.

$$R = \begin{bmatrix} R_1 \\ R_2 \\ \vdots \\ R_n \end{bmatrix} = \begin{bmatrix} r_{11} & r_{12} & \cdots & r_{1m} \\ r_{21} & r_{22} & \cdots & r_{2m} \\ \vdots & \vdots & \vdots & \vdots \\ r_{n1} & r_{n2} & \cdots & r_{nm} \end{bmatrix}.$$

Now we take a suitable ASM_n func $Mn \in \mathcal{M}_n$ and make the multifactorial evaluation:

$$B = (b_1, b_2, \cdots, b_m)$$

$$= \left(M_n\left(r_{11}, \cdots, r_{n1}\right), M_n\left(r_{12}, \cdots, r_{n2}\right), \cdots, M_n\left(r_{1m}, \cdots, r_{nm}\right) \right).$$

Clearly, $B \in \mathcal{F}(E)$. If there exists an index $f_0 \in \{1, 2, \cdots, m\}$ such that

$$b_{j_0} = \max\{b_1, b_2, \cdots, b_m\}$$

then we should adopt the evaluation b_{j_0}.

5.7 A General Model of Multifactorial Decision Making

Normally, a "decision-making" problem is choosing an optimal decision against some goal or objective from the set of all possible alternative decisions. In practical decision problems, the number of goals or objectives under consideration is often more than one. Such problems are referred to as multiple objective decision-making problems (MOD). Since objectives are established on the basis of criteria, the aforementioned decision problems are also referred to as multiple criteria decision-making problems (MCD).

Multiple objective decision-making problems can be classified into two types: Multiple objective programming (MOP) and multiple attribute decision-making (MAD). MOP is a type of optimization problem with infinite alternatives in its constraint region, whereas MAD has finite alternatives. From our factor spaces point of view, both types of decision problems concern decision making with several factors. Therefore, we call these two types of problems multifactorial decision-making problems. We now describe a general framework for modeling a multifactorial decision-making problem.

Let U be a set of strategies or policies and $f_1, f_2, \cdots, f_m$ are mutually independent basic factors of U with $X(f_i)$ denoting the state space of f_i, $i = 1, 2, \cdots, m$. Let's assume

$$\pi = \{f_1, f_2, \cdots, f_m\}$$

to be a family of atomic factors. Define

$$F = \mathcal{P}(\pi), \ \bigvee = \cup, \ \bigwedge = \cap, \ \theta = \phi, \ 1 = \pi, \ and - = \setminus,$$

then $\left(F, \bigvee, \bigwedge, c, \mathbf{0}, \mathbf{1}\right)$ is a complete Boolean algebra. Since F is an atomic lattice, then for any factor $f \in F$ there must exist a family of factors $\{f_{jk}\}_{(1 \leq k \leq r)} \subset \pi$, where $1 \leq r \leq m$ and $f = \bigvee\limits_{k=1}^{r} f_{jk}$. So we may stipulate

$$X(f) = \prod_{j=1}^{r} X(f_{jk}).$$

Consequently, $\{X(f)\}_{(f \in F)}$ forms a factor space; in particular, $X(\mathbf{1}) = \prod\limits_{j=1}^{m} X(f_j)$.

For every strategy $u \in U$, u is completely determined by the state

$$\mathbf{1}(u) = (f_1(u), f_2(u), \cdots, f_m(u))$$

where $\mathbf{1}(u)$ is called a **decision variable**. The state space (complete), $X(\mathbf{1}) = \prod\limits_{j=1}^{m} X(f_j)$ is called the **space of decision variables**. Every factor $f \in F$ is called an **objective** or a **criterion**. **1** is called the **complete objective** or **whole objective** or criterion.

Corresponding to each objective (or criterion) f_j, there is an objective function, for example,

$$\varphi_j : X(f_j) \longrightarrow \mathfrak{R}^+ = \{\text{nonnegative real numbers}\}.$$

Note that $\Re^+$ can be transformed into the closed unit interval $[0, 1]$. Thus we admit

$$\varphi_j : X\left(f_j\right) \longrightarrow [0, 1].$$

From these φ_j we obtain the complete objective (criterion) function:

$$\varphi : X\left(1\right) = \prod_{j=1}^{m} X\left(f_j\right) \longrightarrow [0, 1]^m$$

$$x = (x_1, x_2, \cdots, x_m) \longmapsto \varphi\left(x\right) = \left(\varphi_1\left(x_1\right), \varphi_2\left(x_2\right), \cdots, \varphi_m\left(x_m\right)\right),$$

a vector-valued function.

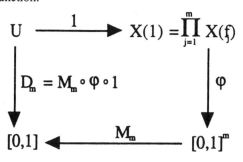

FIGURE 5.3
The decision function D_m.

In this way, we have transformed a decision problem into an optimization problem on $(\varphi \circ 1)\,(U)$. Unfortunately, $\varphi\left(1\left(u\right)\right)$ is not a linear order in U that means difficulties in making comparisons. To get around with this problem, we consider projecting $\varphi\left(1\left(u\right)\right)$ on $[0, 1]$, and this role is performed by the ASM$_m$-funcs. As shown in Figure 5.3, by means of 1, φ, and M_m, we can determine a decision function

$$D_m = M_m \circ \varphi \circ 1 : U \longrightarrow [0, 1]. \tag{5.19}$$

If a strategy (or policy) $u_0 \in U$ satisfies the following condition:

$$D_m\left(u_0\right) = \max\left\{D_m\left(u\right) \mid u \in U\right\},$$

then u_0 is recognized as an optimal solution.

Example 34
Consider the problem of selecting the best student discussed in Example 18. Let $U = \{u_1, u_2, u_3\} = \{$Henry, Lucy, John$\}$ be the set of candidates, and $\pi =$

$\{f_1, f_2, f_3, f_4\} = \{$mathematics, physics, chemistry, foreign language$\}$ be the set of basic factors.

First, we define basic objective functions φ_j (Figure 5.4), $j = 1, 2, 3, 4$ as

$$\varphi_j = \begin{cases} 1, & 90 < x \le 100; \\ \frac{x-80}{10}, & 80 \le x \le 90; \\ 0, & 0 \le x < 80. \end{cases}$$

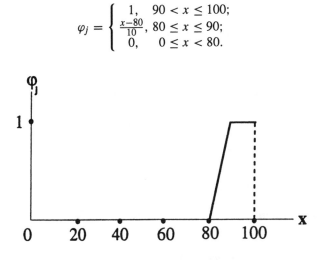

FIGURE 5.4
Basic objective functions, φ_j.

Second, we assume $f_j (u_i)$, and the states of u_i on f_j, are shown in Table 1. The values of their objective functions $\varphi_j \left(f_j (u_i) \right)$ are shown in Table 2.

Table 1   States of u_i on f_j

$u_i \backslash f_j$	f_1	f_2	f_3	f_4
u_1	86	91	95	93
u_2	98	89	93	90
u_3	90	92	85	96

Table 2   Values of objective functions: $\varphi_j \left(f_j (u_i) \right)$

$u_i \backslash f_j$	f_1	f_2	f_3	f_4
u_1	0.6	1	1	1
u_2	1	0.9	1	1
u_3	1	1	0.5	1

Third, we take $M_4 = \sum$ with $a_j = \frac{1}{4}$, $j = 1, 2, 3, 4$. Then we have the decision function D_4 as

$$D_4 (u_i) = \frac{1}{4} \sum_{j=1}^{4} \varphi_j \left(f_j (u_i) \right).$$

Based on this function and the values of Table 2, we obtain

$$D_4(u_1) = \frac{3.6}{4} = 0.9, \quad D_4(u_2) = \frac{3.9}{4} = 0.975, \quad D_4(u_3) = \frac{3.5}{4} = 0.875.$$

We conclude that Lucy is the best student.   ◻

References

[1] Klir, G. J. and Folger, T. A., *Fuzzy Sets, Uncertainty, and Information.* Prentice-Hall, New Jersey, 1988.

[2] Li, H.-X., Multifactorial functions in fuzzy sets theory, *Fuzzy Sets and Systems*, 35(1), 1990, 69–84.

[3] Li, H.-X., *Fuzzy Mathematics Methods in Engineering and Their Applications.* Tianjin Scientific and Technical Press, Tianjin, 1993.

[4] Li, H.-X. and Yen, V. C., Factor spaces and fuzzy decision-making, *Journal of Beijing Normal University*, 30(1), 1994, 41–46.

[5] Li, H.-X. and Wang, P.-Z., Falling shadow representation of fuzzy concepts on factor spaces, *Journal of Yantai University*, No. 2, 1994, 15–21.

[6] Li, H.-X. and Wang, P.-Z., *Fuzzy Mathematics*, National Defense Press, Beijing, 1994.

[7] Li, H.-S. and Yen, V. C., The operations of fuzzy cardinalities, *JMAA*, 182, 1994, 768–778.

[8] Wang, P.-Z., A factor space approach to knowledge representation, *Fuzzy Sets and Systems*, 36, 1990, 113–124.

[9] Wang, P.-Z. and Loe, K. F., (Eds.), *Between Mind and Computer.* World Scientific Publishing, 1993.

[10] Wang, P.-Z. and Li, H.-X., *Mathematical Theory on Knowledge Representation*, Tianjin Scientific and Technical Press, Tianjin, 1994.

[11] Zadeh, L. A., Outline of a new approach to the analysis of complex systems and decision processes, *IEEE Trans. Syst. Man Cybern.*, SMC-1, 1973, 28–44.

[12] Zadeh, L. A. et al. (Eds.), *Fuzzy Sets and Their Applications to Cognitive and Decision Processes*, Academic Press, New York, 1975.

6

Variable Weights Analysis

6.1 Defining the Problem

A common multifactorial function (ASM$_m$-func) M_m used in the additive decision-making systems (cf. Section 5.2) is the mapping (operator) $\sum$ in expression (5.5), that is

$$M_m(x_1, x_2, \cdots, x_m) = \sum(x_1, x_2, \cdots, x_m) \overset{\triangle}{=} \sum_{j=1}^{m} w_j x_j \qquad (6.1)$$

where $w_j \in [0, 1]$, $(j = 1, 2, \cdots, m)$, and $\sum_{j=1}^{m} w_j = 1$. This is the usual weighted mean or weighted average. Since the weights $\{w_j\}$ are constants, the expression represents a constant weight synthesis of factors $\{x_j\}$. Let $W = (w_1, w_2, \cdots, w_m)$. We call W the **constant weight vector**.

A constant weight synthesis of factors provides a measure of combined effects from all the factors in question. The constants reflect the relative strength or importance of related factors. In many situations such an approach is considered reasonable, and it is widely used in practice.

With constant weights, the weight vector W is always fixed, regardless of the underlying structure or configuration of the objective function

$$\varphi(f(u)) = (\varphi_1(f_1(u)), \varphi_2(f_2(u)), \cdots, \varphi_m(f_m(u))).$$

(cf. Section 5.7). By the "structure or configuration" we mean the functional relationship of u and the components of the vector $\varphi(f(u))$. The constant vector W in expression (6.1) does not vary when $X = (x_1, x_2, \cdots, x_m)$ varies. The use of constant weights has its limitations. We illustrate with an example in which it is not appropriate to use the constant vector W for all values of X.

Example 35

Suppose the decision to approve an engineering project is dependent on two factors: f_1 = feasibility and f_2 = necessity. If the two factors are equally important, then we should assign equal weights to each factor, i.e.,

$$W = (w_1, w_2) = (0.5, 0.5).$$

Hence, following expression (6.1), the multifactorial function is

$$M_2 (x_1, x_2) = \sum (x_1, x_2) = 0.5x_1 + 0.5x_2.$$

Consider two cases: (1) the project is entirely feasible, but its necessity is quite low; and (2) the project may be highly necessary, but it is not feasible. Normally we do not approve the project in either case because the "merit" of the combined effect is quite low. Numerically, let $X = (0.1, 0.9) \in X (f_1) \times X (f_2)$ and $X' = (0.5, 0.5)$ $\in X (f_1) \times X (f_2)$. Then we would expect $M_2 (X) \ll M_2 (X')$ in most cases. However, using the constant weight vector, we have

$$M_2 (X) = M_2 (X') = 0.5.$$

This result contradicts common expectations.   ▯

Let us illustrate this example with a graph of a two-dimensional multifactorial function M_2 as given in Figure 6.1.

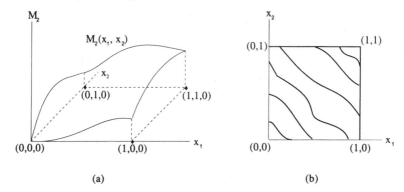

(a)   (b)

FIGURE 6.1
Merit surface and iso-merit curves.

We now analyze the distribution of "iso-merit" curves in a unit square. Let $c \in [0, 1]$ be a constant. Then the function $M_2 (x_1, x_2) = c$, through projection, forms a family of curves in $X_1 \times X_2$ plane for each constant c. When $M_2 (x_1, x_2) = w_1 x_1 + w_2 x_2$, the merit surface M_2 is a plane containing points $(0, 0, 0)$ and

$(1, 1, 1)$. The "slope" or angle of the plane is determined by the weight vector $W = (w_1, w_2)$. The iso-merit curves, in this case, are parallel straight lines; their normal vectors are the weight vector (see Figure 6.2).

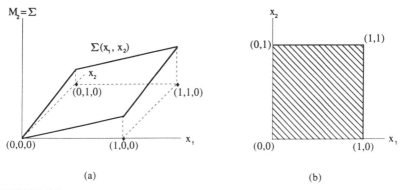

(a)   (b)

FIGURE 6.2
Constant synthetic merit surface and its iso-merit curves.

In the previous example, we must consider not only the relative preference among factors but also the preference of the balance level of state configurations. Generally, the approach is acceptable, and the desire for the optimum merit is sensible if the state configurations are well balanced. Constant weights only reflect the relative preference on each factor; they do not have the restraining power on the state configurations. In the two-dimensional example, if a synthetic function that reflects the preference of the degrees of balance in state configurations, its iso-merit curves should be concave upward curves, not straight lines.

To overcome such deficiencies in the constant weights approach, Wang [9] suggested the use of the variable weights concept, and he also obtained an empirical variable weight formula. We now define variable weights in axiomatic terms.

*DEFINITION 17   A set of m-**dimensional variable weights** is a set of m mappings:*

$$w_j : [0, 1]^m \longrightarrow [0, 1]$$
$$X = (x_1, x_2, \cdots, x_m) \longmapsto w_j(X) = w_j(x_1, x_2, \cdots, x_m)$$
$$j = 1, 2, \cdots, m.$$

These satisfy the following three axioms:
w.1) Normality.

$$\sum_{j=1}^{m} w_j(x_1, x_2, \cdots, x_m) = 1$$

w.2) Continuity. The function w_j is continuous in m-dimensional space.
w.3) Penalty. The function $w_j(x_1, x_2, \cdots, x_m)$ is a monotonically decreasing function of x_j, $j = 1, 2, \cdots, m$.

Let $\{w_j(X)\}_{(1 \leq j \leq m)}$ be a set of m-dimensional variable weights. Define a function $\sum_m^x$:

$$\sum_m^x (X) = \sum_m^x (x_1, x_2, \cdots, x_m)$$

$$= \sum_m^x w_j (x_1, x_2, \cdots, x_m) x_j. \qquad (6.2)$$

Then $\sum_m^x$ is an **ASM$_m$-func**, i.e., $\sum_m^x \in \mathcal{M}_m$. The function $\sum_m^x$ is a (m-dimensional) **variable weight synthetic function**.

6.2   An Empirical Variable Weight Formula

Wang [9] modified the constant weights approach by allowing the use of variables to replace constant weights. This provides a way to reflect preferences on both factors and the degree of balance in state configurations. We now look at a case in two dimensions.

Let $W = (w_1, w_2)$ be a constant weight vector. Define $\lambda = w_2/w_1$. Then

$$\frac{w_2(x_1, x_2)}{w_1(x_1, x_2)} = \lambda \frac{x_1}{x_2} = \frac{w_2 x_1}{w_1 x_2}.$$

From this equation, along with the normality condition, we can simultaneously solve for

$$w_1(x_1, x_2) = \frac{x_2}{\lambda x_1 + x_2} = \frac{w_1 x_2}{w_2 x_1 + w_1 x_2}$$

$$w_2(x_1, x_2) = \frac{\lambda x_1}{\lambda x_1 + x_2} = \frac{w_2 x_2}{w_2 x_1 + w_1 x_2} \qquad (6.3)$$

Figure 6.3 is an illustration of variable weight functions, where the slopes of the arrows indicate the ratio of the variable weight functions.

For m-dimensional variable weights $w_j(x_1, x_2, \cdots, x_m)$, $1 \leq j \leq m$, we can use the following method:

Step 1. Identify the pairwise variable ratios $\eta_{ij}(x_i, x_j)$, where $1 \leq i, j \leq m$.

Let $\{w_j\}_{(1 \leq j \leq m)}$ be a given set of constant weights. We can modify them and obtain two-dimensional variable weights according to the equations in (6.3).

$$w_i(x_i, x_j) = \frac{\lambda_{ij} x_j}{\lambda_{ij} x_j + x_i} = \frac{w_i x_j}{w_j x_i + w_i x_j}$$

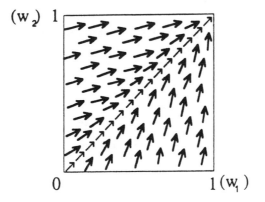

FIGURE 6.3
Slope, the ratio of variable weights.

$$w_j \left(x_i, x_j \right) = \frac{x_i}{\lambda_{ij} x_j + x_i} = \frac{w_i x_i}{w_j x_i + w_i x_j}. \tag{6.4}$$

Therefore, the ratio of variable weights is

$$\eta_{ij} \left(x_i, x_j \right) = \frac{w_i \left(x_i, x_j \right)}{w_j \left(x_i, x_j \right)} = \lambda_{ij} \frac{x_j}{x_i} = \frac{w_i x_j}{w_j x_i}. \tag{6.5}$$

Step 2. Identify variable weights $w_j \left(x_1, x_2, \cdots, x_m \right)$, $1 \le j \le m$.
Since $w_j \left(x_1, x_2, \cdots, x_m \right)$ satisfies

$$\frac{w_i \left(x_1, x_2, \cdots, x_m \right)}{w_j \left(x_1, x_2, \cdots, x_m \right)} = \eta_{ij} \left(x_i, x_j \right) = \frac{w_i x_j}{w_j x_i},$$

and

$$\sum_{j=1}^{m} w_j \left(x_1, x_2, \cdots, x_m \right) = 1.$$

We obtain a system of linear equations:

$$w_1 \left(x_1, x_2, \cdots, x_m \right) - \eta_{11} \left(x_1, x_1 \right) w_1 \left(x_1, x_2, \cdots, x_m \right) = 0$$

$$w_1 \left(x_1, x_2, \cdots, x_m \right) - \eta_{12} \left(x_1, x_2 \right) w_2 \left(x_1, x_2, \cdots, x_m \right) = 0$$

$$\cdots$$

$$w_1 \left(x_1, x_2, \cdots, x_m \right) - \eta_{1m} \left(x_1, x_2 \right) w_m \left(x_1, x_2, \cdots, x_m \right) = 0$$

$$w_2 \left(x_1, x_2, \cdots, x_m \right) - \eta_{21} \left(x_2, x_1 \right) w_1 \left(x_1, x_2, \cdots, x_m \right) = 0$$

$$w_2\,(x_1, x_2, \cdots, x_m) - \eta_{22}\,(x_2, x_2)\,w_2\,(x_1, x_2, \cdots, x_m) = 0$$

$$\cdots$$

$$w_2\,(x_1, x_2, \cdots, x_m) - \eta_{2m}\,(x_2, x_m)\,w_m\,(x_1, x_2, \cdots, x_m) = 0$$

$$\cdots$$

$$w_m\,(x_1, x_2, \cdots, x_m) - \eta_{m1}\,(x_m, x_1)\,w_1\,(x_1, x_2, \cdots, x_m) = 0$$

$$w_m\,(x_1, x_2, \cdots, x_m) - \eta_{m2}\,(x_m, x_2)\,w_2\,(x_1, x_2, \cdots, x_m) = 0$$

$$\cdots$$

$$w_m\,(x_1, x_2, \cdots, x_m) - \eta_{mm}\,(x_m, x_m)\,w_m\,(x_1, x_2, \cdots, x_m) = 0$$

$$w_1\,(x_1, x_2, \cdots, x_m) + w_2\,(x_1, x_2, \cdots, x_m) + \cdots + w_m\,(x_1, x_2, \cdots, x_m) = 1$$

Under the following natural assumptions,

$$\eta_{ij}\,(x_i, x_j) > 0$$
$$\eta_{ii}\,(x_i, x_i) = 1$$
$$\eta_{ij}\,(x_i, x_j) = \frac{1}{\eta_{ji}(x_j, x_i)}$$
$$\eta_{ij}\,(x_i, x_j) = \eta_{ik}\,(x_i, x_k) \cdot \eta_{kj}\,(x_k, x_j)$$

it can be shown that the matrix of this set of homogeneous systems of equations and its augmented matrix have the same rank m. Therefore, there exists a unique solution:

$$w_1\,(x_1, x_2, \cdots, x_m) = \frac{\eta_{1m}\,(x_1, x_m)}{1 + \displaystyle\sum_{i=1}^{m-1} \eta_{im}\,(x_i, x_m)} = \frac{\frac{w_1}{x_1}}{\displaystyle\sum_{j=1}^{m} \frac{w_j}{x_j}},$$

$$w_2\,(x_1, x_2, \cdots, x_m) = \frac{\eta_{2m}\,(x_2, x_m)}{1 + \displaystyle\sum_{i=1}^{m-1} \eta_{im}\,(x_i, x_m)} = \frac{\frac{w_2}{x_2}}{\displaystyle\sum_{j=1}^{m} \frac{w_j}{x_j}},$$

$$\cdots$$

$$w_{m-1}\,(x_1, x_2, \cdots, x_m) = \frac{\eta_{(m-1)m}\,(x_{m-1}, x_m)}{1 + \displaystyle\sum_{i=1}^{m-1} \eta_{im}\,(x_i, x_m)} = \frac{\frac{w_{m-1}}{x_{m-1}}}{\displaystyle\sum_{j=1}^{m} \frac{w_j}{x_j}},$$

$$w_m\,(x_1, x_2, \cdots, x_m) = \frac{1}{1 + \displaystyle\sum_{i=1}^{m-1} \eta_{im}\,(x_i, x_m)} = \frac{\frac{w_m}{x_m}}{\displaystyle\sum_{j=1}^{m} \frac{w_j}{x_j}}.$$

It is simple to show that the set of variable weights just obtained satisfies the variable weights axioms w.1), w.2), and w.3). Note that these variable weights describe just one of the infinite possibilities, and the applications of these weights must be made with great care. The determination of variable weights need to be based on each individual case.

6.3 Principles of Variable Weights

The difference between constant weights and variable weights is that variable weights take both the relative importance of factors and the horizontal configuration of the value of each factor (critical to decision making) into consideration. The simultaneous presence of these two special properties is what makes variable weights valuable.

Next, we study a basic question on variable weights. We ask: What is the nature, or underlying principle, or theory of variable weights? In this section, we discuss the underpinning of the principle of variable weights.

6.3.1 Variable Weights State Vector

If the relative importance of factors has nothing to do with changes of states, then it is appropriate to use a constant weight vector:

$$W = (w_1, w_2, \cdots, w_m), \qquad w_j \in [0, 1], \quad j = 1, 2, \cdots, m$$

$$w_1 + w_2 + \cdots + w_m = 1$$

To avoid getting a useless outcome as pointed out in example 35, namely the unreasonable synthesis due to uneven balance of states, we should apply state dependent weights, that is, these weights should vary as states vary. Such weights form the **variable weight state vector,** and are denoted by

$$S_X \overset{\Delta}{=} (S_1(X), S_2(X), \cdots, S_m(X)),$$

where $X = (x_1, x_2, \cdots, x_m) \in [0, 1]^m$. Its accompanying constant weight vector W is called the **constant weight state vector.**

The variable weight state vector S_X may be viewed as a mapping (or transformation):

$$S_X : [0, 1]^m \longrightarrow [0, 1]^m$$

$$X \longmapsto S_X(X) \overset{\Delta}{=} S_X \circ X$$

$$= \ (S_1\,(X)\,,\,S_2\,(X)\,,\cdots,\,S_m\,(X))\circ(x_1,\,x_2,\cdots,\,x_m)$$

$$\stackrel{\triangle}{=}\ (S_1\,(X)\cdot x_1,\,S_2\,(X)\cdot x_2,\cdots,\,S_m\,(X)\cdot x_m)$$

Where $S_X \circ X$ is a Hardarmard product of two vectors S_X and X. The mapping S_X plays the role of state dependent weights on X; in some sense, it "modifies" and/or " balances" X (see Figure 5.3) . We have a similar diagram as that shown in Figure 6.4. From Figure 6.4, we obtain a **quasi-decision function** D'_m :

$$D'_m = \sum \circ S_X \circ \varphi \circ \mathbf{1}.$$

Suppose we set $M'_m = \sum \circ S_X$ then $D'_m = M'_m \circ \varphi \circ \mathbf{1}$ that is similar to equation (5.19).

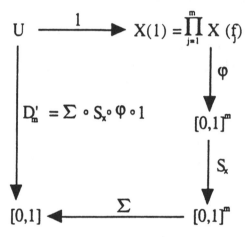

FIGURE 6.4
A quasi-decision function.

For any $u \in U$, we have

$$D'_m = \left(\sum \circ S_X \circ \varphi \circ \mathbf{1}\right)(u) = \left(\sum \circ S_X \circ \varphi\right)(\mathbf{1}\,(u))$$

$$= \left(\sum \circ S_X \circ \varphi\right)(f_1\,(u)\,,\ f_2\,(u)\,,\ \cdots,\ f_m\,(u))$$

$$= \left(\sum \circ S_X\right)(\varphi\,(f_1\,(u)\,,\ f_2\,(u)\,,\ \cdots,\ f_m\,(u)))$$

$$= \left(\sum \circ S_X\right)(\varphi_1\,(f_1\,(u))\,,\ \varphi_2\,(f_2\,(u))\,,\ \cdots,\ \varphi_m\,(f_m\,(u)))\,.$$

Let $x_j \overset{\Delta}{=} \varphi_j \left(f_j \left(u \right) \right)$ and $X = (x_1, x_2, \cdots, x_m)$. Then,

$$D'_m (u) = \left(\sum \circ S_X \right) (X) = \sum (S_X (X)) = \sum (S_X \circ X)$$

$$= \sum (S_1 (X) \cdot x_1, S_2 (X) \cdot x_2, \cdots, S_m (X) \cdot x_m)$$

$$= \sum_{j=1}^{m} w_j \left(S_j (x_1, x_2, \cdots, x_m) \cdot x_j \right)$$

$$= \sum_{j=1}^{m} \left(w_j \cdot S_j (x_1, x_2, \cdots, x_m) \right) \cdot x_j.$$

The reason we call D'_m a quasi-decision function is because M'_m is not an ASM_m-func. Now, let us define

$$M_m : [0, 1]^m \longrightarrow [0, 1], \quad (x_1, x_2, \cdots, x_m) \longmapsto M_m (x_1, x_2, \cdots, x_m)$$

$$M_m (x_1, x_2, \cdots, x_m) \overset{\Delta}{=} \frac{M'_m (x_1, x_2, \cdots, x_m)}{\sum_{j=1}^{m} w_j \cdot S_j (x_1, x_2, \cdots, x_m)}$$

$$= \sum_{j=1}^{m} \frac{w_j \cdot S_j (x_1, x_2, \cdots, x_m)}{\sum_{j=1}^{m} w_j \cdot S_j (x_1, x_2, \cdots, x_m)} x_j$$

If S_X satisfies certain conditions, then M_m will be an ASM_m-func. Here M_m is derived from M'_m and normalization. If we set $D_m \overset{\Delta}{=} M_m \circ \varphi \circ \mathbf{1}$, it takes us right back to equation (5.19) and, moreover, it is a decision function.

We now define the mapping $w_j : [0, 1]^m \longrightarrow [0, 1], \quad j = 1, 2, \cdots, m$, by

$$w_j (x_1, x_2, \cdots, x_m) \overset{\Delta}{=} \frac{w_j \cdot S_j (x_1, x_2, \cdots, x_m)}{\sum_{j=1}^{m} w_j \cdot S_j (x_1, x_2, \cdots, x_m)}. \tag{6.6}$$

If S_X satisfies certain conditions, then $\left\{ w_j (x_1, x_2, \cdots, x_m) \right\}_{(1 \leq j \leq m)}$ is a set of m-dimensional variable weights under definition 17.

In definition 17, let

$$W (X) \overset{\Delta}{=} (w_1 (X), w_2 (X), \cdots, w_m (X))$$

then $W (X) = W (x_1, x_2, \cdots, x_m)$ is called the *variable weight vector*. Now apply Equation (6.6) and we have

$$W (X) = \frac{1}{\sum_{j=1}^{m} w_j \cdot S_j (X)} (w_1 S_1 (X), \cdots, w_m S_m (X))$$

$$= \frac{W \circ S_X}{\sum_{j=1}^{m} w_j \cdot S_j (X)}. \tag{6.7}$$

From Equation (6.7), we obtain an important

THEOREM 19
The variable weight vector W (X) is the normalized Hardarmard product of constant weight vector W and variable weight state vector S_X. That is,

$$W (X) = \frac{W \circ S_X}{\sum_{j=1}^{m} w_j \cdot S_j (x_1, x_2, \cdots, x_m)}.$$

Example 36
Construct a variable weight state vector $S_X = (S_1 (x_1, x_2, \cdots, x_m), \cdots, S_m (x_1, x_2, \cdots, x_m))$ according to

$$S_j (x_1, x_2, \cdots, x_m) = \prod_{i=1, i \neq j}^{m} x_i = x_1 x_2 \cdots x_{j-1} x_{j+1} \cdots x_m.$$

Apply Equation (6.6). Then

$$w_j (x_1, x_2, \cdots, x_m) = \frac{w_j . x_1 x_2 \cdots x_{j-1} x_{j+1} \cdots x_m}{\sum_{j=1}^{m} w_j \cdot x_1 x_2 \cdots x_{j-1} x_{j+1} \cdots x_m}$$

$$= \frac{w_j / x_j}{\sum_{j=1}^{m} w_j / x_j}.$$

▯

This is exactly what we derived earlier—the empirical weight formula that satisfies axioms w.1), w.2), and w.3).

Up to this point, the nature or the underlying principle of variable weights is fully understood. The remaining task is to study the structure of the variable weight state vector S_X.

6.3.2   Axiomatic Definition of Variable Weight State Vectors

DEFINITION 18   *A mapping: $S : [0, 1]^m \longrightarrow [0, 1]^m$ such that*

$$X \longmapsto S (X) \overset{\Delta}{=} S_X \overset{\Delta}{=} (S_1 (X), S_2 (X), \cdots, S_m (X))$$

where $S_j : [0, 1]^m \longrightarrow [0, 1]$, and $X \longmapsto S_j(X)$, $(j = 1, 2, \cdots, m)$ is called an (m-dimensional) **variable weight state vector** *if S satisfies the following axioms:*

s.1) $S\left(\sigma_{ij}(x_1, x_2, \cdots, x_m)\right) = S(x_1, x_2, \cdots, x_m)$;

s.2) $x_i \gg x_j \Longrightarrow S_i(x_1, x_2, \cdots, x_m) \leq S_j(x_1, x_2, \cdots, x_m)$;

s.3) For any variable weight vector obtained from a constant weight, vector W, through Equation (6.7), satisfies axioms w.1), w.2), and w.3);

s.4) $S_j(x_1, x_2, \cdots, x_m)$ *is continuous on each* x_i, $i = 1, 2, \cdots, m$.

Obviously, the function $S_j(x_1, x_2, \cdots, x_m)$ defined in the last example satisfies axioms s.1) through s.4).

Example 37

We now construct a variable weight state vector S_X as follows:

$$S_j(x_1, x_2, \cdots, x_m) \equiv 1, \quad j = 1, 2, \cdots, m. \tag{6.8}$$

S_j satisfies axioms s.1) through s.4). From equation (6.6), we have

$$w_j(x_1, x_2, \cdots, x_m) = w_j, \quad j = 1, 2, \cdots, m.$$

Therefore, $W(X) = W$, which implies that "constant weights" is a special case of "variable weights". ▯

6.3.3 The Balance Function and Its Gradient Vector

In the space of $[0, 1]^m$, the constant weight vector $W = (w_1, w_2, \cdots, w_m)$ is a vector of fixed direction. If we take the following function (an ASM_m-func),

$$\sum(X) = \sum(x_1, x_2, \cdots, x_m) = \sum_{j=1}^{m} w_j x_j \tag{6.9}$$

then its gradient vector is

$$grad \sum(x_1, x_2, \cdots, x_m) = \left(\frac{\partial \sum(X)}{\partial x_1}, \frac{\partial \sum(X)}{\partial x_2}, \cdots, \frac{\partial \sum(X)}{\partial x_m} \right)$$

$$= (w_1, w_2, \cdots, w_m) = W.$$

This explains the fact that a constant weight vector is the gradient vector of a constant weight synthetic function as in Equation (6.9).

Also, note that $grad \sum (x_1, x_2, \cdots, x_m)$ may be written as a Hardarmard product of two vectors:

$$grad \sum (x_1, x_2, \cdots, x_m) = W$$

$$= (w_1, w_2, \cdots, w_m) \circ (1, 1, \cdots, 1)$$

$$= W \circ S_X^0$$

where S_X^0 is the variable weight state vector determined by equation (6.9).

Suppose we define a function $B : [0, 1]^m \longrightarrow [0, 1]$ such that

$$B(X) = B(x_1, x_2, \cdots, x_m) \stackrel{\Delta}{=} \sum_{j=1}^{m} x_j.$$

Then $S_X =$ grad $B(x_1, x_2, \cdots, x_m)$. Thus,

$$grad \sum (x_1, x_2, \cdots, x_m) = W \circ \mathrm{grad} B(x_1, x_2, \cdots, x_m).$$

If the function B is defined by

$$B(x_1, x_2, \cdots, x_m) = \prod_{j=1}^{m} x_j$$

then

$$\mathrm{grad} B(x_1, x_2, \cdots, x_m) = S_X.$$

This follows from the definition of the variable weight state vector in example 36 of this chapter. The components of the gradient vector of B are

$$\frac{\partial B(X)}{\partial x_j} = S_j(X) = x_1 \cdots x_{j-1} x_{j+1} \cdots x_m.$$

From the above discussions, we conclude with a rule: the variable weight state vector is a gradient vector of a certain m-dimensional real function. Such an "m-dimensional real function" can be called a balance function because its gradient vector acts like a balance agent among states. A formal definition follows.

DEFINITION 19   *A mapping $B : [0, 1]^m \longrightarrow \Re$ ($\Re$ is the set of reals) is called a* **balance function** *if it has continuous partial derivatives, and its gradient vector is a variable weight state vector (i.e., satisfies axioms s.1) $\sim$s.4).*

This chapter just begins to explore some of the basic structures of balance functions. Because the structure of balance functions plays an important role in variable weight synthetic functions, it is worth further researching.

References

[1] Dubois, D. and Prade, H., *Fuzzy Sets and Systems*, Academic Press, New York, 1980.

[2] Li, H.-X., Multifactorial analysis, *Fuzzy Systems and Mathematics*, 2(1), 1988, 9–19.

[3] Li, H.-X., Multifactorial functions in fuzzy sets theory, *Fuzzy Sets and Systems*, 35(1), 1990, 69–84.

[4] Li, H.-X., Huang, L., and Yen, V. C., *Factor Spaces and Fuzzy Decision Making*, Proceedings of First Asian Fuzzy Systems Symposium, Singapore, 1993, 484–491.

[5] Li, H.-X., *Fuzzy Mathematics Methods in Engineering and Their Applications*. Tianjin Scientific and Technical Press, Tianjin, 1993.

[6] Li, H.-X. and Wang P.-Z., *Fuzzy Mathematics*, National Defense Press, Beijing, 1994.

[7] Li, H.-X. and Yen, V. C., The operations of fuzzy cardinalities, *JMAA*, 182, 1994, 768-778.

[8] Wang, P.-Z. and Liu, X., Set-valued statistics, *Chinese Journal of Engineering Mathematics*, 1(1), 1984, 43-54.

[9] Wang, P.-Z., *Fuzzy Sets and The Falling Shadow of Random Sets*, Beijing Normal University Press, Beijing, 1985.

[10] Wang, P.-Z., *Fuzzy Engineering—Principles and Methods*, China Productivity Center, Taipei, 1993.

[11] Wang, P.-Z. and Li, H.-X., *Mathematical Theory on Knowledge Representation*, Tianjin Scientific and Technical Press, Tianjin, 1994.

[12] Zimmermann, H. J., *Fuzzy Sets Theory and Its Applications*, Kluwer Academic Publishers, Hingham, 1984.

7

Multifactorial Decision Making with Multiple Objectives

7.1 Background and Models

We discussed certain common synthetic decision models in Section 5.7. These decision models are multifactorial in nature. Relative to the complete factor **1**, there is a unique **complete objective** (factor) **function**:

$$\varphi : X\,(\mathbf{1}) = \prod_{j=1}^{m} X\,(f_j) \longrightarrow [0,1]^m$$

$$(x_1, x_2, \cdots, x_m) \longmapsto \varphi\,(x_1, x_2, \cdots, x_m) = (\varphi_1\,(x_1)\,, \varphi_2\,(x_2)\,, \cdots, \varphi_m\,(x_m))\,.$$

The word "synthetic" used here is relative to the m objectives (factors). The complete objective function φ, for example, is a vector of basic objective functions $\varphi_1,\ \varphi_2,\ \cdots,\ \varphi_m$. However, in many situations, there are more than one complete objective functions, say p of them:

$$\varphi^{(1)} = \left(\varphi_1^{(1)}, \varphi_2^{(1)}, \cdots, \varphi_m^{(1)}\right)$$

$$\varphi^{(2)} = \left(\varphi_1^{(2)}, \varphi_2^{(2)}, \cdots, \varphi_m^{(2)}\right)$$

$$\vdots$$

$$\varphi^{(p)} = \left(\varphi_1^{(p)}, \varphi_2^{(p)}, \cdots, \varphi_m^{(p)}\right).$$

This type of decision models is referred to as **multiple (complete) objective syn-**

thetic decision models. We now construct a basic prototype for this class of models.

Let U be a set of decision alternatives and let $\pi = \{f_1, f_2, \cdots, f_m\}$ be a family of basic factors (atomic factors) of U. Set $F = \mathcal{P}(\pi)$. Then the following section 5.7, $(F, \bigvee, \bigwedge, c, \mathbf{0}, \mathbf{1})$ forms a complete Boolean algebra, and $\{X(1)\}_{(f \in F)}$ constitutes a factor space. For each decision alternative $u \in U$, the decision variable $\mathbf{1}(u)$ (the state of the complete factor or objective) is determined by the states of atomic factors (basic objectives), i.e., $\mathbf{1}(u) = (f_1(u), f_2(u), \cdots, f_m(u))$.

Suppose we have p complete objective statements or sentences: $e_1, e_2, \cdots, e_p$. The statement e_k is the kth objective expressed in words or sentences. Let $E = \{e_1, e_2, \cdots, e_p\}$. The set E is called the **set of complete objective statements**. The modeling or design of the aforementioned p complete objective functions should conform to its set of complete objective statements.

According to section 5.7, for every complete objective function,

$$\varphi^{(k)} (k = 1, 2, \cdots, p)$$

there is a decision function (see Figure 7.1) $D_m^{(k)}$:

$$D_m^{(k)} = M_m \circ \varphi^{(k)} \circ 1, \quad k = 1, 2, \cdots, p. \tag{7.1}$$

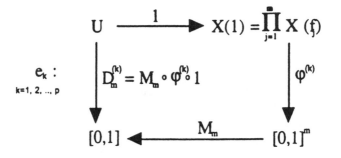

FIGURE 7.1

The correspondence between e_k and $D_m^{(k)}$.

Since for every decision alternative $u \in U$ and every decision function $D_m^{(k)}$, the functional value $D_m^{(k)}(u)$ is defined, we can construct a mapping:

$$D^{(u)} : E \longrightarrow [0, 1]$$

$$e_k :\longmapsto D^{(u)}(e_k) \overset{\triangle}{=} D_m^{(k)}(u) \tag{7.2}$$

The mapping can be viewed as a fuzzy set on E, i.e., $D^{(u)} \in \mathcal{F}(E)$. Since E is finite, the fuzzy set $D^{(u)}$ can be expressed in vector form:

$$D^{(u)} = \left(D^{(u)}(e_1), D^{(u)}(e_2), \cdots, D^{(u)}(e_p) \right)$$

$$= \left(D_m^{(u)}(e_1), D_m^{(u)}(e_2), \cdots, D_m^{(u)}(e_p) \right).$$

If there exists an index $k_0 \in \{1, 2, \cdots, p\}$ such that

$$D_m^{(u)}(e_{k_0}) = \max \left\{ D^{(u)}(e_1), D^{(u)}(e_2), \cdots, D^{(u)}(e_p) \right\}$$

then according to the principle of the highest (maximum) membership, u is recognized as satisfying the complete objective statement e_{k_0}.

Example 38

In the problem of evaluating student academic achievement (cf., example 34 of Chapter 5), let $U = \{u_1, u_2, u_3\}$ be a set of candidates for evaluation, where u_1 =Henry, u_2 =Lucy, and u_3 =John; let $E = \{e_1, e_2, e_3, e_4\}$ be a set of objective statements (linguistic grades), where e_1 =excellent, e_2 =good, e_3 =fair, and e_4 =poor; and let $\pi = \{f_1, f_2, f_3, f_4\}$ be the family of basic factors, where f_1 =mathematics, f_2 =physics, f_3 =chemistry, and f_4 =foreign language. For each linguistic grade e_k ($k = 1, 2, 3, 4$), there is a complete objective function:

$$\varphi^{(1)} = \left(\varphi_1^{(1)}, \varphi_2^{(1)}, \varphi_3^{(1)}, \varphi_4^{(1)} \right)$$

$$\varphi^{(2)} = \left(\varphi_1^{(2)}, \varphi_2^{(2)}, \varphi_3^{(2)}, \varphi_4^{(2)} \right)$$

$$\varphi^{(3)} = \left(\varphi_1^{(3)}, \varphi_2^{(3)}, \varphi_3^{(3)}, \varphi_4^{(3)} \right)$$

$$\varphi^{(4)} = \left(\varphi_1^{(4)}, \varphi_2^{(4)}, \varphi_3^{(4)}, \varphi_4^{(4)} \right).$$

Let $\varphi_j^{(k)}$, ($k, j = 1, 2, 3, 4$) be defined as follows:

$$\varphi_j^{(1)}(x) = \begin{cases} 1, & 90 < x \le 100 \\ \frac{x-80}{10}, & 80 \le x \le 90 \\ 0, & 0 \le x < 80 \end{cases}$$

$$\varphi_j^{(2)}(x) = \begin{cases} \frac{100-x}{10}, & 90 \le x \le 100 \\ 1, & 80 \le x < 90 \\ \frac{x-70}{10}, & 70 \le x < 80 \\ 0, & 0 \le x < 70 \end{cases}$$

$$\varphi_j^{(3)}(x) = \begin{cases} 0, & 90 \le x \le 100 \\ \frac{90-x}{10}, & 80 < x < 90 \\ 1, & 70 \le x \le 80 \\ \frac{x-60}{10}, & 60 \le x < 70 \\ 0, & 0 \le x < 60 \end{cases}$$

$$\varphi_j^{(4)}(x) = \begin{cases} 0, & 70 < x \le 100 \\ \frac{70-x}{10}, & 60 \le x \le 70 \\ 1, & 0 \le x < 60 \end{cases}.$$

The graphs of $\varphi_j^{(1)}$ are the same as those in Figure 5.4. The graphs of $\varphi_j^{(2)}$, $\varphi_j^{(3)}$, and $\varphi_j^{(4)}$ are given in Figure 7.2 , Figure 7.3, and Figure 7.4, respectively. Assume

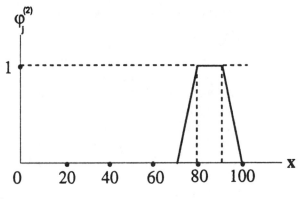

FIGURE 7.2

that the states (scores) of each factor (subject) of u_j have values as given in Table 1. Then we can calculate the respective objective function value $\varphi_j^{(k)}\left(f_j\left(u_i\right)\right)$ as in Table 2 through Table 5.   ▯

Table 1   The Value of States

$f_j(u_i)$	f_1	f_2	f_3	f_4
u_1	85	90	95	75
u_2	70	80	65	60
u_3	90	60	70	85

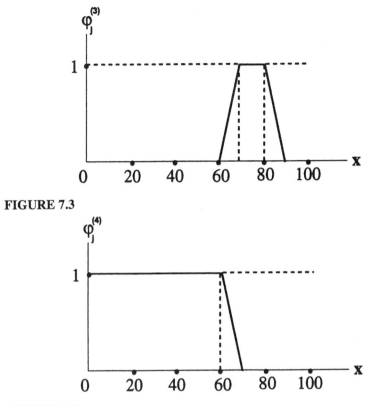

FIGURE 7.3

FIGURE 7.4

Table 2 The Value of the Objective Function $\varphi_j^{(1)}$

$\varphi_j^{(1)}(f_j(u_i))$	f_1	f_2	f_3	f_4
u_1	0.5	1	1	0
u_2	0	0	0	0
u_3	1	0	0	0.5

Take $M_4 = \sum$ and w_j (or a_j)= $\frac{1}{4}$, ($j = 1, 2, \cdots,$). Then the decision function $D_4^{(k)}(u_i)$ is

$$D_4^{(k)}(u_i) = \frac{1}{4}\sum_{j=1}^{4}\varphi_j^{(k)}(f_j(u_i)), \quad i = 1, 2, 3 \text{ and } j = 1, 2, 3, 4.$$

Based on Table 2 through Table 5, we obtain the values of $D_4^{(k)}(u_i)$ as shown in Table 6.

Table 3   The Value of the Objective Function $\varphi_j^{(2)}$

$\varphi_j^{(2)}\left(f_j\left(u_i\right)\right)$	f_1	f_2	f_3	f_4
u_1	1	1	0.5	0.5
u_2	0	1	0	0
u_3	1	0	0	1

Table 4   The Value of the Objective Function $\varphi_j^{(3)}$

$\varphi_j^{(3)}\left(f_j\left(u_i\right)\right)$	f_1	f_2	f_3	f_4
u_1	0.5	0	0	1
u_2	1	1	0.5	0
u_3	0	0	0	0.5

Table 5   The Value of the Objective Function $\varphi_j^{(4)}$

$\varphi_j^{(4)}\left(f_j\left(u_i\right)\right)$	f_1	f_2	f_3	f_4
u_1	0	0	0	0
u_2	0	0	0.5	1
u_3	0	1	0	0

The table also defines the following fuzzy sets on $E = \{e_1, e_2, e_3, e_4\}$:

$$D^{(u_1)} = (0.63, 0.75, 0.38, 0.00)$$

$$D^{(u_2)} = (0.00, 0.25, 0.63, 0.38)$$

$$D^{(u_3)} = (0.38, 0.50, 0.38, 0.25)$$

Finally, judging according to the principle of the maximum membership, we have evaluations for three students: Henry gets a "good" mark, Lucy gets a "fair" mark, and John gets a "good" mark.

7.2   Multifactorial Evaluation

Multifactorial evaluation is a special case of multiple objective multifactorial decision-making. Its purpose is to provide a synthetic evaluation of an object relative to an objective in a fuzzy decision environment with many factors.

Let U be a set of objects for evaluation, let $\pi = \{f_1, f_2, \cdots, f_m\}$ be the set of basic factors in the evaluation system (or process), and let $E = \{e_1, e_2, \cdots, e_p\}$ be a set of letter grades or qualitative classes used in the evaluation. According to

Table 6 The Values of Decision Functions.

$D_4^{(k)}(u_i)$	e_1	e_2	e_3	e_4
u_1	0.63	0.75	0.38	0
u_2	0	0.25	0.63	0.38
u_3	0.38	0.5	0.38	0.25

Section 7.1, for every object $u \in U$, there are $m \times p$ values of objective functions:

$$\varphi_j^{(k)}\left(f_j(u)\right), \quad k = 1, 2, \cdots, p; \quad j = 1, 2, \cdots, m.$$

We express the $m \times p$ values in the matrix form:

$$\begin{bmatrix} \varphi_1^{(1)}(f_1(u)) & \varphi_1^{(2)}(f_1(u)) & \cdots & \varphi_1^{(p)}(f_1(u)) \\ \varphi_2^{(1)}(f_2(u)) & \varphi_2^{(2)}(f_2(u)) & \cdots & \varphi_2^{(p)}(f_2(u)) \\ \vdots & \vdots & \cdots & \vdots \\ \varphi_m^{(1)}(f_m(u)) & \varphi_m^{(2)}(f_m(u)) & \cdots & \varphi_m^{(p)}(f_m(u)) \end{bmatrix}.$$

Let $r_{ij}(u) \overset{\triangle}{=} \varphi_j^{(k)}\left(f_j(u)\right)$. Then the above matrix can be written as

$$R^{(u)} = \begin{bmatrix} r_{11}(u) & r_{12}(u) & \cdots & r_{1p}(u) \\ r_{21}(u) & r_{22}(u) & \cdots & r_{2p}(u) \\ \vdots & \vdots & \cdots & \vdots \\ r_{m1}(u) & r_{m2}(u) & \cdots & r_{mp}(u) \end{bmatrix}. \tag{7.3}$$

The matrix $R^{(u)}$ may also be viewed as a fuzzy relation between π and E, i.e., $R^{(u)} \in \mathcal{F}(\pi \times E)$. Define

$$R_j^{(u)} = \left(r_{j1}(u), r_{j2}(u), \cdots, r_{jp}(u)\right). \tag{7.4}$$

Then this is the degree of membership of the object u with respect to a factor f_j on the set of letter grades $\{e_1, e_2, \cdots, e_p\}$. We call $R_j^{(u)}$ the **single-factor evaluation vector**. Since the matrix $R^{(u)}$ consists of $R_1^{(u)}$, $R_2^{(u)}$, $\cdots$, $R_m^{(u)}$ row vectors, we may write

$$R^{(u)} = \begin{bmatrix} R_1^{(u)} \\ R_2^{(u)} \\ \vdots \\ R_m^{(u)} \end{bmatrix}. \tag{7.5}$$

Therefore, we call $R^{(u)}$ the **single-factor evaluation matrix** of object u.

Form the expression (7.2), for any $u \in U$ and define

$$d_k(u) \overset{\triangle}{=} D^{(u)}(e_k), \quad k = 1, 2, \cdots, p. \tag{7.6}$$

Then $D^{(u)} = \left(d_1(u), d_2(u), \cdots, d_p(u)\right)$, and the decision function of (7.1) becomes

$$d_k(u) = \left(M_m \circ \varphi^{(k)} \circ 1\right)(u) = \left(M_m \circ \varphi^{(k)}\right)(1(u))$$

$$= \left(M_m \circ \varphi^{(k)}\right)(f_1(u), f_2(u), \cdots, f_m(u))$$

$$= M_m\left(\varphi^{(k)}(f_1(u), f_2(u), \cdots, f_m(u))\right)$$

$$= M_m\left(\varphi_1^{(k)}(f_1(u)), \varphi_2^{(k)}(f_2(u)), \cdots, \varphi_m^{(k)}(f_m(u))\right)$$

$$= M_m(r_{1k}(u), r_{2k}(u), \cdots, r_{mk}(u)).$$

Take M_m to be the $\sum$ operator, i.e.,

$$M_m(x_1, x_2, \cdots, x_m) = \sum(x_1, x_2, \cdots, x_m) = \sum_{j=1}^{m} w_j x_j.$$

Then $d_k(u)$ has the following form:

$$d_k(u) = \sum_{j=1}^{m} w_j r_{jk}(u), \tag{7.7}$$

where $W = (w_1, w_2, \cdots, w_m)$ is a constant weight vector. Hence, we have an important representation:

$$D^{(u)} = W \circ R^{(u)}. \tag{7.8}$$

The product between the vector W and the matrix $R^{(u)}$ follows equation (7.7).

Equation (7.8) is the fundamental formula in multifactorial evaluation. If M_m is defined by

$$M_m(x_1, x_2, \cdots, x_m) = \bigvee_{j=1}^{m} w_j r_{jk}(u)$$

then $d_k(u)$ has the following form:

$$d_k(u) = \bigvee_{j=1}^{m} w_j r_{jk}(u). \tag{7.9}$$

This time the product ∘ in expression (7.8) is defined by Expression (7.9).

Similarly, if M_m is taken to be as in Equation (5.8), then $d_k(u)$ is a commonly used expression:

$$d_k(u) = \bigvee_{j=1}^{m} \left(w_j \wedge r_{jk}(u) \right). \tag{7.10}$$

The product ∘ in expression (7.8) is now defined by equation (7.10).

We now proceed to further extend the preceding development. Let T be a triangular norm in $\mathcal{T}(2)$ and T^* be a complementary triangular norm in $\mathcal{T}^*(2)$. We will define the product in equation (7.8) by T and T^*. However, that product requires guarantee from the following.

PROPOSITION 32

Let $W = (w_1, w_2, \cdots, w_m)$ be a constant weight vector. T and T^* are given triangular and complementary triangular norms (both are not necessarily related), respectively. Notice that $T(x, y) = xTy$ and $T^*(x, y) = xT^*y$. Define

$$M_m(X) \overset{\Delta}{=} \overset{m}{\underset{j=1}{T^*}} \left(w_j T x_j \right) = (w_1 T x_1) \, T^* \, (w_2 T x_2) \, T^* \cdots T^* \, (w_m T x_m). \tag{7.11}$$

Then M_m is an ASM_m-func, i.e., $M_m \in \mathcal{M}_m$.

The proof is straightforward and hence omitted.
If M_m has the form of Expression (7.11), then

$$d_k(u) = \overset{m}{\underset{j=1}{T^*}} \left(w_j T r_{jk}(u) \right). \tag{7.12}$$

In this case, the product in the Expression (7.8) is defined by Equation (7.12).

If we denote a multifactorial evaluation model by $M(T, T^*)$, then $M(\bigvee, \bigwedge)$ is the model defined by Expression (7.10), and $M(\oplus, \cdot)$ is the model defined by Expression (7.7).

Notice that the constant weight vector satisfies the normality condition, i.e., $\sum_{j=1}^{m} w_j = 1$. Hence,

$$d_k(u) = \sum_{j=1}^{m} w_j r_{jk}(u) = \bigoplus_{j=1}^{m} \left(w_j r_{jk}(u) \right).$$

This means that $\oplus$ has degenerated to +.

To summarize, a multifactorial evaluation model requires three basic elements:

1. A family of basic factors, $\pi = \{f_1, f_2, \cdots, f_m\}$;
2. A set of evaluation phrases (or verbal grades), $E = \{e_1, e_2, \cdots, e_p\}$;
3. For every object $u \in U$, there is a single-factor evaluation matrix $R^{(u)} = (r_{jk}(u))_{m \times p}$.

With the preceding three elements, for a given $u \in U$, its evaluation result $D^{(u)} \in \mathcal{F}(E)$ can be derived as in Figure 7.5.

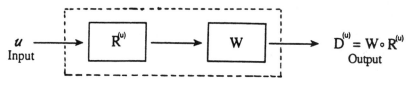

Transformer

FIGURE 7.5
A system of multifactorial evaluation model.

Since, for a given u, $R^{(u)}$ becomes a fixed fuzzy relation in $\mathcal{F}(\pi \times E)$ and the weight vector W can be viewed as a fuzzy set in $\mathcal{F}(\pi)$, for a given "input" W, $R^{(u)}$ acts as a transformer that turns W into an "output" $D^{(u)}$ (see Figure 7.6).

FIGURE 7.6
A partial multifactorial evaluation model (1).

In addition, for a fixed $u \in U$, regarding $R^{(u)}$ as the input and W the transformer, we then have the illustration in Figure 7.7.

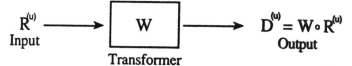

FIGURE 7.7
A partial multifactorial evaluation model (2).

Figure 7.5 suggests that we can define a mapping as follows:

$$\xi : U \longrightarrow \mathcal{F}(E)$$

$$u \longmapsto \xi(u) \overset{\Delta}{=} D^{(u)} = W \circ R^{(u)}. \tag{7.13}$$

Figure 7.6 suggests that we can define a transform as follows:

$$\eta^{(u)} : \mathcal{F}(\pi) \longrightarrow \mathcal{F}(E)$$

$$W \longmapsto \eta^{(u)}(W) \overset{\triangle}{=} W \circ R^{(u)}. \qquad (7.14)$$

Moreover, Figure 7.7 suggests that we can also define a transform in these terms:

$$\zeta^{(u)} : \mathcal{F}(\pi \times E) \longrightarrow \mathcal{F}(E)$$

$$R^{(u)} \longmapsto \zeta^{(u)}\left(R^{(u)}\right) \overset{\triangle}{=} W \circ R^{(u)}. \qquad (7.15)$$

Example 39

A Cloth Selection Problem.

Assume the basic factors of interest in the cloth selection consist of f_1 =style, f_2 =quality, and f_3 =price, i.e., $\pi = \{f_1, f_2, f_3\}$. The verbal grades used for the selection are $e_1 = $ best, e_2 =good, e_3 =fair, and e_4 =poor, i.e., $E = \{e_1, e_2, e_3, e_4\}$. For a particular piece of cloth, u, the single-factor evaluation may be carried out by professionals or customers. For example, if the survey results on the "style" factor are 70% for the best, 20% for the good, 10% for the fair, and none for the poor, then the single-factor evaluation vector $R_1^{(u)}$ is

$$R_1^{(u)} = (0.7, 0.2, 0.1, 0.0).$$

Similarly, we can obtain the following single-factor evaluation vectors for f_2, and f_3 :

$$R_2^{(u)} = (0.2, 0.4, 0.3, 0.1)$$

and

$$R_3^{(u)} = (0.1, 0.3, 0.4, 0.2).$$

Now we have the following single-factor evaluation matrix:

$$R^{(u)} = \begin{bmatrix} R_1^{(u)} \\ R_2^{(u)} \\ R_3^{(u)} \end{bmatrix} = \begin{bmatrix} 0.7 & 0.2 & 0.1 & 0.0 \\ 0.2 & 0.4 & 0.3 & 0.1 \\ 0.1 & 0.3 & 0.4 & 0.2 \end{bmatrix}.$$

If a customer's weight vector with respect to the three factors is

$$W = (0.5, 0.3, 0.2)$$

and the multifactorial evaluation model is $M\left(\bigvee, \bigwedge\right)$, then we can compute the multifactorial evaluation vector as:

$$D^{(u)} = W \circ R^{(u)} = (0.5, 0.3, 0.2) \circ \begin{bmatrix} 0.7\ 0.2\ 0.1\ 0.0 \\ 0.2\ 0.4\ 0.3\ 0.1 \\ 0.1\ 0.3\ 0.4\ 0.2 \end{bmatrix}$$

$$= (0.5, 0.3, 0.3, 0.2).$$

Because the largest component of $D^{(u)}$ is $d_1(u) = 0.5$, this piece of cloth received the "best" rating from the customers. □

Example 40

A Teaching Evaluation Problem.

Assume the basic factors that influence students' teaching evaluation are f_1 =clarity and understandability, f_2 =proficiency in teaching material, f_3 =liveliness and stimulation, and f_4 =writing neatness (or clarity), i.e., $\pi = \{f_1, f_2, f_3, f_4\}$. Let $E = \{e_1, e_2, e_3, e_4\}$ = {excellent, very good, good, poor} be the verbal grade set. We now evaluate teacher u. By selecting an appropriate group of students and faculty, we can have them respond with their ratings on each factor and then obtain the single-factor evaluation on each factor. As in the previous example, we have a single-factor evaluation matrix:

$$R^{(u)} = \begin{bmatrix} 0.4\ 0.5\ 0.1\ 0.0 \\ 0.6\ 0.3\ 0.1\ 0.0 \\ 0.1\ 0.2\ 0.6\ 0.1 \\ 0.1\ 0.2\ 0.5\ 0.2 \end{bmatrix}.$$

For a specific weight vector $W = (0.5, 0.2, 0.2, 0.1)$, and with the evaluation model $M\left(\bigvee, \bigwedge\right)$, it is easy to find

$$D^{(u)} = W \circ R^{(u)} = (d_1(u), d_2(u), d_3(u), d_4(u))$$

$$= (0.4, 0.5, 0.2, 0.1),$$

where $d_1(u) = (w_1 \wedge r_{11}(u)) \vee (w_2 \wedge r_{21}(u)) \vee (w_3 \wedge r_{31}(u)) \vee (w_4 \wedge r_{41}(u))$
$= (0.5 \wedge 0.4) \vee (0.2 \wedge 0.6) \vee (0.2 \wedge 0.1) \vee (0.1 \wedge 0.1)$
$= 0.4 \vee 0.2 \vee 0.1 \vee 0.1$
$= 0.4.$

Similarly, we can find the values for $d_2(u)$, $d_3(u)$, and $d_4(u)$. From our results, we conclude that teacher u should be rated as "very good". □

7.3 The Multifactorial Evaluation Approach to the Classification of Quality

Let U be a set of objects for evaluation, e.g., material, products, enterprises, colleges, employees, ..., etc. Let $\pi = \{f_1, f_2, \cdots, f_m\}$ be a set of basic factors that determine the quality of objects under evaluation, and let $E = \{e_1, e_2, \cdots, e_p\}$ be a set of verbal evaluation outcomes, where e_k represents quality class k. In general, there is a unified standard on each quality factor, and it is normally expressed in numerical values. Hence the evaluation criteria can be presented in the form of Table 7 and Table 8. These tables are derived by partitioning the factor states.

Table 7   Indices of Quality Classes

Factor\Class	e_1	e_2	$\cdots$	e_p
f_1	a_{11}	a_{12}	$\cdots$	a_{1p}
f_2	a_{21}	a_{22}	$\cdots$	a_{2p}
$\vdots$	$\vdots$	$\vdots$	$\vdots$	$\vdots$
f_m	a_{m1}	a_{m2}	$\cdots$	a_{mp}

Table 8   Quality Classes by Index Interval

Factor\Class	e_1	e_2	$\cdots$	e_p
f_1	$a_{10} - a_{11}$	$a_{11} - a_{12}$	$\cdots$	$a_{1(p-1)} - a_{1p}$
f_2	$a_{20} - a_{21}$	$a_{21} - a_{22}$	$\cdots$	$a_{2(p-1)} - a_{2p}$
$\vdots$	$\vdots$	$\vdots$	$\cdots$	$\vdots$
f_m	$a_{m0} - a_{m1}$	$a_{m1} - a_{m2}$	$\cdots$	$a_{m(p-1)} - a_{mp}$

Note. The value a_{jk} used in Table 7 means that the index of the jth quality factor assigned to the class e_k is either greater than a_{jk} or less than a_{jk}, that is, a_{jk} acts as a dividing line. The difference $a_{j(k-1)} - a_{jk}$ means that the index of the jth quality factor assigned to the class e_k is in that range.

For any object u under evaluation, if u is assigned to the same class e_k uniformly across all factors, then u belongs to the class e_k. But, normally each factor will have a different impact on u. For example, u belongs to e_2 under f_1; u belongs to e_4 under f_2, and so on. If we take all factors into consideration, then to what class does u belong? In order to answer this question, we first "soften" or make "elastic" the absolute boundaries and intervals in Table 6 and Table 7. In other words, for every factor f_j, we will construct a fuzzy class e_k for all $k \in \{1, 2, \cdots, p\}$. Since the fuzzy class e_k is a fuzzy set that is induced by f_j, we can denote the fuzzy set by $A_{\sim jk}$. Next, we define the objective function $\varphi_j^{(k)}(x)$ to be the membership function: $\varphi_j^{(k)}(x) = A_{\sim jk}(x)$ as laid out below.

1. Relative to Table 7, we construct membership functions as follows:

a. When a_{jk}, the index of factor f_j assigned to the quality class e_k, is *greater than* a_{jk}, for $(j = 1, 2, \cdots, m)$ and $(k = 1, 2, \cdots, p)$, then define

$$\varphi_j^{(1)}(x) = \begin{cases} 1, & x \geq a_{j1} \\ \frac{a_{j2}-x}{a_{j2}-a_{j1}}, & a_{j1} > x \geq a_{j2} \\ 0, & x < a_{j2} \end{cases} \quad j = 1, 2, \cdots, m;$$

$$\varphi_j^{(k)}(x) = \begin{cases} \frac{a_{jk-1}}{x}, & x \geq a_{jk-1} \\ 1, & a_{jk-1} > x \geq a_{jk} \\ \frac{a_{jk+1}-x}{a_{jk+1}-a_{jk}}, & a_{jk} > x \geq a_{jk+1} \\ 0, & x \leq a_{jk+1} \end{cases}$$

$$j = 1, 2, \cdots, m;$$
$$k = 2, \cdots, p-1;$$

$$\varphi_j^{(p)}(x) = \begin{cases} \frac{a_{jp-1}}{x}, & x \geq a_{jp-1} \\ 1, & a_{jp-1} > x \geq a_{jp} \\ \frac{x}{a_{jp}}, & x < a_{jp} \end{cases} \quad j = 1, 2, \cdots, m.$$

b. When a_{jk}, the index of factor f_j assigned to the quality class e_k, is *less than* a_{jk}, for $(j = 1, 2, \cdots, m)$ and $(k = 1, 2, \cdots, p)$, then define

$$\varphi_j^{(1)}(x) = \begin{cases} 1, & x \leq a_{j1} \\ \frac{a_{j2}-x}{a_{j2}-a_{j1}}, & a_{j1} < x \leq a_{j2} \\ 0, & x > a_{j2} \end{cases} \quad j = 1, 2, \cdots, m;$$

$$\varphi_j^{(k)}(x) = \begin{cases} \frac{x}{a_{jk-1}}, & x \leq a_{jk-1} \\ 1, & a_{jk-1} < x \leq a_{jk} \\ \frac{a_{jk+1}-x}{a_{jk+1}-a_{jk}}, & a_{jk} < x \leq a_{jk+1} \\ 0, & x > a_{jk+1} \end{cases}$$

$$j = 1, 2, \cdots, m;$$
$$k = 2, \cdots, p-1;$$

$$\varphi_j^{(p)}(x) = \begin{cases} \frac{x}{a_{jp-1}}, & x \leq a_{jp-1} \\ 1, & a_{jp-1} < x \leq a_{jp} \\ \frac{a_{jp}}{x}, & x > a_{jp} \end{cases} \quad j = 1, 2, \cdots, m.$$

2. For the Table 8, we define the membership function as follows:

$$\varphi_j^{(1)}(x) = \begin{cases} 1, & a_{j0} \leq x < a_{j1} \\ \frac{a_{j2}-x}{a_{j2}-a_{j1}}, & a_{j1} < x \leq a_{j2} \\ 0, & a_{j2} \leq x \leq a_{jm} \end{cases} \quad j = 1, 2, \cdots, m;$$

$$\varphi_j^{(k)}(x) = \begin{cases} 0, & a_{j0} \leq x \leq a_{jk-2} \\ \frac{x-a_{jk-2}}{a_{jk-1}-a_{jk-2}}, & a_{jk-2} < x < a_{jk-1} \\ 1, & a_{jk-1} \leq x < a_{jk} \\ \frac{a_{jk+1}-x}{a_{jk+1}-a_{jk}}, & a_{jk} \leq x < a_{jk+1} \\ 0, & a_{jk+1} \leq x \leq a_{j-p} \end{cases}$$

$$j = 1, 2, \cdots, m;$$
$$k = 2, \cdots, p-1;$$

$$\varphi_j^{(p)}(x) = \begin{cases} 0, & a_{j0} \leq x < a_{jp-2} \\ \frac{x-a_{jp-2}}{a_{jp-1}-a_{jp-2}}, & a_{jp-2} \leq x \leq a_{jp-1} \\ 1, & a_{jp-1} \leq x \leq a_{jp} \end{cases} \quad j = 1, 2, \cdots, m.$$

3. For every $u \in U$, there is a corresponding index (or state) vector (obtained via a survey sampling):

$$1(u) = (f_1(u), f_2(u), \cdots, f_m(u)).$$

By substituting these membership functions, we have the single-factor evaluation matrix

$$R^{(u)} = (r_{jk}(u))_{m \times p} = \left(\varphi_j^{(k)}(f_j(u))\right)_{m \times p}.$$

4. For a given set of objects U, the relative importance between quality factors varies. Therefore, we have to find a weight vector $W = (w_1, w_2, \cdots, w_m)$ before the evaluation. Then, according to the model $M(\bigvee, \cdot)$, we find $D^{(u)} = W \circ R^{(u)}$, where

$$d_k(u) = \bigvee_{j=1}^{m} w_j \cdot r_{jk}(u), \quad k = 1, 2, \cdots, p.$$

Example 41
Evaluation of Quality in the Textile Industry.
Data used in the quality evaluation may be given in the form of Table 7. Here we will grade the combed polyester and cotton blended yarn (containing 60% or more of polyester). The technical standards of the yarn are defined in Table 9.

Table 9   Indices of Technical Standards for Yarn Classification

Factor\Class	e_1 First	e_2 Second	e_3 Third	e_4 Fourth
f_1 : breaking point strength* gf/Tex	≥ 17	≥ 17	≥ 17	≥ 17
f_2 : tension* coefficient of variation (%)	≤ 8.5	≤ 10	≤ 11.5	≤ 13.5
f_3 : weight coefficient of variation (%)	≤ 1.5	≤ 2	≤ 2.5	≤ 3.5
f_4 : naps per gram	≤ 7	≤ 10	≤ 13	≤ 16

*These are measured on a single sliver basis.

From this table, factor f_1 can be considered later because its standard is the same across the four classes. Let's assume $W = (0.3, 0.3, 0.4)$ to be a weight distribution on factors f_1, f_2, and f_3. Let u denote the kind of yarn for evaluation with state values $f_1(u) = 18$, $f_2(u) = 9.6$, $f_3(u) = 1.4$, and $f_4(u) = 10$. Then,

$$R^{(u)} = \begin{bmatrix} 0.47 & 1 & 0.96 & 0.83 \\ 1 & 0.93 & 0.7 & 0.56 \\ 0.3 & 1 & 1 & 0.77 \end{bmatrix}.$$

We find that

$$D^{(u)} = W \circ R^{(u)} = (0.56, 0.98, 0.90, 0.73).$$

This indicates that, on the basis of factors two, three, and four, the yarn is rated as "second class"; also, since it satisfies the condition on factor one, we conclude that the yarn should be rated as such.

Suppose u' represents a different kind of yarn, and its state values are $f_1(u') = 16.5$, $f_2(u') = 11$, $f_3(u') = 1.4$, and $f_4(u) = 10$. Then

$$R^{(u')} = \begin{bmatrix} 0.125 & 0.360 & 1 & 0.960 \\ 1 & 0.93 & 0.7 & 0.56 \\ 0.3 & 1 & 1 & 0.77 \end{bmatrix}.$$

We have

$$D^{(u')} = W \circ R^{(u')} = (0.46, 0.79, 0.91, 0.76).$$

Therefore, on the basis of factors f_2, f_3, and f_4 the yarn should be rated as "class three"; however, since its factor one index is below 17, the rating in this case should be decreased to "class four" instead. $\square$

7.4 Incomplete Multifactorial Evaluation

We have mentioned previously that there were three basic elements in multifactorial evaluation:

1. A family of basic factors, $\pi = \{f_1, f_2, \cdots, f_m\}$;
2. A set of evaluation phrases (or verbal grades), $E = \{e_1, e_2, \cdots, e_p\}$;
3. For every object $u \in U$, there is a single-factor evaluation matrix

$$R^{(u)} = \left(r_{jk}(u) \right)_{m \times p}.$$

However, in complex real world problems, it is common that certain basic factors may not be fully understood at the time of evaluation. This means that the family of basic factors may be incomplete. We call this kind of problem an **evaluation with partial factors** or **incomplete factorial evaluation** problem.

In an incomplete factorial evaluation problem, an important question is how to construct a family of basic factors π. Is there a way to make the *incomplete* factorial evaluation problem *complete*? We will show that under certain conditions this problem can be solved.

Let u be an object for evaluation, e.g., material, products, students, employees, etc. then u is called a **manifested evaluation object** if it satisfies the following three conditions:

1) Observability — If it is possible to conduct simple evaluations by using instruments or direct human observations and contacts.

2) Separability — If u is regarded as a whole by certain measurement (e.g., area, weight, volume, total counts, etc.), then u can be arbitrarily divided into subbodies (or subdivisions) in the sense of that measurement.

3) Comparability — If u' is a subbody derived from u, then there exists a ratio between u' and u in the chosen measurement, and the ratio is a number between 0 and 1.

The evaluation system with these conditions on u is referred to as a **manifested evaluation system.**

We now illustrate a dissection method and explain how that method can complete manifested evaluation systems. The role of the dissection method is to simultaneously construct the family of basic factors π and the weight vector W. The procedure of the dissection method is as follows:

Step 1. Building the family of basic factors π.

(1). Divide u into m_1 equal subparts and select a subpart f_1 from them according to the selection criteria β; the ratio between f_1 and u is designated by k_1.

(2). Divide u into m_2 equal subparts ($m_2 < m_1$); then select a subpart f_2 from them according to the selection criteria β; the ratio between f_2 and u is designated by k_2.

...

Continue this process.

...

(m-1). Divide u into m_{m-1} equal subparts ($m_{m-1} < m_{m-2}$); then select a subpart f_{m-1} from them according to the selection criteria β; the ratio between f_{m-1} and u is designated by k_{m-1}.

(m). Define $f_m = u$. Obviously the ratio between f_m and u is $k_m = 1$. Thus, we have a family of basic factors $\pi = \{f_1, f_2, \cdots, f_m\}$.

Step 2. Calibrating the weight vector $W = (w_1, w_2, \cdots, w_m)$. The components of W are set as

$$w_j = k_j / \sum_{i=1}^{m} k_i, \quad j = 1, 2, \cdots, m.$$

Note. Let $w_{j1} = \max \{w_1, w_2, \cdots, w_m\}$ and $w_{j2} = \min \{w_1, w_2, \cdots, w_m\}$. To avoid the case $w_{j1} \gg w_{j2}$, we can define an "adjusted" mapping thus:

$$\varphi : [0, 1] \longrightarrow [0, 1], \quad x \longmapsto \varphi(x),$$

such that φ is monotonic, i.e., $x \le y \Longrightarrow \varphi(x) \le \varphi(y)$ (or $\varphi(x) \le \varphi(y)$). Then, set

$$w_j = \frac{\varphi(k_j)}{\sum_{i=1}^{m} \varphi(k_i)}, \quad j = 1, 2, \cdots, m.$$

Example 42

Quality Inspection on the Coating of Capsules.

The color on the coating of capsules used in certain pills is inspected and classified into four categories:

e_1 = unevenly colored
e_2 = partially uneven colored
e_3 = slightly uneven colored
e_4 = evenly colored

Hence, we have the set $E = \{e_1, e_2, e_3, e_4\}$.

Notice that the factors that influence the coloring are too complex to study and, therefore, basically are unknown. Consequently, this is an example of the incomplete evaluation problem. It is also easy to recognize that the capsule is the *manifested evaluation object*; hence the dissection method applies.

We proceed as follows. First, we take a random sample of 100 capsules from a batch of capsules (denoted by u) just produced. Then we divide the surface area (not the physical capsule itself) of each capsule into subdivisions as in Figure 7.8.

Our criterion β is to "rate the capsule category on the basis of the worst unevenly colored subdivision".

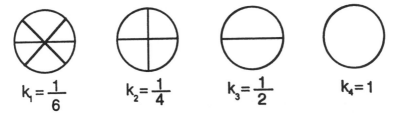

Each circle is equally divided into parts.

FIGURE 7.8
The dissection of object u.

First, we inspect the 100 capsules with respect to factor f_1 (i.e., a subdivision of one-sixth). Suppose 10 were found "unevenly colored", 15 were found "partially uneven colored", 20 were found "slightly uneven colored", and 55 were found "evenly colored", then we have found the single-factor (i.e., f_1) evaluation vector

$$R_1^{(u)} = (0.10, 0.15, 0.20, 0.55).$$

Similarly, relative to each factor f_2 (a subdivision of one-fourth), f_3 (a subdivision of one-half), and f_4 (the whole), we obtain a corresponding single-factor evaluation vector:

$$R_2^{(u)} = (0.00, 0.10, 0.30, 0.60)$$

$$R_3^{(u)} = (0.00, 0.00, 0.20, 0.80)$$

$$R_4^{(u)} = (0.00, 0.00, 0.15, 0.85).$$

Therefore, the single-factor evaluation matrix is

$$R^{(u)} = \begin{bmatrix} 0.10 & 0.15 & 0.10 & 0.55 \\ 0.00 & 0.10 & 0.30 & 0.60 \\ 0.00 & 0.00 & 0.20 & 0.80 \\ 0.00 & 0.00 & 0.15 & 0.85 \end{bmatrix}.$$

The weight vector W can be found easily; it is

$$W = (0.08, 0.11, 0.23, 0.45).$$

From these values, the multifactorial evaluation vector is found to be (under the model $M\left(\bigvee, \bigwedge\right)$)

$$D^{(u)} = W \circ R^{(u)} = (0.08, 0.10, 0.20, 0.45).$$

We can conclude that the color of capsules is "even" and, hence, it passes the inspection. ▯

7.5 Multilevel Multifactorial Evaluation

When the evaluation system is very complex, a large number of factors, normally, must be taken into consideration. Then we may face two problems. First, is the difficulty in ascertaining the weights. Second, even though there is no difficulty in obtaining weights, the weights will be very small numerically because of the normality condition. The evaluation vector $D^{(u)}$ is the result of $W \circ R^{(u)}$.

When a common model $M\left(\bigvee, \bigwedge\right)$) is adopted, then $d_k(u) \le \bigvee_{j=1}^{m} w_j$. Information contained in smaller weights will be partially or totally lost after performing the "$\bigwedge$" operation. An example follows.

Example 43

Suppose we are evaluating the quality of a batch of products u. There are nine basic factors in the family π, i.e., $\pi = \{f_1, f_2, \cdots, f_9\}$. There are four classes of verbal evaluations, i.e., $E = \{e_1 = $ excellent, $e_2 = $ good, $e_3 = $ fair, $e_4 = $ poor$\}$. An evaluation team consists of experts, inspectors, and consumers; they will evaluate the products against three factors, respectively. For example, experts are assigned to $E_1 = \{f_1, f_2, f_3\}$; inspectors are assigned to $E_2 = \{f_4, f_5, f_6\}$; and consumers are assigned to $E_3 = \{f_7, f_8, f_9\}$. We obtain three single-factor evaluation matrices:

$$R_{(1)}^{(u)} = \begin{bmatrix} 0.36 & 0.24 & 0.13 & 0.27 \\ 0.20 & 0.32 & 0.25 & 0.23 \\ 0.40 & 0.22 & 0.26 & 0.12 \end{bmatrix},$$

$$R_{(2)}^{(u)} = \begin{bmatrix} 0.30 & 0.28 & 0.24 & 0.18 \\ 0.26 & 0.36 & 0.12 & 0.20 \\ 0.22 & 0.42 & 0.16 & 0.10 \end{bmatrix},$$

$$R_{(3)}^{(u)} = \begin{bmatrix} 0.38 & 0.24 & 0.08 & 0.20 \\ 0.34 & 0.25 & 0.30 & 0.11 \\ 0.24 & 0.28 & 0.30 & 0.18 \end{bmatrix}.$$

The combined single-factor evaluation matrix is

$$R^{(u)} = \begin{bmatrix} R^{(u)}_{(1)} \\ R^{(u)}_{(2)} \\ R^{(u)}_{(3)} \end{bmatrix} = \begin{bmatrix} 0.36 & 0.24 & 0.13 & 0.27 \\ 0.20 & 0.32 & 0.25 & 0.23 \\ 0.40 & 0.22 & 0.26 & 0.12 \\ 0.30 & 0.28 & 0.24 & 0.18 \\ 0.26 & 0.36 & 0.12 & 0.20 \\ 0.22 & 0.42 & 0.16 & 0.10 \\ 0.38 & 0.24 & 0.08 & 0.20 \\ 0.34 & 0.25 & 0.30 & 0.11 \\ 0.24 & 0.28 & 0.38 & 0.18 \end{bmatrix}.$$

Assume that the constant weight vector is known as

$$W = (0.10, 0.12, 0.07, 0.07, 0.16, 0.10, 0.10, 0.10, 0.18).$$

Then we find the evaluation vector

$$D^{(u)} = W \circ R^{(u)} = (0.18, 0.18, 0.18, 0.18).$$

This does not permit us to draw conclusions. ▯

Let's take a closer look at the computation of $d_1(u)$:

$$\begin{aligned} d_1(u) &= (w_1 \wedge r_{11}(u)) \vee (w_2 \wedge r_{21}(u)) \vee \cdots \vee (w_9 \wedge r_{91}(u)) \\ &= (0.10 \wedge 0.36) \vee (0.12 \wedge 0.20) \vee \cdots \vee (0.18 \wedge 0.24) \\ &= 0.10 \vee 0.12 \vee 0.07 \vee 0.07 \vee 0.16 \vee 0.10 \vee 0.10 \vee 0.10 \vee 0.18 \\ &= 0.18. \end{aligned}$$

We find that the elements in the first column of the matrix $R^{(u)}$ are irrelevant after the "min" operation. Of course, this is caused by the smaller values of w_j. To solve this problem, we use the concept of "levels".

In situations where a large number of factors is present, it is common to group factors into categories according to some attributes or properties. For example, in rank ordering the best ten business schools in the U.S., one may consider such factors as: teaching, research, program design, employment prospects, etc. There is a weight distribution among these factors. Hence, we can proceed with the multifactorial evaluation. However, each single-factor evaluation here is the result of a multifactorial evaluation from a level below that factor. For example, factors that influence teaching evaluations, such as quality of faculty, quality of students, teaching facilities, etc., are below the level of "teaching". Similarly, we can determine the next level of factors below the "quality of faculty" level. For this type of multilevel factorial structure, we have developed an evaluation model.

Here are the steps of the multilevel multifactorial evaluation procedure:

Step 1. Classify the family of basic factors for $\pi = \{f_1, f_2, \cdots, f_m\}$ into s subsets according to certain attributes

$$\pi_i = \left\{f_{i_1}, f_{i_2}, \cdots, f_{i_{m_i}}\right\}, \quad i = 1, 2, \cdots, s,$$

and they satisfy

(a) $m_1 + m_2 + \cdots + m_s = m$;
(b) $\pi_1 + \pi_2 + \cdots + \pi_s = \pi$; and
(c) $(\forall i, j) \left(i \neq j \Longrightarrow \pi_i \cap \pi_j = \Phi\right)$.

Step 2. For every factor subset π_i, find its multifactorial (level-1) evaluation. Let $E = \left\{e_1, e_2, \cdots, e_p\right\}$ be the set of verbal grades used in the evaluation, and let $W_i = \left\{w_{i_1}, w_{i_2}, \cdots, w_{i_{m_i}}\right\}$ be the weight vector for the subset π_i, where $w_{i_1} + w_{i_2} + \cdots + w_{i_{m_i}} = 1$. Further assume $R_{(i)}^{(u)}$ to be the single-factor evaluation matrix from π_i. Then we have the following level-1 evaluation vector :

$$D_{(i)}^{(u)} = W_i \circ R_{(i)}^{(u)} = \left(d_{i1}(u), d_{i2}(u), \cdots, d_{ip}(u)\right), \quad i = 1, 2, \cdots, s.$$

Step 3. View each π_i as a factor. Then

$$\pi = \{\pi_1, \pi_2, \cdots, \pi_s\}$$

is again a family of factors. The single-factor evaluation matrix with respect to π is

$$R^{(u)} = \begin{bmatrix} D_{(1)}^{(u)} \\ D_{(2)}^{(u)} \\ \vdots \\ D_{(s)}^{(u)} \end{bmatrix} = \begin{bmatrix} d_{11}(u) & d_{12}(u) & \cdots & d_{1p}(u) \\ d_{21}(u) & d_{22}(u) & \cdots & d_{2p}(u) \\ \vdots & \vdots & \cdots & \vdots \\ d_{s1}(u) & d_{s2}(u) & \cdots & d_{sp}(u) \end{bmatrix}.$$

Since each π_i is an attribute of π, the relative importance among π_i gives rise to these weights:

$$W = (w_1, w_2, \cdots, w_s).$$

Thus we find the level-2 evaluation vector

$$D^{(u)} = W \circ R^{(u)} = \left(d_1^{(u)}, d_2^{(u)}, \cdots, d_m^{(u)}\right),$$

where

$$d_k^{(u)} = \overset{s}{\underset{j=1}{T^*}} \left(w_j T d_{jk}(u)\right), \quad k = 1, 2, \cdots, p.$$

Here (T^*, T) represents two general operators. The choice of operators such as $(\vee, \wedge)$, $(\vee, \cdot)$, etc. will depend upon the problem at hand. Figure 7.9 gives a straightforward illustration of a 2-level multifactorial evaluation.

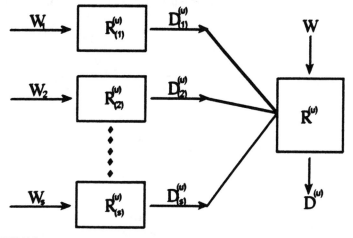

FIGURE 7.9
A 2-level multifactorial evaluation model.

If one or more families of factors π_i contain many factors, then they can be similarly divided into another layer of subsets that leads to the level-3 evaluation model. The process can go on to as many levels as it is appropriate.

Example 44
We now proceed to take care of the remaining issues in the last example. First, we classify the family of basic factors π into three subsets: $\pi_1 = \{f_1, f_2, f_3\}$, $\pi_2 = \{f_4, f_5, f_6\}$, $\pi_3 = \{f_7, f_8, f_9\}$. Let $R_{(1)}^{(u)}$, $R_{(2)}^{(u)}$, $R_{(3)}^{(u)}$ be the corresponding single-factor evaluation matrix. The weight vectors of π_1, π_2, and π_3 are

$$W_1 = (0.30, 0.42, 0.28),$$

$$W_2 = (0.20, 0.50, 0.30),$$

and

$$W_3 = (0.30, 0.30, 0.40).$$

We find the evaluation vectors:

$$D_{(1)}^{(u)} = W_1 \circ R_{(1)}^{(u)} = (0.30, 0.32, 0.26, 0.27)$$

$$D_{(2)}^{(u)} = W_2 \circ R_{(2)}^{(u)} = (0.26, 0.26, 0.20, 0.20)$$

$$D_{(3)}^{(u)} = W_3 \circ R_{(3)}^{(u)} = (0.30, 0.28, 0.30, 0.20).$$

If we combine the three single-factor evaluation matrices (i.e., level-2 single-factor evaluation matrices), we have

$$R^{(u)} = \begin{bmatrix} R_{(1)}^{(u)} \\ R_{(2)}^{(u)} \\ R_{(3)}^{(u)} \end{bmatrix} = \begin{bmatrix} 0.30 & 0.32 & 0.26 & 0.27 \\ 0.26 & 0.26 & 0.20 & 0.20 \\ 0.30 & 0.28 & 0.30 & 0.20 \end{bmatrix}.$$

If we assume that $W = (0.20, 0.35, 0.45)$ is the weight vector for the family of three factors $\{\pi_1, \pi_2, \pi_3\}$, then we find that the level-2 evaluation vector is

$$D^{(u)} = W \circ R^{(u)} = (0.30, 0.35, 0.30, 0.20).$$

We used $(\bigvee, \bigwedge)$ in the above computation. Now our evaluation indicates that this batch belongs to the "good" class. $\Box$

7.6 An Application of Multifactorial Evaluation in Textile Engineering

In this section, we provide a real world application of multifactorial evaluation of the quality of the raw sliver in textile engineering (see Ma [1]). By "raw sliver" we mean the cotton sliver produced by carding machines; its quality is closely related to the yarn and its final product — cloth. For evaluating the quality of the raw sliver, factories may use these five indices: f_1 = stretchability, f_2 = degree of separation, f_3 = evenness, f_4 = weight unevenness, and f_5 = number of cotton naps; these five indices are used here, and they form the basic family of factors $\pi = \{f_1, f_2, f_3, f_4, f_5\}$. The verbal evaluation has these three classes: e_1 = excellent, e_2 = good, and e_3 = poor. Table 10 was established from random samples obtained from the carding machines of the first branch factory of the Tianjin Number One Textile Factory.

Table 10 Standards of Quality for Raw Slivers.

Class\Factor	f_1	f_2	f_3	f_4	f_5
e_1 : excellent	$66 \sim 70$	$48 \sim 54$	$9 \sim 10$	$2.9 \sim 3.1$	$45 \sim 50$
e_2 : good	$63 \sim 66$	$43 \sim 48$	$10 \sim 12$	$3.1 \sim 3.5$	$50 \sim 55$
e_3 : poor	$60 \sim 63$	$41 \sim 43$	$12 \sim 14$	$3.5 \sim 4.8$	$55 \sim 65$

Since we only have five basic factors, we can use a one-level multifactorial evaluation model. Suppose a group of experts have agreed to use the following weights:

$$W = (0.23, 0.25, 0.15, 0.15, 0.22),$$

we can construct objective functions $\varphi_j^{(k)}(x)$ according to Table 10 as follows:

$$\varphi_1^{(1)}(x) = \begin{cases} 1, & 66 \le x \le 70 \\ \frac{1}{3}(x - 63), & 63 \le x \le 66 \\ 0, & 60 \le x < 63 \end{cases}$$

$$\varphi_1^{(2)}(x) = \begin{cases} \frac{1}{4}(70 - x) & 66 < x \le 70 \\ 1, & 63 \le x \le 66 \\ \frac{1}{3}(x - 60), & 60 \le x < 63 \end{cases}$$

$$\varphi_1^{(3)}(x) = \begin{cases} 0, & 66 \le x \le 70 \\ \frac{1}{3}(66 - x), & 63 < x < 66 \\ 1, & 60 \le x \le 63 \end{cases}$$

$$\varphi_2^{(1)}(x) = \begin{cases} 1, & 48 \le x \le 54 \\ \frac{1}{5}(x - 43), & 43 \le x < 48 \\ 0, & 41 \le x \le 43 \end{cases}$$

$$\varphi_2^{(2)}(x) = \begin{cases} \frac{1}{6}(54 - x), & 48 < x \le 54 \\ 1, & 43 \le x < 48 \\ \frac{1}{2}(x - 41), & 41 \le x < 43 \end{cases}$$

$$\varphi_2^{(3)}(x) = \begin{cases} 0, & 48 < x \le 54 \\ \frac{1}{5}(48 - x), & 43 < x < 48 \\ 1, & 41 \le x \le 43 \end{cases}$$

$$\varphi_3^{(1)}(x) = \begin{cases} 1, & 9 \le x \le 10 \\ \frac{1}{2}(12 - x), & 10 < x \le 12 \\ 0, & 12 < x \le 14 \end{cases}$$

$$\varphi_3^{(2)}(x) = \begin{cases} x - 9, & 9 \le x < 10 \\ 1, & 10 \le x \le 12 \\ \frac{1}{2}(14 - x), & 12 < x \le 14 \end{cases}$$

$$\varphi_3^{(3)}(x) = \begin{cases} 0, & 9 \le x < 10 \\ \frac{1}{2}(x - 10), & 10 \le x \le 12 \\ 1, & 12 \le x \le 14 \end{cases}$$

$$\varphi_4^{(1)}(x) = \begin{cases} 1, & 2.9 \le x \le 3.1 \\ \frac{5}{2}(3.5 - x), & 3.1 < x \le 3.5 \\ 0, & 3.5 < x \le 4.8 \end{cases}$$

$$\varphi_4^{(2)}(x) = \begin{cases} 5(x - 2.9), & 2.9 \le x < 3.1 \\ 1, & 3.1 \le x \le 3.5 \\ \frac{10}{15}(4.8 - x), & 3.5 < x \le 4.8 \end{cases}$$

$$\varphi_4^{(3)}(x) = \begin{cases} 0, & 2.9 \le x < 3.1 \\ \frac{5}{2}(x - 3.1), & 3.1 \le x < 3.5 \\ 1, & 3.5 \le x \le 4.8 \end{cases}$$

$$\varphi_5^{(1)}(x) = \begin{cases} 1, & 45 \le x \le 50 \\ \frac{1}{5}(55 - x), & 50 < x \le 55 \\ 0, & 55 < x \le 65 \end{cases}$$

$$\varphi_5^{(2)}(x) = \begin{cases} \frac{1}{5}(x - 45), & 45 \le x < 50 \\ 1, & 50 \le x \le 55 \\ \frac{1}{10}(65 - x), & 55 < x \le 65 \end{cases}$$

$$\varphi_5^{(3)}(x) = \begin{cases} 0, & 45 \le x \le 50 \\ \frac{1}{5}(x - 55), & 50 < x < 55 \\ 1, & 55 \le x \le 65 \end{cases}$$

We now proceed with the multifactorial evaluation on the quality of a raw sliver from a carding machine. First, we must obtain measurements of the raw sliver on all five factors. These values are

$$f_1(u) = 64.8, \quad f_2(u) = 50, \quad f_3(u) = 11.2, \quad f_4(u) = 3.6, \quad \text{and} \quad f_5(u) = 52.4.$$

From here, we find the values of all objective functions: $\varphi_j^{(k)}(x)\left(f_j(u)\right) = \gamma_{jk}(u)$, and they are shown in the following single-factor evaluation matrix:

$$R^{(u)} = \left(\gamma_{jk}(u)\right)_{5\times 3} = \begin{bmatrix} 0.6 & 1 & 0.4 \\ 1 & 0.67 & 0 \\ 0.4 & 1 & 0.6 \\ 0 & 0.92 & 1 \\ 0.52 & 1 & 0.48 \end{bmatrix}.$$

Finally, we find the evaluation vector:

$$D^{(u)} = W \circ R^{(u)} = (0.25, 0.23, 0.15).$$

We conclude that the quality of the raw sliver from the carding machine should be rated as "excellent".

References

[1] Ma, H.-Y., A method for the synthetic evaluation on card sliver quality, *Journal of Tianjing College of Textile Technology*, 5(1), 1986, 102–107. (In Chinese.)

[2] Li, H.-X., Multifactorial fuzzy sets and multifactorial degree of nearness, *Fuzzy Sets and Systems*, 19(3), 1986, 291–297.

[3] Li, H.-X., A fuzzy mathematical model of grading quality, *Mathematics in Practice and Theory*, No.2 (1986), 9–13.

[4] Li, H.-X., Multifactorial analysis, *Fuzzy Systems and Mathematics*, 2(1), 1988, 9–19.

[5] Li, H.-X., Multifactorial functions in fuzzy sets theory, *Fuzzy Sets and Systems*, 35(1), 1990, 69–84.

[6] Li, H.-X., *Fuzzy Mathematics Methods in Engineering and Their Applications*, Tianjin Scientific and Technical Press, Tianjin, 1993. (In Chinese.)

[7] Li, H.-X. and Wang, P.-Z., *Fuzzy Mathematics*, National Defense Press, Beijing, 1994. (In Chinese.)

[8] Li, H.-X. and Yen, V. C., The operations of fuzzy cardinalities, *JMAA*, 182(1994), 768–778.

[9] Li, H.-X. and Yen, V. C., Factor spaces and fuzzy decision making, *Journal of Beijing Normal University*, 30(1), 1994, 41–46.

[10] Wang, P.-Z., *Fuzzy Set Theory and Its Applications*, Shanghai Scientific and Technical Press, Shanghai, 1984. (In Chinese.)

[11] Wang, P.-Z., *Fuzzy Sets and The Falling Shadow of Random Sets*, Beijing Normal University Press, Beijing, 1985. (In Chinese.)

[12] Wang, P.-Z., *Fuzzy Engineering — Principles and Methods*, China Productivity Center, Taipei, 1993. (In Chinese.)

8

Set-Valued Statistics and Degree Analysis

In traditional statistics, an outcome is always a point in the sample space of an experiment. If we relax this condition by admitting subsets or fuzzy subsets of the sample space as outcomes of experiments, then we have the **set-valued statistics** (or **set-valued statistical experiments**). The extension of traditional statistical methods to the set-valued statistical methods has real and practical significance because it can greatly expand the domain of traditional statistical applications, including, but not limited to, such areas as economics and social and behavioral sciences.

8.1 Fuzzy Statistics and Random Sets

The concept of the degree of membership in fuzzy set theory is fundamental in real world applications. People have applied statistical methods for the construction of membership functions. In Section 4.1, we introduced fuzzy statistical methods in which every outcome of the experiment is a subset of the universe U. Hence, it is an example of **set-valued statistics**.

The subjects used in traditional statistical experiments often are physical objects with little or no psychological dependence. Fuzzy statistics, however, are closely related to psychology because psychological tests frequently use them as a basis for further analysis. In physical psychology, repetitive experiments have shown that there exists an accurate law, in the form of a power function, between the psychological responses gained through various senses (vision, hearing, smelling, tasting, feeling) and the amount of stimuli from the environment. This explains why scientific psychological measurements can objectively reveal the underlying reality. Psychological measurements are important today because there are many such measurements routinely conducted, published, and applied by social, economic, and political professionals. Therefore, the inclusion of psychological measurements in fuzzy statistics is an added advantage over the traditional statistics, especially, when such measurements cannot be overlooked from analysis.

It is interesting that there exists a kind of "duality" between statistics and fuzzy statistics. Here is an analogy: if, "the fixed circle (the sample space) and indefinite points (outcomes)" are the bases of traditional statistical experiments, then "the fixed point and indefinite circles" are the bases of fuzzy statistical experiment. Is there a transformation between the two models? The answer is affirmative.

Figure 8.1 shows that the "circle" in X is a "point" in the power set $\mathcal{P}(X)$. The "point" x in X corresponds to the "circle" $\{x\}$ in $\mathcal{P}(X)$. If X is changed to $\mathcal{P}(X)$, then "point" and "circle" are interchanged. The set $\{x\}^0$ means

$$\{x\}^0 = \{\beta \in \mathcal{P}(X) \mid \beta \supset \{x\}\}.$$

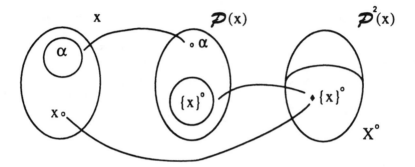

FIGURE 8.1
The roles of points and circles.

This provides a means for transforming a fuzzy statistical model on X to a traditional statistical model on $\mathcal{P}(X)$.

According to statistics, a sample outcome is a realization of a random variable. Thus, it is necessary to define measurable structures and random variables on $\mathcal{P}(X)$. Denote

$$X^0 \overset{\triangle}{=} \left\{\{x\}^0 \mid x \in X\right\}.$$

If $\mathcal{B}$ is a σ-algebra containing X^0, then $(\mathcal{P}(X), \mathcal{B})$ is a measurable space. A random variable is a mapping defined from the probability field $(\Omega, \mathcal{A}, p)$ to the measurable space $(\mathcal{P}(X), \mathcal{B})$ such that

$$\xi : \Omega \longrightarrow \mathcal{P}(X)$$

and

$$\xi^{-1}\left(\underset{\sim}{C}\right) = \left\{\omega \in \Omega \mid \xi(\omega) \in \underset{\sim}{C}\right\} \in \mathcal{A}, \qquad \left(\forall \underset{\sim}{C} \in \mathcal{B}\right).$$

The measurable space $(\mathcal{P}(X), \mathcal{B})$ may be viewed as a hyper-measurable structure on X. The random variable ξ is a random set on X (a rigorous definition should be given under the hyper-measurable structure [9]). We define $\Xi\,(\mathcal{A},\,\mathcal{B})$ to be the set of all random sets from $(\Omega,\,\mathcal{A})$ to $(\mathcal{P}\,(X)\,,\,\mathcal{B})$. In other words, fuzzy statistical experiments are realizations of random sets.

8.2 The Falling Shadow of Random Sets

Although fuzzy statistical models can be converted to traditional statistical models, they have their own special characteristics. The probability distribution of the random set ξ, $\left\{p_\xi\left(\underset{\sim}{C}\right)\right\}_{\left(\underset{\sim}{C}\in\mathcal{B}\right)}$, for example, is difficult to state explicitly. However, it is easier to represent the restriction of p_ξ on X^0.

Let ξ be a random set on X, i.e., $\xi : \Omega \longrightarrow \mathcal{P}\,(X)$ (measurable with respect to $\mathcal{B}$). Denote

$$\mu_\xi\,(x) \overset{\triangle}{=} p\,\{\omega \mid \xi\,(\omega) \ni x\}\,, \quad x \in X$$

and call it the **falling shadow** of ξ (a formal definition is given in Reference 9). Also, we can rewrite the above expression as

$$\mu_\xi\,(x) = p\,\left\{\omega \mid \xi\,(x) \in \{x\}^0\right\} = p_\xi\left(\{x\}^0\right)\,, \quad x \in X.$$

This explains that μ_ξ is the restriction of p_ξ on X^0. It is a real function defined on X, and it is an important new class of numerical values. We shall make this point clear after the following propositions.

Let $(\mathcal{P}\,(X)\,,\,\mathcal{B}_1)$ and $(\mathcal{P}\,(X)\,,\,\mathcal{B}_2)$ be two hyper-measurable structures on X and Y, respectively. Also, let $\xi \in \Xi\,(\mathcal{A},\,\mathcal{B}_1)$ and $\eta \in \Xi\,(\mathcal{A},\,\mathcal{B}_2)$ and define

$$\mu_{(\xi,\eta)}\,(x,\,y) \overset{\triangle}{=} p\,\{\omega \mid \xi\,(\omega) \ni x,\, \eta\,(\omega) \ni y\}\,.$$

Then it is called the **joint falling shadow** of ξ and η. If $\mu_\xi\,(x) > 0$, and we denote

$$\mu_{\eta|\xi}\,(y \mid x) \overset{\triangle}{=} p\,\{\eta \ni x \mid \xi \ni x\}\,,$$

then it is called the **conditional falling shadow** of η given $\xi \ni x$. Obviously,

$$\mu_{\eta|\xi}\,(y \mid x) = \mu_{(\xi,\eta)}\,(x,\,y)\,/\mu_\xi\,(x)\,.$$

We denote random sets ξ and η as independent if for any $\underset{\sim_i}{C} \in \mathcal{B}_i$ $(i = 1, 2)$, the following always holds:

$$p\left\{\omega \mid \xi(\omega) \in \underset{\sim_1}{C}, \eta(\omega) \in \underset{\sim_2}{C}\right\}$$

$$= p\left\{\omega \mid \xi(\omega) \in \underset{\sim_1}{C}\right\} \cdot p\left\{\omega \mid \eta(\omega) \in \underset{\sim_2}{C}\right\}.$$

We omit the definition of independence for a family of more than two random sets.

PROPOSITION 33

A necessary condition for two random sets to be independent is

$$\mu_{(\xi,\eta)}(x, y) = \mu_\xi(x) \cdot \mu_\eta(y).$$

Let m be a measure on the measurable space $(X, \mathcal{B})$. If the falling shadow μ_ξ of the random set ξ on X is measurable with respect to $\mathcal{B}$, then we can define

$$\overline{m}(\xi) \overset{\Delta}{=} \int_X \mu_\xi(x)\, m(dx).$$

Similarly, we can define $\overline{m}(\eta \mid \xi \ni x)$. The following three propositions are valid if all terms are well defined.

PROPOSITION 34
(The Marginal Falling Shadow Formula)

$$\mu_\eta(y) = \frac{\int_X \mu_{(\xi,\eta)}(x, y)\, m(dx)}{\overline{m}(\xi \mid \eta \ni y)}.$$

PROPOSITION 35
(The Full Falling Shadow Formula)

$$\mu_\eta(y) = \frac{\int_X \mu_\xi(x)\, \mu_{\eta|\xi}(y \mid x)\, m(dx)}{\overline{m}(\xi \mid \eta \ni y)}.$$

PROPOSITION 36
(Bayes Formula)

$$\mu_{\xi|\eta}(x \mid y) = \frac{\mu_\xi(x) \cdot \mu_{\eta|\xi}(y \mid x) \cdot \overline{m}(\xi \mid \eta \ni y)}{\int_X \mu_\xi(u)\, \mu_{\eta|\xi}(y \mid u)\, m(du)}.$$

These formulas show that we can find the counterparts of fundamental laws on random variables through the falling shadow concept in the random set theory. When fuzzy sets are viewed as the falling shadow of random sets, then it becomes a powerful working tool for dealing with fuzzy sets. Conversely, the generalization of the falling shadow concept provides fuzzy set mathematics with an important representation method for random set theory.

8.3   Set-Valued Statistics

For simplicity, we first discuss set (non-fuzzy) outcomes in set-valued statistical experiments. A set-valued statistical experiment involves repetitive trials (and realizations) of a random set. The falling shadow could be a membership function (in a fuzzy statistical experiment). Therefore, set-valued statistics are more general than fuzzy statistics. The functions of set-valued statistics are to perform estimation and inference on falling shadows.

Given $\xi \in \Xi (\mathcal{A}, \mathcal{B})$, we make n independent trials and obtain the following n sample observations:

$$\xi_1, \xi_2, \cdots, \xi_n, \qquad (\xi_i \in \mathcal{P}(X)).$$

Look at the sample from an abstract point of view. This is a set of independent random sets with the same distribution ξ. For any $x \in X$, denote

$$\overline{\xi}(x) = \frac{1}{n} \sum_{i=1}^{n} \mathcal{X}_{\xi_i}(x)$$

then this is called the **covering frequency** of ξ with respect to x. We can use it for the estimation of the value of the falling shadow at x. The function $\overline{\xi}$ is called the **estimation function** of μ_ξ. We can use the law of large numbers to illustrate the sufficiency of the estimation.

THEOREM 20

(Law of Large Numbers on Falling Shadows) Let $\xi_i \in \Xi (\mathcal{A}, \mathcal{B})$, $(i = 1, 2, \cdots,$ $n, \cdots)$ be a set of independent and identically distributed random sets with $\mu_{\xi_i}(x)$ $= \mu(x)$. Then

$$\overline{\xi}_n(x, \omega) \longrightarrow \mu(x) \qquad a.e. \quad (n \longrightarrow \infty).$$

PROOF   For every $x \in X$, define

$$\xi_i^x (\omega) \overset{\Delta}{=} \mathcal{X}_{\xi_i(\omega)} (x) .$$

Then, $\xi_1^x, \xi_2^x, \cdots, \xi_n^x, \cdots$ is a set of independent and identically distributed random variables whose expected values are

$$E\left(\xi_n^x\right) = \int_\Omega \mathcal{X}_{\xi_n} (x) \, p \, (d\omega) = \int_{\{\xi_n \ni x\}} p \, (d\omega)$$

$$= p\left\{w \mid \xi_n \ni x\right\} = \mu \, (x) .$$

By Kolmogorov's law of large numbers, we can conclude the validity of the theorem.   ∎

For a random set ξ, $\overline{m} \, (\xi)$ represents the area under the curve μ_ξ, that is a very important characteristic of μ_ξ.

Let $\left(X, \underset{\sim}{B}\right)$ be a measurable space. Denote $\mathcal{X} \, (x, \omega) \overset{\Delta}{=} \mathcal{X}_{\xi(\omega)} (x)$, and set

$$\Xi_0 \, (\mathcal{A}, \mathcal{B}) \overset{\Delta}{=} \left\{\xi \in \Xi \, (\mathcal{A}, \mathcal{B}) \mid \mathcal{X} \, (x, \omega) \text{ is measurable in } \underset{\sim}{B} \times \mathcal{A}\right\} .$$

THEOREM 21

Let $\left(X, \underset{\sim}{B}\right)$ be a measurable space and let m be a positive measure on $\underset{\sim}{B}$. If $\xi \in \Xi_0 \, (\mathcal{A}, \mathcal{B})$, then

$$\overline{m} \, (\xi) = E \, (m \, (\xi \, (\omega))) .$$

PROOF   By Fubini's theorem,

$$\overline{m} \, (\xi) = \int_X \mu_\xi \, (x) \, m \, (dx) = \int_X p \, (\xi \ni x) \, m \, (dx)$$

$$= \int_X \left(\int_\Omega \mathcal{X}_{\xi(\omega)} (x) \, p \, (d\omega)\right) m \, (dx)$$

$$= \int_X \left(\int_\Omega \mathcal{X} \, (x, \omega) \, p \, (d\omega)\right) m \, (dx)$$

$$= \int_X \left(\int_\Omega \mathcal{X} \, (x, \omega) \, p \, (d\omega)\right) p \, (\omega)$$

$$= \int_{\Omega} m\left(\xi\left(\omega\right)\right) p\left(d\omega\right) = E\left(m\left(\xi\right)\right).$$

Are there any relationships and differences between set-valued statistics and traditional statistics? What are the relationships between the falling shadow of random sets and distributions of random variables? The function $\overline{m}\left(\xi\right)$ contains important information for the above questions.

PROPOSITION 37

Let $X = \{x_1, x_2, \cdots, x_k, \cdots\}$, $\underset{\sim}{B} = \mathcal{P}\left(X\right)$, $m\left(\alpha\right)$ be the number of elements in α $\left(\alpha \in \underset{\sim}{B}\right)$ and $\xi \in \Xi_0\left(\mathcal{A}, \mathcal{B}\right)$. If ξ is a nonempty set, then ξ is essentially degenerate if and only if $\overline{m}\left(\xi\right) = 1$. Under these conditions, ξ is the falling shadow when it is viewed as a random set, and μ_ξ is the distribution of ξ when it is viewed as a random variable, i.e.,

$$\mu_\xi\left(x_k\right) = p\left(\xi = \{x\}\right).$$

PROOF   Define $\Gamma = \{\omega \mid m\left(\xi\left(\omega\right)\right) = 1\}$. Because ξ is a nonempty set,

$$\Gamma^c = \{\omega \mid m\left(\xi\left(\omega\right)\right) \geq 2\}.$$

If ξ is essentially degenerate, then $p\left(\Gamma^c\right) = 0$ and

$$\overline{m}\left(\xi\right) = \int_{\Gamma} m\left(\xi\left(\omega\right)\right) p\left(d\omega\right) + \int_{\Gamma^c} m\left(\xi\left(\omega\right)\right) p\left(d\omega\right)$$

$$= \int_{\Gamma} pd\left(\omega\right) = p\left(\Gamma\right) = 1.$$

Conversely, if $p\left(\Gamma^c\right) > 0$, then

$$\overline{m}\left(\xi\right) = \int_{\Gamma} m\left(\xi\left(\omega\right)\right) p\left(d\omega\right) + \int_{\Gamma^c} m\left(\xi\left(\omega\right)\right) p\left(d\omega\right)$$

$$\geq p\left(\Gamma\right) + 2p\left(\Gamma^c\right) \geq 1 + p\left(\Gamma^c\right) > 1.$$

Up to this point, we know that $p\left(\Gamma^c\right) = 0$ if and only if $\overline{m}\left(\xi\right) = 1$. When $p\left(\Gamma^c\right) = 0$, then

$$\mu_\xi\left(x_k\right) = p\left(\omega \mid \xi\left(\omega\right) \ni x_k\right)$$

$$= p \left(\xi = \{x\} \right) + p \left(\Gamma^c \cap \{ \omega \mid \xi \left(\omega \right) \ni x_k \} \right)$$

$$= p \left(\xi = \{x\} \right).$$

∎

PROPOSITION 38

Let $X = \Re$ (the real number system), $\mathcal{B}$ a Borel field, m a Lebesque measure on $\mathcal{B}$, $\xi \in \Xi_0 \left(\mathcal{A}, \mathcal{B} \right)$, and ξ a nonempty set. Then ξ is essentially degenerate if and only if $\overline{m} \left(\xi \right) = 0$, (that also implies $\mu_{\xi} \left(x \right) \equiv 0$).

PROOF   Since $\overline{m} \left(\xi \right) = \int_{\Omega} m \left(\xi \left(\omega \right) \right) p \left(d\omega \right) = 0$ if and only if $m \left(\xi \left(\omega \right) \right) = 0$ $(a.e.p)$. For ξ is not an empty set, hence $\overline{m} \left(\xi \right) = 0$ if and only if ξ is essentially degenerate. If $\overline{m} \left(\xi \right) = 0$, this obviously implies $\mu_{\xi} \left(x \right) \equiv 0$.   ∎

The above two propositions indicate that, under degenerate conditions, when X is a discrete set, the results hold; when X is the set of reals and m is a Lebesque measure, then the falling shadow of a nonempty random set is zero.

Let $\{\alpha_1, \alpha_2, \cdots, \alpha_n\}$ be a set of samples of ξ. Define

$$\overline{m} \left(\alpha_1, \alpha_2, \cdots, \alpha_n \right) \stackrel{\Delta}{=} \frac{1}{n} \sum_{i=1}^{n} m \left(\alpha_i \right).$$

This function can be used as an estimator for $\overline{m} \left(\xi \right)$. Applying Kolmogorov's law of large numbers, we obtain

PROPOSITION 39

Let $\overline{m} \left(\xi \right) < \infty$, and $\xi, \xi_1, \xi_2, \cdots, \xi_n, \cdots$ be independent and identically distributed random sets. When $n \longrightarrow \infty$, then

$$\overline{m} \left(\xi_1, \xi_2, \cdots, \xi_n \right) = \frac{1}{n} \sum_{i=1}^{n} m \left(\xi_i \right) \longrightarrow \overline{m} \left(\xi \right), \quad (a.e.p).$$

8.4   Degree Analysis

Applications of set-valued statistics may be most hopeful in areas where psychological measurements are used. There exists a broad array of such measurements for the purposes of estimating or evaluating the degrees of satisfaction to an objective or requirement. Some examples of measurements are "degrees of satisfaction", "degrees of credibility", "degrees of coordination and cooperation", "degrees of stability", "degrees of reliability", "degrees of user friendliness", etc. These measurements are desirable indicators in real life; however, they lack mathematical methods for supporting their analysis. An approach to this issue by using the set-valued statistical method is called the **degree analysis**.

We can roughly describe the degree analysis as follows. If the estimating "degree" must rely upon psychological measurements, then a set of selected representative experts and professionals will carry out a well-planned experiment. There are several such experimental methods:

1. The **interval method**.

The degree of satisfaction may be expressed as a number between 0 and 1, with 0 meaning unsatisfactory and 1 meaning extremely satisfactory, as shown in Figure 8.2 a. Each participant in the experiment determines 3 to 5 values of the degree of satisfaction and then marks them on the line segment; the left-most mark is denoted as coordinate x and the right-most mark is denoted as coordinate y. Hence, this results in an interval $[x, y]$ (Figure 8.2 b). The collection of all experimental intervals from the participants forms a set of samples $\{(x_i, y_i), i = 1, 2, \cdots, n\}$. By the expression (8.1), we can find $\bar{\xi}(x)$ that represents a fuzzy degree of satisfaction, as shown in Figure 8.2 c. Next, compute

$$a = \frac{1}{n} \sum_{i=1}^{n} \frac{x_i + y_i}{2}$$

and

$$\overline{m} = \frac{1}{n} \sum_{i=1}^{n} (y_i - x_i).$$

The value a is the **point estimation** of the degree of satisfaction, and $\overline{m}$ is called the **estimation blindness**. The smaller $\overline{m}$ value means the greater certainty or precision of the estimation when $\overline{m} = 0$ means absolute certainty.

2. The **confidence (point) method**.

In this experiment, each subject is asked to mark a point x on the interval $[0, 1]$ and write a positive integer $k, 5 \leq k \leq 10$ above the mark x (as shown in Figure 8.3), signifying the subject's **confidence level** on the mark x. The confidence level may be interpreted in percentages. Care must be made to distinguish between the underlying meanings of the point x and the confidence level k.

The interval method and the point method are interchangeable. This is because there exists a positive proportion (correlation) between the level of confidence in the point method and the degree of concentration of points in the interval method. The approximate functional relationship can be written as

$$\rho = f(\theta)$$

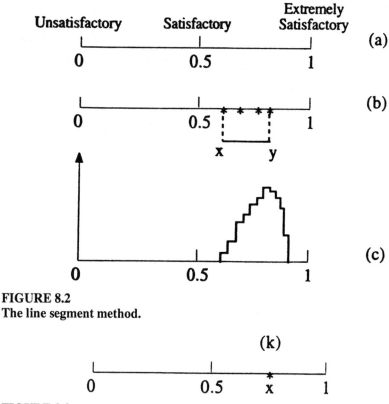

FIGURE 8.2
The line segment method.

FIGURE 8.3
The confidence level k.

where θ is the confidence level and ρ is the estimated radius of interval estimation. Suppose $\{(x_i, \theta_i)\}$ is a set of sample obtained via the confidence method. Then, its "interval" equivalent is

$$[x_i - f(\theta_i), x_i - f(\theta_i)] \cap [0, 1].$$

Conversely, given $\{[x_i, y_i]\}$, we can transform it into the confidence levels by

$$\left(\frac{x_i + y_i}{2}, f^{-1}\left(\frac{y_i - x_i}{2}\right)\right).$$

As to the approximate function f itself, this is found through well-established statistical methods.

The interchange between the interval method and the confidence method has significant implications. It suggests that the set-valued statistics may become a kind of statistics where sample numerical observations are not equally valued, i.e., each sample has a degree of "qualification" for being in that sample state. Thus, we have the so-called colored data. Some real world applications, such as the weighted function regression analysis in mathematical statistics and Krige's method in geological statistics, use weighted data in their analysis.

3. The simplified interval-confidence method.

As shown in Figure 8.4 a, each subject of the experiment marks a point of satisfaction x_i on the interval [0, 1]; next, the same subject marks a point a_i reflecting the degree of confidence as shown in Figure 8.4 b. Thus, after n experiments we have n pairs of (x_i, a_i). A simple estimate of the degree of satisfaction is by

$$a = \frac{\sum_{i=1}^{n} a_i x_i}{\sum_{i=1}^{n} a_i}.$$

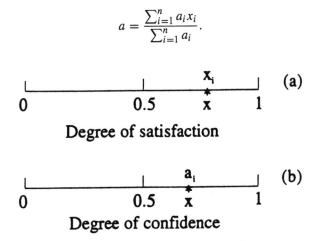

Degree of satisfaction

Degree of confidence

FIGURE 8.4
The simplified interval-confidence method.

4. The multistage estimation method.

This method requires each subject of the experiment to make one and only one check sign in each column of a table such as in Table 1, which provides measures of confirmation on each category of satisfaction. For example, on the "very unsatisfactory" column of Table 1, the level of confirmation is "median agree"; on the "slightly unsatisfactory" column, the level of confirmation is "strongly agree", etc.

For convenience, we can simplify Table 1 to Table 2, that, in turn, is plotted in Figure 8.5. Each check mark in Table 2 corresponds to a point in the figure. On the scale of [0, 1], the five check marks (from the left to the right) have the following coordinates (degree of satisfaction, degree of confidence): $(0, 0.75)$, $(0.25, 1)$, $(0.5, 0.75)$, $(0.75, 0.5)$, and $(1, 0)$.

The piecewise linear curve plotted from the five check points represents a fuzzy set on [0, 1]. Since the response from each subject of the experiment is a fuzzy set, the multistage estimation method is a set-valued statistic.

Table 1 Estimation Worksheet.

	Extremely unsatisfactory	Slightly unsatisfactory	Satisfactory	Very satisfactory	Extremely satisfactory
Strongly agree					
Agree	√	√	√		
Weakly agree					
Weakly disagree				√	
Disagree					
Strongly disagree					√

Table 2 Estimation Worksheet.

	Extremely unsatisfactory	Slightly unsatisfactory	Satisfactory	Very satisfactory	Extremely satisfactory
Strongly agree					
Agree	√	√	√		
Neutral				√	
Disagree					
Strongly disagree					√

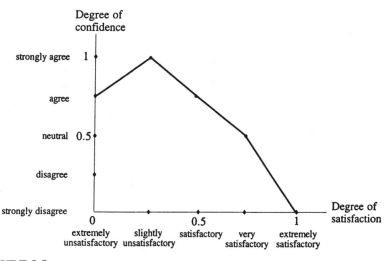

FIGURE 8.5
A piecewise linear curve of a multistage estimation (a membership function).

Assume the response of a subject from the previous experiment is represented as a five-dimensional vector $(e_1, e_2, e_3, e_4, e_5)$, where e_i is the second coordinate of the i-th point. Then in this notation the piecewise linear curve formed by the five points can be expressed as $(0.75, 1, 0.75, 0.5, 0)$. Let

$$\left(e_1^i, e_2^i, e_3^i, e_4^i, e_5^i \right), \quad i = 1, 2, \cdots, n$$

be the set of sample experiments from n subjects. Define

$$\bar{e}_j = \frac{1}{n} \sum_{i=1}^{n} e_j^i, \quad j = 1, 2, 3, 4, 5.$$

The vector $(\bar{e}_1, \bar{e}_2, \bar{e}_3, \bar{e}_4, \bar{e}_5)$ is called the **fuzzy falling shadow vector.** A point estimate for the degree of satisfaction in the multistage estimation method is

$$a = 0.25\bar{e}_2 + 0.5\bar{e}_3 + 0.75\bar{e}_4 + \bar{e}_5.$$

Define

$$\theta = \frac{1}{5} \sum_{j=1}^{5} \bar{e}_j.$$

We call θ the **mean (average) degree of confidence.**

8.5   Random and Set-Valued Experiments

The usefulness of set-valued statistical experiments is also demonstrated in situations where physical measurements were employed. This is because physical measurements are always subject to errors. A common method of reporting physical measurements is in the form of $x \pm \Delta$; i.e., an interval $[x - \Delta, x + \Delta]$. Hence, a random experiment can result in a set-valued statistical experiment.

Let ξ and η be independent and real-valued random experiments. Assume $p\,(\eta > 0) = 1$. Define $\zeta \overset{\Delta}{=} [\xi - \eta, \xi + \eta]$. Under properly defined measurable structures, ζ is a random set and its falling shadow exhibits a simple form:

$$\mu_\zeta\,(x) = p\,(\xi \ni x) = p\,(|\,\xi - x\,| \le \eta)$$

$$= 1 - p\,(x < \eta) - p\,(\xi + \eta < x)$$

$$= p\,(\xi - \eta \le x) - p\,(\xi + \eta < x)\,.$$

Consequently,
$$\mu_\zeta\,(x) = F_{\xi-\eta}\,(x) - F_{\xi+\eta}\,(x - 0)\,, \tag{8.1}$$

where the function $F_\theta \overset{\Delta}{=} p\,(\theta \le x)$ is the distribution function of the random variable θ.

If $\xi \sim N\,(a, \sigma^2)$, $\eta \sim N\,(b, \gamma^2)$, $b > 0$, and $\gamma \ll b$, then $p\,(\eta > 0) \approx 1$. For $\zeta \overset{\Delta}{=} [\xi - \eta, \xi + \eta]$, it follows from the last equation that

$$\mu_\zeta\,(x) = \Phi\left(\frac{x - (a - b)}{\sqrt{\sigma^2 + \gamma^2}}\right) - \Phi\left(\frac{x - (a + b)}{\sqrt{\sigma^2 + \gamma^2}}\right), \tag{8.2}$$

where
$$\Phi\,(x) = \frac{1}{\sqrt{2\pi}} \int_{-\infty}^{x} e^{-\frac{u^2}{2}}\, du.$$

We call $\zeta \overset{\Delta}{=} [\xi - \eta, \xi + \eta]$ the random set formed by ξ and η; ξ is the center of ζ and η is the radius of ζ. We can derive the following:

PROPOSITION 40
If the falling shadow of the random set ζ is

$$\mu_\zeta\,(x) = \Phi\left(\frac{x - c}{\rho}\right) - \Phi\left(\frac{x - d}{\rho}\right), \quad (c < d)\,, \tag{8.3}$$

then ζ can be constructed from the two random variables ξ and η with

$$\xi \sim N\left(\frac{d+c}{2}, \sigma^2\right), \quad and \ \eta \sim N\left(\frac{d-c}{2}, \rho^2 - \sigma^2\right), \quad (\sigma \le \rho),$$

and furthermore,

$$\overline{m}(\zeta) = d - c. \tag{8.4}$$

In Proposition 40, the decomposition of ζ is not unique. Also, under the condition $\sigma^2 + \gamma^2 = \rho^2$, when $\sigma = \rho$ and $\gamma = 0$, then η is a constant; when $\sigma = 0$ and $\gamma = \rho$, then ξ is a constant.

If the universe $U = \mathfrak{R}$ (the set of reals), we adopt the following operation of the linear combination of intervals:

$$\alpha [a_1, b_1] + \beta [a_2, b_2] \overset{\Delta}{=} \{\alpha x + \beta y \mid x \in [a_1, b_1], \quad y \in [a_2, b_2]\}.$$

Given a set of samples $\alpha^{(1)}, \alpha^{(2)}, \cdots, \alpha^{(n)}$ of the random set of a random variable, then

$$\overline{\alpha} \overset{\Delta}{=} \frac{1}{n}\left(\alpha^{(1)} + \alpha^{(2)} + \cdots + \alpha^{(n)}\right)$$

may serve as an estimate of the expected value of the center random variable ξ. From the following proposition, we find that $\overline{\alpha}$ is a sufficient estimator.

PROPOSITION 41

Assume $\zeta_1, \zeta_2, \cdots, \zeta_n, \cdots$ and ζ are independent and identically distributed random sets. Let $\zeta = [\xi - \eta, \xi + \eta]$, $E\xi = a$, $E\eta = \delta$. Then, for every $x \in R \backslash \{a - \delta, a + \delta\}$, it follows that

$$\chi_{\frac{1}{n}\left(\sum_{i=1}^{n} \zeta_i(\omega)\right)}(x) \longrightarrow \chi_{[a-\delta, a+\delta]}(x), \quad (a.e.p.) \quad (n \to \infty).$$

PROOF   Let ξ_n and η_n represent the center random variable and the radius random variable of the random set η_n, respectively. Then $\frac{1}{n}\sum_{i=1}^{n}\xi_i(\omega)$ and $\frac{1}{n}\sum_{i=1}^{n}\eta_i(\omega)$ are the center and the radius of $\frac{1}{n}\sum_{i=1}^{n}\zeta_i(\omega)$, respectively. The sets $\{\xi_n\}$ and $\{\eta_n\}$ are independent sequences of random variables. Also,

$$\overline{\xi}_n = \frac{1}{n}\sum_{i=1}^{n}\xi_i \longrightarrow a \quad (a.e.p.),$$

$$\overline{\eta}_n = \frac{1}{n}\sum_{i=1}^{n}\eta_i \longrightarrow \delta \quad (a.e.p.).$$

For any $x \in (a - \delta, a + \delta)$, and $\varepsilon = \delta - |x - a|$, there exists an integer N, such that, when $n \geq N$,

$$|\bar{\xi}_n - a| < \frac{\varepsilon}{2}, \text{ and } |\bar{\xi}_n - \delta| < \frac{\varepsilon}{2}.$$

Note that

$$|\bar{\xi}_n - x| \leq |\bar{\xi}_n - a| + |x - a| < \delta - \frac{\varepsilon}{2} \leq \bar{\eta}_n.$$

Hence,

$$X_{\frac{1}{n}\left(\sum_{i=1}^{n} \zeta_i(\omega)\right)}(x) = 1.$$

Therefore the proposition is true.

For any $x \notin [a - \delta, a + \delta]$, we do not lose generality to assume that $x > a + \delta$. If $\varepsilon = |x - a| - \delta$, then there exists an inter N such that when $n \geq N$,

$$|\bar{\xi}_n - x| > x - \left(a + \frac{\varepsilon}{2}\right) = \delta + \frac{\varepsilon}{2} \geq \bar{\eta}_n.$$

This implies that

$$X_{\frac{1}{n}\left(\sum_{i=1}^{n} \zeta_i(\omega)\right)}(x) = 0.$$

The proposition is again true and hence completes the proof. ∎

When $U = \Re$, and all of the random sets are the same set $\zeta = [\xi - \eta, \xi + \eta]$, then the falling shadow function of ζ can be expressed in the convolution form.

PROPOSITION 42

1. If $\zeta = [\xi - \eta, \xi + \eta]$, and the random variables ξ and η are independent, then

$$\mu_\xi(x) = \int_{-\infty}^{+\infty} \mu_{\bar{\eta}}(u - x) \, dF_\xi(u),$$

where $\bar{\eta} = [-\eta, \eta]$, $\left(\text{it follows that } \mu_{\bar{\eta}}(x) = p(\eta > |x|)\right)$ and $F_\xi(u) = p(\xi \leq u)$.
2. If ξ and η are integer random variables, then

$$\mu_\xi(k) = \sum_{i=-\infty}^{+\infty} \mu_{\bar{\eta}}(i - k) \, p_\xi(i),$$

where $p_\xi(i) = p(\xi = i)$.

3. Assuming ξ and η are integer random variables, take n and m as independent observations on each random variable, respectively. Let the frequency of $\xi = k$ be n_k $\left(\sum_k n_k = n\right)$, the frequency of $\eta = k$ be m_k $\left(\sum_k m_k = m\right)$, and define

$$\mu = \mu_{\zeta-i} = \sum_{j \geq i} \frac{m_j}{m}, \quad (i \geq 0) \tag{8.5}$$

then,

$$\bar{\alpha}_k = \frac{1}{n} \sum_{i=-\infty}^{+\infty} \mu_i n_{k+1}, \quad (k = 0, \pm 1, \pm 2, \cdots)$$

is a sufficient estimator of $\mu_\xi (k)$.

The proof is omitted.

8.6 A Mathematical Model for Employee Evaluation

In this section, we apply the methods discussed previously to a real world problem — employee evaluation. This problem is an important one in human resource management. At the center of the problem is the question of how to measure and evaluate employees. In this regard, the degree analysis may prove to be an effective tool.

8.6.1 Single-Factor Evaluation of Quality

Let $\pi = \{f_1, f_2, \cdots, f_n\}$ be a family of basic factors relevant to the evaluation of a group of professionals, e.g., teachers, managers, engineers, sportsmen, etc. The factors are determined by the management personnel, a priori. Suppose an evaluation committee consists of personnel from different ranks of the organization, say m ranks. Let

$$E_q = \left\{e_{q1}, e_{q2}, \cdots, e_{qk_q}\right\}, \quad q = 1, 2, \cdots, m$$

be the set of evaluators of rank (or level) q in an evaluation committee of m ranks.

Suppose an employee β is evaluated by e_{qj}, the j-th evaluator of rank q; then the evaluator will mark x_{iqj} the "merit", and mark a_{iqj} the "degree of confidence" with respect to each factor f_i on their scales as shown in Figure 8.6.

The collection of merit values and degree of confidence values from all evaluators of rank q on the single factor f_i can be used as a point estimator of the merit value

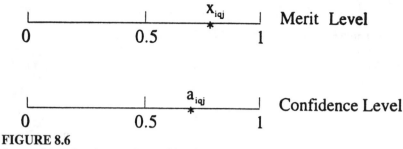

FIGURE 8.6
A sample evaluation on factor i by the evaluator qi.

of factor f_i for employee β. This is found by computing the weighted average below:

$$\alpha_{iq} = \frac{\sum_{j=1}^{k_q} a_{iqj} x_{iqj}}{\sum_{j=1}^{k_q} a_{iqj} x_{iqj}}. \tag{8.6}$$

Let $b_1, b_2, \cdots, b_m \left(b_q \geq 0, \ \sum_{q=1}^{m} b_q = 1 \right)$ be a weight distribution over the set $\{E_i\}$ of groups of rank i in the evaluation committee, then

$$\alpha_i = \sum_{q=1}^{m} b_q \alpha_{iq} \tag{8.7}$$

is a combined evaluation from all rank groups on factor f_i for employee β. Denote

$$A = (\alpha_1, \alpha_2, \ \cdots, \alpha_n). \tag{8.8}$$

This is the single-factor evaluation vector — our basis of evaluation.

8.6.2 Synthetic Evaluation of Quality

Let $W = \{w_1, w_2, \cdots, w_n\}$ be a weight vector for the set of factors $\{f_1, f_2, \cdots, f_n\}$. Construct a synthetic function:

$$M_n (x_1, x_2, \cdots, x_n) = \sum_{i=1}^{n} w_i x_i. \tag{8.9}$$

If the single-factor evaluation vector $A = (\alpha_1, \alpha_2, \ \cdots, \alpha_n)$ is given, then by substituting A into the above function, the result

$$\alpha = M_n (\alpha_1, \alpha_2, \ \cdots, \alpha_n)$$

is a point estimate with all factors considered. The synthetic function used here just serves as an example; it is not limited to this particular function.

8.6.3 Determination of Weights

In addition to the method used in Section 4.6, we can use the method of degree analysis to determine the weights among ranks in the weight vector $B = (b_1, b_2, \cdots, b_m)$. Here is an example.

Suppose the weights in $B = (b_1, b_2, \cdots, b_m)$ are determined by p persons. The j-th person will make four independent (no memory, uncorrelated) marks on b_i, for example, one in the morning, one in the afternoon, one the next morning, and one the next afternoon. The result is shown in the Figure 8.7.

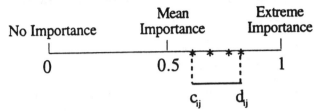

FIGURE 8.7
Four independent marks of importance.

The marks on b_i by the j-th evaluator consolidates an interval $\left[c_{ij}, d_{ij}\right]$. Using all p persons' intervals, compute

$$b'_i = \frac{1}{p} \sum_{j=1}^{p} \frac{c_{ij} + d_{ij}}{2}, \qquad m_i = \frac{1}{p} \sum_{j=1}^{p} \left(d_{ij} - c_{ij}\right)$$

and

$$b_i = \frac{b'_i \left(1 - m_i\right)}{\sum_{i=1}^{a} b'_i \left(1 - m_i\right)}. \tag{8.10}$$

This finds the components of vector B.

8.6.4 Classification of Talents

For managerial purposes, it is useful to know which employee has what talent. The classification of employees into talent or skill groups according to a set of characteristics (this is also called clustering) will facilitate the effective use of people by the management.

Let $\{\beta_1, \beta_2, \cdots, \beta_r\}$ be r candidates for classification. Assume each β_i has a corresponding single-factor evaluation vector:

$$A_i = (\alpha_{i1}, \alpha_{i2}, \cdots, \alpha_{in}), \quad i = 1, 2, \cdots, r.$$

The components of A_i can be regarded as the state of n characteristics. From here, we can calculate the similarity coefficient r_{ij}, and then obtain a fuzzy similarity matrix $R = \left(r_{ij}\right)$; next, we can transform R into a fuzzy equivalent matrix R^*, and finally, we can find the clustering graph according to R^*.

8.6.5   Horizontal Comparisons

The factors or criteria used by a committee in the evaluation of personnel may depend upon the type of organization, the geographic location, and the environment. Some factors used in one type of organization may not be comparable in another organization. How do we evaluate someone who comes from diverse organizations across the country?

Suppose we have k different types of organizations: $d_1, d_2, \cdots, d_k$; let $h_1, h_2, \cdots, h_t$ be the factors that make these organizations different or distinguishable, and $v_1, v_2, \cdots, v_t$ be the corresponding weights of the factors. Each evaluator of the p evaluators will mark on a unit interval three to five times to express the degree of satisfaction on each factor (that makes organizations different). Using a method similar to that shown in Figure 8.7, an interval $\left[c_{ijs}, d_{ijs}\right]$ can be determined from the evaluator s on factor i and organization type j. Define

$$r_j = \frac{1}{t} \sum_{i=1}^{t} v_i \left(\frac{1}{p} \sum_{s=1}^{p} \frac{c_{ijs} + d_{ijs}}{2} \right). \tag{8.11}$$

The r_j, $(j = 1, 2, \cdots, k)$ is called the **horizontal adjustment factor**. It is capable of adjusting disparate values of evaluation into one horizontal level and making them comparable.

Assume organization i recommends one person whose multifactorial evaluation is α^i, $i = 1, 2, \cdots, k$. Define

$$\eta^i = r_i \cdot \alpha^i \tag{8.12}$$

then η^i is the adjusted value. We can rank order values of η^i from the smallest to the largest:

$$\eta^{i_1}, \ \eta^{i_2}, \ \cdots, \ \eta^{i_k}.$$

This enables us to select the best candidate.

8.6.6   Representation of Marginal Values

The outputs or accomplishments of a person are normally proportional to the amount of effort he or she invests. If taking this factor into consideration, we expect an increase in the evaluation score for those who put in extra effort. Before developing the representation, we define the concept of the "gain function".

DEFINITION 20   *Let p be a natural number and $p \gg 1$. A mapping $\zeta_p : [0.1] \longrightarrow [0, 1]$ is called a* **gain function** *if it satisfies the following:*

1) ζ_p is continuous and piecewise differentiable;
2) $x_1 \geq x_2 \Longrightarrow \left(\zeta_p(x_1) \geq \zeta_p(x_2), \quad \zeta_p'(x_1) \geq \zeta_p'(x_2)\right)$, and
3) $\zeta_p(0) = 0, \quad \zeta_p(1) = 1, \quad \zeta_p(0.5) \leq 0.5$.
(ζ_p' is the derivative of ζ_p).

Example 45
The following mapping $\zeta_p : [0.1] \longrightarrow [0, 1]$

$$\zeta_p(x) = \begin{cases} 0, & 0 \leq x \leq 0.5 \\ p \cdot \left(\frac{x-0.5}{0.5}\right)^k, & 0.5 < x \leq 1 \end{cases}$$

is a gain function, where k is a real number.

We now apply the concept of the gain function to multifactorial evaluations. First, we construct a multifactorial function:

$$G(x_1, x_2, \cdots, x_n) = \frac{1}{p+1} \sum_{i=1}^{n} \left(x_i + \zeta_p(x_i)\right) w_i$$

where $W = (w_1, w_2, \cdots, w_n)$ is a weight vector. The function ζ_p can be the one in the preceding example with $p = 2$ and $k = 4$. If $A = (\alpha_1, \alpha_2, \cdots, \alpha_n)$ is a known single-factor evaluation vector, then after substituting into G, the resulting value

$$\alpha = G(\alpha_1, \alpha_2, \cdots, \alpha_n)$$

is the multifactorial evaluation with the notion of "gain". ⬚

8.6.7 Recognition of Controversial Type of Persons

By "controversial type" of persons, we mean those people who receive about half and half on the "for" votes and "against" votes. In this case, their evaluation scores are polarized. People such as "open-minded" persons, and "revolutionary-minded" persons, may very well fit into this type. These people should be recognized and used accordingly.

Let $\lambda \in (0.5, 1)$ and $\tau \in (0, 0.5)$. Define

$$A_\lambda \overset{\Delta}{=} \{j \mid x_{iqj} \geq \lambda\},$$

$$B\tau \overset{\Delta}{=} \{j \mid x_{iqj} \leq \tau\},$$

and

$$C_{\lambda\tau} = \{j \mid \lambda < x_{iqj} < \tau\}.$$

By using an upper threshold λ and lower threshold τ, we can obtain a group A_λ of "for's", a group $B\tau$ of "against's", and a group $C_{\lambda\tau}$ of "neutrals". Let

$$\eta_{iq}(\lambda) = \begin{cases} \dfrac{\sum_{j \in A_\lambda}(1-a_{iqj}\cdot x_{iqj})}{(1-|A_\lambda|)}\left(1 - \dfrac{|A_\lambda|}{k_q}\right), & A_\lambda \neq \Phi; \\ 1, & A_\lambda = \Phi; \end{cases}$$

and

$$\delta_{iq}(\tau) = \begin{cases} \dfrac{\sum_{j \in B_\tau}a_{iqj}x_{iqj}}{\tau|B_\tau|}\left(1 - \dfrac{|B_\tau|}{k_q}\right), & B_\tau \neq \Phi; \\ 1, & B_\tau = \Phi. \end{cases}$$

We call $\eta_{iq}(\lambda)$ and $\delta_{iq}(\tau)$ the λ-deviation and the τ-deviation of the i-th factor on the q-th level. The smaller the λ-deviation is, the more noticeable the merit will be. On the other hand, the smaller the τ-deviation is, the more noticeable the deficiencies will be.

Assume $A_\lambda \neq \Phi$ and $B_\tau \neq \Phi$, and also define

$$\nu_{\lambda\tau} = \begin{cases} |A_\lambda|/|B\tau|, & |A_\lambda| \leq |B\tau|; \\ |B\tau|/|A_\lambda|, & |A_\lambda| > |B\tau|, \end{cases}$$

and

$$\theta_{iq}(\lambda, \tau) = \begin{cases} \nu_{\lambda\tau}\dfrac{|A_\lambda|+|B\tau|}{k|C_{\lambda\tau}|}, & 0 < \dfrac{|A_\lambda|+|B\tau|}{k|C_{\lambda\tau}|} \leq 1, \quad and \quad C_{\lambda\tau} \neq \Phi; \\ \nu_{\lambda\tau}, & \text{otherwise.} \end{cases}$$

We call $\theta_{iq}(\lambda, \tau)$ the degree of controversy of the i-th factor f_i and the q-th level. In personnel evaluation, we first look at the value $\theta_{iq}(\lambda, \tau)$, and next analyze $\eta_{iq}(\lambda)$ and $\delta_{iq}(\tau)$.

Note. If $A_\lambda = \Phi$ or $B_\tau = \Phi$, or $A_\lambda = B_\tau = \Phi$, then there is no controversy relative to λ and τ. Also, it is necessary that λ and τ be measured according to the proper experiments and requirements of the organization. If we compute the following:

$$\eta_i(\lambda) = \sum_{q=1}^{m} b_q \eta_{iq}(\lambda),$$

$$\delta_i(\tau) = \sum_{q=1}^{m} b_q \delta_{iq}(\tau),$$

and

$$\theta_i(\lambda, \tau) = \sum_{q=1}^{m} b_q \theta_{iq}(\lambda, \tau),$$

that is, if we use all levels of evaluation, we obtain the combined λ-deviation, the combined τ-evaluation, and the combined degree of controversy of factors f_i.

References

[1] Dubois, D. and Prade, H., *Fuzzy Sets and Systems*, Academic Press, New York, 1980.

[2] Li, H.-X., Mathematical models for evaluating quality of cadres, *Mathematics in Practice and Theory*, 3, 1987, 11–16.

[3] Li, H.-X., *Fuzzy Mathematical Methods in Engineering and Their Applications*, Tianjing Scientific and Technical Press, Tianjing, 1993.

[4] Li, H.-X. and Wang, P.-Z., *Fuzzy Mathematics*, National Defense Industry Press, Beijing, 1994.

[5] Li, H.-X. and Yen, V. C., et al., The Operations of Fuzzy Cardinalities, *JMMA*, 182, 1994, 768–778.

[6] Luo, C.-Z., *Introduction to Fuzzy Sets*, Beijing Normal University Press, Beijing, 1993.

[7] Shafer, G., *A Mathematical Theory of Evidence*, Princeton University Press, 1976.

[8] Wang, P.-Z., Set-Valued Statistics, *Chinese Journal of Engineering Mathematics*, 1(1), 1984, 43–54.

[9] Wang, P.-Z., *Fuzzy Sets and Falling Shadow of Random Sets*, Beijing Normal University Press, Beijing, 1985.

[10] Wang, P.-Z., *Fuzzy Engineering — Principles and Methods*, China Productivity Center, Taipei, 1993.

[11] Wang, P.-Z. and Li, H.-X., *Fuzzy Mathematical Theory and Its Applications*, Science Press, Beijing, 1994.

[12] Zimmermann, H. J., *Fuzzy Sets Theory and Its Applications*, Kluwer Academic Publishers, Hingham, 1984.

9

Refinements of Fuzzy Operators

In certain applications, Zadeh's operators "∨" and "∧" appear to be quite rough. Many people have proposed refinements of these operators. In this chapter, we first introduce the axiomatic structure of Zadeh's operators and then discuss other commonly used operators. Finally, we illustrate the operations of fuzzy sets based on the fuzzy falling shadow concept.

9.1   The Axiomatic Structure of Zadeh's Operators

The operations of fuzzy sets can be carried out by using "∨" and "∧" operators on the respective membership functions. A problem might be raised here: Why do people choose these operators over the other operators? In 1973, Bellman and Giertz [1] , made a comment on this issue from the axiomatic point of view. They compared logic operations to fuzzy set operations by recognizing the "intersection" and "union" of fuzzy sets as the logical "and", and the logical "or" operations; and the fuzzy set $\underset{\sim}{A}$ as a proposition ("an element x belongs to $\underset{\sim}{A}$") that can be accepted as *more or less* true. Considering two propositions, S and T, their truth values are $\mu_S \in [0, 1]$ and $\mu_T \in [0, 1]$, respectively. The truth values of composite propositions of S and T formed by "and" and "or", denoted by $\mu_{(S \text{ and } T)}$ and $\mu_{(S \text{ or } T)}$, should be in the range [0, 1]; in addition, these values can be regarded as the values of membership functions of the intersection and union of S and T, respectively.

What is needed here are two real-valued functions f and g from $[0, 1]^2$ to $[0, 1]$ such that

$$\mu_S \text{ and } \mu_T = f(\mu_S, \mu_T),$$

and

$$\mu_S \text{ or } \mu_T = g(\mu_S, \mu_T).$$

Bellman and Giertz regard the following restrictions on f and g as reasonable:

1) f and g are continuous and nondecreasing functions in μ_S and μ_T;

2) f and g are symmetrical, i.e.,

$$f(\mu_S, \mu_T) = f(\mu_T, \mu_S) \quad and \quad g(\mu_S, \mu_T) = g(\mu_T, \mu_S);$$

3) $f(\mu_S, \mu_S)$ and $g(\mu_S, \mu_S)$ are strictly increasing in μ_S;

4) $f(\mu_S, \mu_S) \leq \min\{\mu_S, \mu_T\}$, $g(\mu_S, \mu_T) \geq \max\{\mu_S, \mu_T\}$; (This means that the truth value of "S and T" is no greater than the truth value of S or the truth value of T; and the truth value of "S or T" is at least as great as the truth value of S or the truth value of T.)

5) $f(1, 1) = 1$, and $g(0, 0) = 0$.

6) Since logically equivalent propositions must assume the same truth value, by implication, fuzzy sets with the same content (concept) must have the same membership function. For example, if the proposition "S_1 and (S_2 or S_3)" is logically equivalent to the proposition "(S_1 and S_2) or (S_1 and S_3)", their truth values must be equal.

By using the symbol "$\wedge$" to represent "and", "$\vee$" to represent "or", Bellman and Giertz formalized the aforementioned conditions into the set of axioms that follows. The two operations $\vee$ and $\wedge$ are, in fact, binary operations with values in [0, 1], and satisfy associative, commutative, and distributive laws.

1) $\mu_S \wedge \mu_T$ and $\mu_S \vee \mu_T$ are continuous and nondecreasing functions in μ_S and μ_T;

2) $\mu_S \wedge \mu_T = \mu_T \wedge \mu_S$, $\mu_S \vee \mu_T = \mu_T \vee \mu_S$;

3) $\mu_S \wedge \mu_S$ and $\mu_S \vee \mu_S$ are strictly increasing in μ_S;

4) $\mu_S \wedge \mu_T \leq \min\{\mu_S, \mu_T\}$, $\mu_S \vee \mu_T \geq \max\{\mu_S, \mu_T\}$;

5) $1 \wedge 1 = 1$, $0 \vee 0 = 0$;

6) $(\mu_S \wedge \mu_T) \wedge \mu_Q = \mu_S \wedge (\mu_T \wedge \mu_Q)$, $(\mu_S \vee \mu_T) \vee \mu_Q = \mu_S \vee (\mu_T \vee \mu_Q)$;

7) $\mu_S \wedge (\mu_T \vee \mu_Q) = (\mu_S \wedge \mu_T) \vee (\mu_S \wedge \mu_Q)$;

   $\mu_S \vee (\mu_T \wedge \mu_Q) = (\mu_S \vee \mu_T) \wedge (\mu_S \vee \mu_Q)$.

In addition, Bellman and Giertz proved mathematically the following result:

$$\mu_{S \wedge T} = \min\{\mu_S, \mu_T\}, \quad and \quad \mu_{S \vee T} = \max\{\mu_S, \mu_T\}.$$

The complement of a fuzzy set should satisfy the following: if the proposition S is true, then its complement "not S" (denoted by $\neg S$) is false. In another words, if $\mu_S = 1$, then $\mu_{\neg S} = 0$, and vice versa. The complementary function, denoted by h, and defined from [0, 1] to [0, 1], should be continuous, monotonically decreasing, and idempotent (that is the complement of the complement is itself). Because of this requirement, Bellman and Giertz added another condition:

$$h\left(\frac{1}{2}\right) = \frac{1}{2}.$$

We summarize the above discussion into the following two theorems.

THEOREM 22

Let $f, g : [0, 1] \times [0, 1] \longrightarrow [0, 1]$ be two binary operations that satisfy the following:

1) f and g are continuous and nondecreasing functions;
2) $f(x, y) = f(y, x)$, $g(x, y) = g(y, x)$;
3) $u(x) = f(x, x)$, and $v(x) = g(x, x)$ are strictly increasing in x;
4) $f(x, y) \leq \min\{x, y\}$, $g(x, y) \geq \max\{x, y\}$;
5) $f(1, 1) = 1$, $g(0, 0) = 0$;
6) f and g satisfy the associative law, i.e.,

$$f(x, f(y, z)) = f(f(x, y), z), \quad g(x, g(y, z)) = g(g(x, y), z);$$

7) f and g satisfy the distributive law, i.e.,

$$f(x, g(y, z)) = g(f(x, y), f(x, z))$$

and

$$g(x, f(y, z)) = f(g(x, y), g(x, z)).$$

Then f and g are uniquely determined and they are

$$f(x, y) = \min\{x, y\} = x \wedge y,$$

and

$$g(x, y) = \max\{x, y\} = x \vee y.$$

PROOF

a) We prove that both $u(x)$ and $v(x)$ are bijections from $[0, 1]$ to $[0, 1]$. First, conditions 4) and 5) imply that $u(0) = 0$ and $u(1) = 1$. Next, from conditions 1) and 2), $u(x)$ is a strictly increasing continuous function. Hence $u(x)$ is a bijection from $[0, 1]$ to $[0, 1]$. The same arguments apply to $v(x)$.

b) We prove that for any $x \in [0, 1]$, x satisfies

$$x = f(x, g(x, x)), \quad \text{and} \quad x = g(x, f(x, x)). \tag{9.1}$$

Let $u(x) = a$. From conditions 4), 6), and 7), we have

$$u(x) = f(x, x) = a \leq \max\{a, f(a, a)\}$$

$$\leq g\,(a,f\,(a,a)) = f\,(g\,(a,a)\,,g\,(a,a))$$

$$= u\,(g\,(a,a))\,.$$

Because $u\,(x)$ is strictly increasing, this means $x \leq g\,(a,a)$. Also,

$$g\,(a,a) = g\,(u\,(x)\,,u\,(x)) = g\,(f\,(x,x)\,,f\,(x,x))$$

$$= f\,(x,g\,(x,x)) \leq \min\{x,g\,(x,x)\} \leq x.$$

It follows that $x = g\,(a,a)$ and $x = f\,(x,g\,(x,x))$.
The same proof applies to $x = g\,(x,f\,(x,x))$.
c) We prove that for any $a \in [0,1]$, a satisfies

$$f\,(a,a) = a,\ \text{and}\ g\,(a,a) = a. \tag{9.2}$$

From b), we find

$$f\,(a,a) = f\,(f\,(a,a)\,,g\,(f\,(a,a)\,,f\,(a,a)))$$

$$= f\,(f\,(a,a)\,,f\,(a,f\,(a,a)))$$

$$= f\,(f\,(a,a)\,,a)\,.$$

It follows that

$$f\,(a,a) = f\,(f\,(f\,(a,a)\,,a)\,,a) = f\,(f\,(a,a)\,,f\,(a,a))\,,$$

that is,

$$u\,(a) = u\,(f\,(a,a))\,.$$

From a) we conclude that $a = f\,(a,a)$.
The same proof applies to $a = g\,(a,a)$.
d) We prove that for any a, $b \in [0,1]$,

$$f\,(a,g\,(a,b)) = g\,(a,f\,(a,b)) = a.$$

From condition 4) or part a) just proved, we have

$$a \leq \max\{a,f\,(a,b)\} \leq g\,(a,f\,(a,b))$$

$$= f\left(g\left(a, a\right), g\left(a, b\right)\right) = f\left(a, g\left(a, b\right)\right)$$

$$\leq \min\left\{a, g\left(a, a\right)\right\} \leq a.$$

Therefore, $f\left(a, g\left(a, b\right)\right) = a$. The same proof applies to $g\left(a, f\left(a, b\right)\right) = a$.
e) We prove that for any $a, b \in [0, 1]$,

$$f\left(a, b\right) = \min\left\{a, b\right\}, \text{ and } g\left(a, b\right) = \max\left\{a, b\right\}. \qquad (9.3)$$

From condition 2), we can assume that $a \leq b$. Define

$$k\left(a, y\right) = g\left(a, y\right).$$

This implies that
$$k\left(a, a\right) = g\left(a, a\right) = a,$$

and
$$k\left(a, 1\right) = g\left(a, 1\right) \geq \max\left\{a, 1\right\} = 1.$$

Hence, $k\left(a, 1\right) = 1$. Since, for a fixed a, $k\left(a, y\right)$ is a continuous function form $[a, 1]$ to $[a, 1]$, then for $b \geq a$, there exists c such that $c \geq a$, and

$$k\left(a, c\right) = g\left(a, c\right) = b.$$

It follows that

$$f\left(a, b\right) = f\left(a, g\left(a, c\right)\right) = g\left(f\left(a, a\right), f\left(a, c\right)\right)$$

$$= g\left(a, f\left(a, c\right)\right) = a = \min\left\{a, b\right\}.$$

Similarly, $g\left(a, b\right) = \max\left\{a, b\right\}.$ ∎

THEOREM 23
If a function $h : [0, 1] \longrightarrow [0, 1]$ satisfies the following conditions:
1) $h\left(0\right) = 1$, $h\left(1\right) = 0$;
2) h is a continuous and strictly decreasing function;
3) $(\forall x \in [0, 1])\left(h\left(h\left(x\right)\right) = x\right)$; and
4) $(\forall x \in [0, 1])\left(h\left(1 - x\right) = 1 - h\left(x\right)\right),$
then
$$h\left(x\right) = 1 - x.$$

PROOF   When $x = 0$, $\frac{1}{2}$, and 1, $h(x) = 1 - x$ is valid. If there exists $x_0 \in [0, 1] \setminus \left\{0, \frac{1}{2}, 1\right\}$ such that $h(x_0) = y_0 \neq 1 - x_0$ (without loss of generality, we assume $y_0 > 1 - x_0$), then

$$y_1 = h(x_1) = h(1 - x_0) = 1 - h(x_0) < 1 - (1 - x_0) = x_0,$$

where $x_1 = 1 - x_0$ and $h(x_1) = y_1$.

It follows that

$$1 - x_0 < h(x_0) < h(y_1) = x_1 = 1 - x_0.$$

Thus we have a contradiction, so the theorem is proved.   ∎

9.2   Common Fuzzy Operators

9.2.1   Probability Operators "$\cdot$" and "$\overset{\wedge}{+}$"

For any $A, B \in \mathcal{F}(U)$, the probability operators "$\cdot$" and "$\overset{\wedge}{+}$" are defined thus: for any $x, y \in [0, 1]$,

$$\left(A \cap B\right)(u) \overset{\Delta}{=} A(u) \cdot B(u) \quad \text{(the usual multiplication)},$$

and

$$\left(A \cup B\right)(u) \overset{\Delta}{=} A(u) + B(u) - A(u) \cdot B(u).$$

These satisfy the following:

(1) **Commutativity:** $x \overset{\wedge}{+} y = y \overset{\wedge}{+} x$; and $x \cdot y = y \cdot x$.

Since $x \overset{\wedge}{+} y = x + y - x \cdot y = y + x - y \cdot x = y \overset{\wedge}{+} x$.

(2) **Associativity:** $\left(x \overset{\wedge}{+} y\right) \overset{\wedge}{+} z = x \overset{\wedge}{+} \left(y \overset{\wedge}{+} z\right)$ and $(x \cdot y) \cdot z = x \cdot (y \cdot z)$.

PROOF   Since

$$\left(x \overset{\wedge}{+} y\right) \overset{\wedge}{+} z = (x + y - x \cdot y) \overset{\wedge}{+} z$$
$$= (x + y - x \cdot y) + z - (x + y - x \cdot y) \cdot z$$
$$= x + y + z - x \cdot y - x \cdot z - y \cdot z + x \cdot y \cdot z$$

On the other hand,

$$x \overset{\wedge}{+} \left(y \overset{\wedge}{+} z \right) = x + \left(y \overset{\wedge}{+} z \right) - x \cdot \left(y \overset{\wedge}{+} z \right)$$
$$= x + (y + z - y \cdot z) - x \cdot (y + z - y \cdot z)$$
$$= x + y + z - y \cdot z - x \cdot y - x \cdot z + x \cdot y \cdot z$$
$$= x + y + z - x \cdot y - x \cdot z - y \cdot z + x \cdot y \cdot z$$

Therefore, the operator "$\overset{\wedge}{+}$" is associative. Similarly, one can prove the same for the operator "$\cdot$". ∎

(3) **De Morgan's laws:** $\left(x \overset{\wedge}{+} y \right)^c = x^c \cdot y^c$; and $x^c \overset{\wedge}{+} y^c = (x \cdot y)^c$.

PROOF Since

$$\left(x \overset{\wedge}{+} y \right)^c = 1 - \left(x \overset{\wedge}{+} y \right)$$

$$= 1 - (x + y - x \cdot y)$$

$$= 1 - x - y + x \cdot y$$

$$= (1 - x)(1 - y)$$

$$= x^c \cdot y^c.$$

(Note: The complementary operator "c" on $[0, 1]$ is defined by $x^c = 1 - x$.)
For the second identity,

$$x^c \overset{\wedge}{+} y^c = (1 - x) \overset{\wedge}{+} (1 - y)$$

$$= (1 - x) + (1 - y) - \overset{\bullet}{(1 - x)}(1 - y)$$

$$= 2 - x - y - (1 - x - y + x \cdot y)$$

$$= 1 - x \cdot y$$

$$= (x \cdot y)^c.$$

∎

(4) **0-1 Law:** $x \overset{\wedge}{+} 1 = 1$; $x \overset{\wedge}{+} 0 = x$; $x \cdot 1 = x$; and $x \cdot 0 = 0$.

Since $x \overset{\wedge}{+} 1 = x + 1 - x \cdot 1 = 1$, and $x \overset{\wedge}{+} 0 = x + 0 - x \cdot 0 = x$.

(5) **Reflexivity:** $(x^c)^c = x$.

This is obviously true.

However, the "$\overset{\wedge}{+}$" and "$\cdot$" operators behave differently in the following laws.

Idempotency is not valid, i.e., $x \overset{\wedge}{+} x \neq x$. Because

$$x \overset{\wedge}{+} x = x + x - x \cdot x = 2x - x^2 = x(2 - x)$$

if we set $x(2 - x) = x$ and when $x > 0$, $2 - x = 1$ or $x = 1$. Hence, when $x \in (0, 1)$, $x \overset{\wedge}{+} x \neq x$.

Distributivity is not valid, i.e., $\left(x \overset{\wedge}{+} y\right) \cdot z \neq x \cdot \hat{z} + y \cdot z$.

Since $\left(x \overset{\wedge}{+} y\right) \cdot z = (x + y - xy) \cdot z = x \cdot z + y \cdot z - x \cdot y \cdot z$; but $x \cdot \hat{z} + y \cdot z = x \cdot z + y \cdot z - x \cdot y \cdot z^2$, so they are not equal.

The complementary law is not valid, i.e., $x \overset{\wedge}{+} x^c \neq 1$.

Since $x \overset{\wedge}{+} x^c = x + (1 - x) - x(1 - x) = 1 - x(1 - x) \neq 1$.

9.2.2   Bounded Operators "⊖" and "⊕"

The operations of the **bounded sum** or addition "⊕" and the **bounded difference** or subtraction "⊖" are defined in

$$\left(A_{\sim} \cup B_{\sim}\right)(u) \overset{\Delta}{=} A_{\sim}(u) \oplus B_{\sim}(u) \overset{\Delta}{=} \min\left\{A_{\sim}(u) + B_{\sim}(u), 1\right\}$$

and

$$\left(A_{\sim} \cap B_{\sim}\right)(u) \overset{\Delta}{=} A_{\sim}(u) \ominus B_{\sim}(u) \overset{\Delta}{=} \max\left\{A_{\sim}(u) + B_{\sim}(u) - 1\right\}.$$

They satisfy the following:

(1) Associativity: $(x \oplus y) \oplus z = x \oplus (y \oplus z)$.

PROOF   For $(x \oplus y) \oplus z = [(x + y) \wedge 1] \oplus z = (((x + y) \wedge 1) + z) \wedge 1$,

and $x \oplus (y \oplus z) = x \oplus (((y + z) \wedge 1)) = (x + ((y + z) \wedge 1)) \wedge 1.$
Case 1: $x + y \leq 1$, and $y + z \leq 1$. Then

$$(x \oplus y) \oplus z = (x + y + z) \wedge 1 = x \oplus (y \oplus z).$$

Case 2: $x + y > 1$, and $y + z > 1$. Then

$$(x \oplus y) \oplus z = (x + z) \wedge 1 = 1 = (x + 1) \wedge 1 = x \oplus (y \oplus z).$$

Case 3: $x + y \leq 1$, and $y + z > 1$. Then

$$(x \oplus y) \oplus z = (x + y + z) \wedge 1 == 1 = (x + 1) \wedge 1 = x \oplus (y \oplus z).$$

Case 4: $x + y \leq 1$, and $y + z \leq 1$. Then

$$(x \oplus y) \oplus z = (x + z) \wedge 1 = 1 = (x + y + z) \wedge 1 = x \oplus (y \oplus z).$$

We can show $(x \ominus y) \ominus z = x \ominus (y \ominus z)$ in a similar manner.
This completes the proof. ∎

(2) Commutativity. Obviously valid.
(3) Reflexivity. Obviously valid.
(4) Complementary law: $x \oplus x^c = 1$; and $x \ominus x^c = 0$.
     Since $x \oplus x^c = x \oplus (1 - x) = [x + (1 - x)] \wedge 1 = 1$ and
        $x \ominus x^c = x \ominus (1 - x) = [x + (1 - x) - 1] = 0.$
(5) De Morgan's laws: $(x \oplus y)^c = x^c \ominus y^c$; and $(x \ominus y)^c = x^c \oplus y^c.$

PROOF Since

$$(x \oplus y)^c = [(x + y) \wedge 1]^c$$

$$= (x + y)^c \vee 0 = (1 - x - y) \vee 0$$

and

$$x^c \ominus y^c = (1 - x) \ominus (1 - y)$$

$$= [(1 - x) + (1 - y) - 1] \vee 0$$

$$= (1 - x - y) \vee 0,$$

the first identity is proved, and the second one can be proven similarly. ∎

(6) Polarity: $x \oplus 0 = x$; $x \oplus 1 = 1$; $x \ominus 0 = 0$; and $x \ominus 1 = x$.
Since $x \oplus 0 = (x + 0) \wedge 1 = x$; $x \oplus 1 = (x + 1) \wedge 1 = 1$;
$$x \ominus 0 = (x + 0 - 1) \vee 0 = 0; \text{ and } x \ominus 1 = (x + 1 - 1) \vee 0 = x.$$
However, the two operations $\oplus$ and $\ominus$ have different properties in the following:
(7) Idempotency is invalid, i.e., $x \oplus x \neq x$.
For example, when $x \in (0.5, 1)$,

$$x \oplus x = \min \{x + x, 1\} = 1 \neq x.$$

(8) Distributivity is invalid, i.e., $(x \oplus y) \ominus z \neq (x \ominus z) \oplus (y \ominus z)$.

PROOF   From the left-hand side,

$$(x \oplus y) \ominus z = (((x + y) \wedge 1) + z - 1) \vee 0;$$

from the right-hand side,

$$(x \ominus z) \oplus (y \ominus z) = [((x + z - 1) \vee 0) + ((y + z - 1) \vee 0)] \wedge 1.$$

Now let $x = 0.4$, $y = 0.5$, and $z = 0.6$, then

$$(x \oplus y) \ominus z = 0.5,$$

but

$$(x \ominus z) \oplus (y \ominus z) = 0.1.$$

This completes the proof.   ∎

(9) Absorption is invalid, i.e., $(x \ominus y) \oplus x \neq x$.
Since $(x \ominus y) \oplus x = (((x + y - 1) \vee 0) + x) \wedge 1$, when $x = 0.5$ and $y = 0.6$, then
$$(x \ominus y) \oplus x = 0.6 \wedge 1 = 0.6 \neq x.$$

9.2.3   Einstein's Operators: $\dot{\varepsilon}$ and $\overset{+}{\varepsilon}$

The operations of **Einstein's operators** $\dot{\varepsilon}$ and $\overset{+}{\varepsilon}$ are defined by:

$$\left(\underset{\sim}{A} \cap \underset{\sim}{B} \right) (u) \overset{\triangle}{=} \underset{\sim}{A} (u) \, \dot{\varepsilon} \underset{\sim}{B} (u) \overset{\triangle}{=} \frac{\underset{\sim}{A} (u) \cdot \underset{\sim}{B} (u)}{1 - \left(1 - \underset{\sim}{A} (u) \right) \left(1 - \underset{\sim}{B} (u) \right)}$$

and,

$$\left(\underset{\sim}{A} \cup \underset{\sim}{B}\right)(u) \overset{\Delta}{=} \underset{\sim}{A}(u) \overset{+}{\varepsilon} \underset{\sim}{B}(u) \overset{\Delta}{=} \frac{\underset{\sim}{A}(u) + \underset{\sim}{B}(u)}{1 + \underset{\sim}{A}(u) \cdot \underset{\sim}{B}(u)}.$$

These two operators satisfy the following:
(1) Commutativity. (Obvious)
(2) Associativity: $\left(x \overset{+}{\varepsilon} y\right) \overset{+}{\varepsilon} z = x \overset{+}{\varepsilon} \left(y \overset{+}{\varepsilon} z\right)$; and $\left(x \overset{\cdot}{\varepsilon} y\right) \overset{\cdot}{\varepsilon} z = x \overset{\cdot}{\varepsilon} \left(y \overset{\cdot}{\varepsilon} z\right)$.

PROOF　We prove the first identity; the second follows similarly.
From the left-hand side,

$$\left(x \overset{+}{\varepsilon} y\right) \overset{+}{\varepsilon} z = \frac{x + y}{1 + xy} \overset{+}{\varepsilon} z = \frac{\frac{x+y}{1+xy} + z}{1 + \frac{(x+y)z}{1+xy}} = \frac{x + y + z + xyz}{1 + xy + xz + yz}.$$

From the right-hand side,

$$x \overset{+}{\varepsilon} \left(y \overset{+}{\varepsilon} z\right) = \frac{x + y + z + xyz}{1 + xy + xz + yz}.$$

Since both sides are identical, the result is proved.
(3) Polarity: $x \overset{+}{\varepsilon} 0 = x$; $x \overset{+}{\varepsilon} 1 = 1$; $x \overset{\cdot}{\varepsilon} 0 = 0$; and $x \overset{\cdot}{\varepsilon} 1 = x$.
　　Since

$$x \overset{+}{\varepsilon} 0 = \frac{x + 0}{1 + x \cdot 0} = x;$$

$$x \overset{+}{\varepsilon} 1 = \frac{x + 1}{1 + x \cdot 1} = 1;$$

$$x \overset{\cdot}{\varepsilon} 0 = \frac{x \cdot 0}{1 + (1 - x)(1 - 1)} = 0;$$

and

$$x \overset{\cdot}{\varepsilon} 1 = \frac{x \cdot 1}{1 + (1 - x)(1 - 1)} = x.$$

(4) Reflexivity. (Obvious)
(5) De Morgan's laws: $\left(x \overset{+}{\varepsilon} y\right)^c = x^c \overset{+}{\varepsilon} y^c$; and $\left(x \overset{\cdot}{\varepsilon} y\right)^c = x^c \overset{\cdot}{\varepsilon} y^c$. ∎

PROOF　We will prove the first identity, the second follows similarly.

Since

$$\left(x \overset{+}{\varepsilon} y\right)^c = 1 - \frac{x+y}{1+xy} = \frac{1-x-y+xy}{1+xy} = x^c \overset{+}{\varepsilon} y^c.$$

■

However, it is easy to show that Einstein's operators do not satisfy the idempotent law, the absorption law, the distributive law, or the complementary law.

9.2.4   Hamacher's Operators "$\dot{v}$" and "$\overset{+}{v}$"

The operations of **Hamacher's operators** "$\dot{v}$" and "$\overset{+}{v}$" are defined by:

$$\left(\underset{\sim}{A} \cap \underset{\sim}{B}\right)(u) \overset{\Delta}{=} \underset{\sim}{A}(u) \,\dot{v}\, \underset{\sim}{B}(u) \overset{\Delta}{=} \frac{\underset{\sim}{A}(u) \cdot \underset{\sim}{B}(u)}{r + (1-r)\left(\underset{\sim}{A}(u) \overset{\wedge}{+} \underset{\sim}{B}(u)\right)}$$

and

$$\left(\underset{\sim}{A} \cup \underset{\sim}{B}\right)(u) \overset{\Delta}{=} \underset{\sim}{A}(u) \,\overset{+}{v}\, \underset{\sim}{B}(u) \overset{\Delta}{=} \frac{\underset{\sim}{A}(u) \overset{\wedge}{+} \underset{\sim}{B}(u) - (1-r)\,\underset{\sim}{A}(u) \cdot \underset{\sim}{B}(u)}{r + (1-r)\left(1 - \underset{\sim}{A}(u) \cdot \underset{\sim}{B}(u)\right)},$$

where r is a parameter and $r \geq 1$. When $r = 1$, Hamacher's operators become probability operators, and when $r = 2$, Hamacher's operators are Einstein's operators.

9.2.5   Yager's Operators "$\dot{y}$" and "$\overset{+}{y}$"

The operations of **Yager's operators** "$\dot{y}$" and "$\overset{+}{y}$" are defined by:

$$\left(\underset{\sim}{A} \cap \underset{\sim}{B}\right)(u) \overset{\Delta}{=} \underset{\sim}{A}(u) \,\dot{y}\, \underset{\sim}{B}(u) = 1 - \min\left\{1, \left[\left(1 - \underset{\sim}{A}(u)\right)^p\right.\right.$$

$$\left.\left. + \left(1 - \underset{\sim}{B}(u)\right)^p\right]^{1/p}\right\}$$

and

$$\left(A_{\sim} \cup B_{\sim}\right)(u) \stackrel{\triangle}{=} A_{\sim}(u) \stackrel{+}{y} B_{\sim}(u) = \min\left\{1, \left[\left(A_{\sim}(u)\right)^p + \left(B_{\sim}(u)\right)^p\right]^{1/p}\right\},$$

where p is a parameter and $p \geq 1$. When $p = 1$, Yager's operators become the bounded operators, and when $p = \infty$, Yager's operators are Zadeh's operators.

9.3 Generalized Fuzzy Operators

In the previous section, we discussed several commonly used fuzzy operators. For the purpose of differentiating them from Zadeh's operators, we call the former operators the **generalized fuzzy operators**. The axiomatic form of the generalized fuzzy operators is the triangular norm T and the complementary triangular norm T^* (cf. Section 3.4). For the generalized fuzzy operators, the triangular norm T is the "and" operator and the complementary triangular norm T^* is the "or" operator. We define operational notations for T and T^* as "$*$" and "$\stackrel{+}{*}$", respectively. It follows that for any fuzzy sets, $A_{\sim}$, $B_{\sim} \in \mathcal{F}(U)$, generally, they satisfy

$$\left(A_{\sim} \cup B_{\sim}\right)(u) = A_{\sim}(u) \stackrel{+}{*} B_{\sim}(u)$$

and

$$\left(A_{\sim} \cap B_{\sim}\right)(u) = A_{\sim}(u) * B_{\sim}(u).$$

Example 46

Define two operators "$\dot{p}$" and "$\stackrel{+}{p}$" as follows:

$$x \dot{p} y = \max\left\{0, \left(x^{2p-1} + y^{2p-1} - 1\right)^{\frac{1}{2p-1}}\right\}$$

and

$$x \stackrel{+}{p} y = 1 - \max\left\{0, \left((1-x)^{2p-1} + (1-y)^{2p-1}\right)^{\frac{1}{2p-1}}\right\},$$

where $p = 1, 2, \cdots$.

We can verify that "$\dot{p}$" and "$\overset{+}{p}$" are in fact the "and" and "or" operators of the generalized fuzzy operators. In the special cases where $p = 1$, $x \overset{.}{p} y = \max\{0, x + y - 1\} = x \ominus y$ and when $p = \infty$,

$$x \overset{.}{p} y = \begin{cases} 0, & x < 1, y < 1; \\ y, & x = 1; \\ x & y = 1. \end{cases}$$

☐

Next, we analyze the problem of "crisp domains" of fuzzy operators. This is needed for the purpose of comparisons among operators. Because fuzzy operators are binary functions from $[0, 1] \times [0, 1] \longrightarrow [0, 1]$, first we study those points in the domain whose functional value is 0 or 1. We call those points crisp points since they indicate clearly whether they belong to or do not belong to a set.

Given a fuzzy operator $*$ ($*$ represents either "$\dot{*}$" or "$\overset{+}{*}$"), we define

$$\sigma(*) \overset{\triangle}{=} \{(x, y) \in [0, 1] \times [0, 1] \mid x * y = 0 \text{ or } 1\}$$

and call it the **crisp domain** of the fuzzy operator $*$. We can easily verify the following properties:

1) $(x, y) \in \sigma(*) \Longrightarrow (y, x) \in \sigma(*)$;
2) $\{(0, 0), (1, 1)\} \subset \sigma(*) \subset [0, 1] \times [0, 1]$.

Since the operators "$\dot{*}$" and "$\overset{+}{*}$" are symmetrical, we limit our discussions in the following to "$\dot{*}$" only. From the definition of the "$\dot{*}$" operator, we have

$$(\{0\} \times [0, 1]) \cup ([0, 1] \times \{0\}) \cup \{(1, 1)\} \subset \sigma\left(\dot{*}\right) \subset [0, 1] \times [0, 1].$$

PROPOSITION 43

Let $\sigma_m \overset{\triangle}{=} (\{0\} \times [0, 1]) \cup ([0, 1] \times \{0\}) \cup \{(1, 1)\}$. *Then*

$$\sigma(\wedge) = \sigma\left(\dot{\vee}\right) = \sigma_m. \tag{9.4}$$

PROOF   For any $(x, y) \in \sigma_m$, then x and y satisfy $x \wedge y = x \dot{\vee} y = 0$ or 1. Thus, $(x, y) \in \sigma(\wedge)$ and $(x, y) \in \sigma\left(\dot{\vee}\right)$. We can conclude that $\sigma_m \subset \sigma(\wedge)$ and $\sigma_m \subset \sigma\left(\dot{\vee}\right)$.

Conversely, if $(x, y) \notin \sigma_m$, then $x \wedge y \in (0, 1)$ and $x \overset{.}{v} y \in (0, 1)$. Thus, $(x, y) \notin \sigma (\wedge)$ and $(x, y) \in \sigma \left(\overset{.}{v} \right)$. We then conclude that $\sigma_m \supset \sigma (\wedge)$ and $\sigma_m \supset \sigma \left(\overset{.}{v} \right)$. This completes the proof. ∎

PROPOSITION 44

$\sigma \left(\overset{.}{y} \right) = \left\{ (x, y) \in [0, 1] \times [0, 1] \mid (1 - x)^p + (1 - y)^p \geq 1 \right\} \cup \{(1, 1)\}.$

PROOF Since

$$x \overset{.}{y} y = 1 \iff \min \left\{ 1, \left[(1 - x)^p + (1 - y)^p \right]^{1/p} \right\} = 0$$

$$\iff \left[(1 - x)^p + (1 - y)^p \right]^{1/p} = 0$$

$$\iff x = y = 1.$$

Also,

$$x \overset{.}{y} y = 0 \iff \min \left\{ 1, \left[(1 - x)^p + (1 - y)^p \right]^{1/p} \right\} = 1$$

$$\iff \left[(1 - x)^p + (1 - y)^p \right]^{1/p} \geq 1$$

$$\iff (1 - x)^p + (1 - y)^p \geq 1.$$

∎

Figure 9.2 shows the curve $\sigma \left(\overset{.}{y} \right)$ under different values of p. If $p = 1$, this corresponds to the operator $\ominus$ that has a larger crisp domain than other operators already discussed previously, and that has an area of size $1/2$. There exists operators with greater crisp domains than the $\ominus$ operator, e.g., the $\overset{.}{p}$ operator used in the first example of this section.

PROPOSITION 45

$\sigma \left(\overset{.}{p} \right) = \left\{ (x, y) \mid x^{2p-1} + y^{2p-1} \leq 1 \right\} \cup \{(1, 1)\}.$

PROOF The proof is omitted since it is similar to the last one. ∎

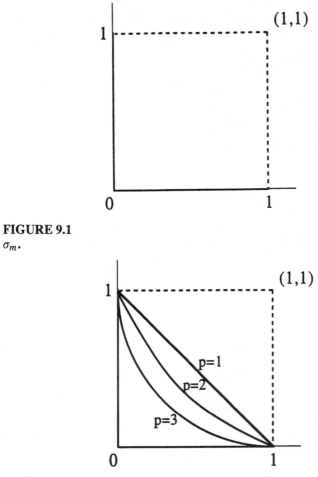

FIGURE 9.1

σ_m.

FIGURE 9.2

$\sigma\left(\dot{y}\right)$.

For different values of p, Figure 9.3 shows the behaviors of the curve $\sigma\left(\dot{p}\right)$.

As we can see from the Figure 9.2 and Figure 9.3, the curve $\sigma\left(\dot{p}\right)$ behaves in the opposite direction from the curve $\sigma\left(\dot{y}\right)$. That is, as p increases, $\sigma\left(\dot{p}\right)$ also increases, and when $p = \infty$,

$$\sigma\left(\dot{p}\right) = ([0, 1) \times [0, 1)) \cup \{(1, 1)\} .$$

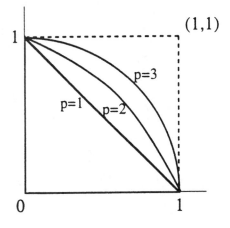

FIGURE 9.3

$\sigma\left(\dot{p}\right)$.

This is the largest crisp domain for a fuzzy "and" operator; its area is 1. We denote it by

$$\sigma_M = ([0, 1) \times [0, 1)) \cup \{(1, 1)\} = [0, 1]^2 .$$

PROPOSITION 46

$$\sigma\left(\dot{v}\right) \subset \sigma\left(\dot{y}\right) \subset \sigma\left(\dot{p}\right).$$

PROOF   Since $\sigma\left(\dot{v}\right) = \sigma_m$, by implication, $\sigma\left(\dot{v}\right) \subset \sigma\left(\dot{y}\right)$. Therefore, we only need to prove

$$\sigma\left(\dot{y}\right) \subset \sigma\left(\dot{p}\right).$$

For any $(x, y) \in \sigma\left(\dot{y}\right)$, according to Proposition 44, we have

$$x = y = 1 \quad or \quad (1 - x)^p + (1 - y)^p \geq 1.$$

If $x = y = 1$, then $(x, y) \in \sigma\left(\dot{p}\right)$.

If $(1 - x)^p + (1 - y)^p \geq 1$, then $(1 - x) + (1 - y) \geq (1 - x)^p + (1 - y)^p \geq 1$. This implies

$$(1 - x) + (1 - y) \geq 1 \text{ or } x + y \leq 1.$$

Therefore, for any p', it follows that

$$x^{2p'-1} + y^{2p'-1} \leq x + y \leq 1.$$

By the last proposition, we conclude that $(x, y) \in \sigma\left(\dot{p}\right)$. This completes the proof. ∎

PROPOSITION 47

Let $\underset{\sim}{A}, \underset{\sim}{B} \in \mathcal{F}(U)$ and also let the operation of $\underset{\sim}{A} \cap \underset{\sim}{B}$ be defined by the "$\dot{*}$". If $\sigma\left(\dot{*}\right) = \sigma_m$, then

$$Supp\left(\underset{\sim}{A} \cap \underset{\sim}{B}\right) = \left(Supp\,\underset{\sim}{A}\right) \cap \left(Supp\,\underset{\sim}{B}\right).$$

When $\underset{\sim}{A} = \underset{\sim}{B}$, then

$$Supp\left(\underset{\sim}{A} \cap \underset{\sim}{B}\right) = Supp\,\underset{\sim}{A}.$$

PROOF For

$$u \in Supp\left(\underset{\sim}{A} \cap \underset{\sim}{B}\right) \Longleftrightarrow \left(\underset{\sim}{A} \cap \underset{\sim}{B}\right)(u) > 0$$

$$\Longleftrightarrow \underset{\sim}{A}(u) > 0 \quad and \quad \underset{\sim}{B}(u) > 0$$

$$\Longleftrightarrow u \in \left(Supp\,\underset{\sim}{A}\right) \cap \left(Supp\,\underset{\sim}{B}\right).$$

∎

This proposition explains that when $\sigma\left(\dot{*}\right) = \sigma_m$, the supports of fuzzy sets do not change under the operator "$\dot{*}$". In general, when $\sigma\left(\dot{*}\right) \neq \sigma_m$, the support of the fuzzy set derived from the operation "$\dot{*}$" of a fuzzy set with itself will be a smaller set.

9.4   The Strength of Fuzzy Operators "AND" and "OR"

In this section we discuss the concept of the **strength of the fuzzy operator** "and" (similar for the operator "or"). Chen [2] has made a significant contribution in this area.

We know that the generalized fuzzy operators "$\overset{.}{*}$" and "$\overset{+}{*}$" satisfy

$$\underset{\sim}{A}\ (u)\ \overset{.}{*}\underset{\sim}{B}\ (u) \leq \underset{\sim}{A}\ (u) \wedge \underset{\sim}{B}\ (u)$$

and

$$\underset{\sim}{A}\ (u)\ \overset{+}{*}\underset{\sim}{B}\ (u) \geq \underset{\sim}{A}\ (u) \vee \underset{\sim}{B}\ (u).$$

This means that Zadeh's $\wedge$ operator is the roughest of all "intersection" operators and Zadeh's $\vee$ operator is the roughest of all "union" operators. Being the roughest operator does not imply that it is a bad operator, and likewise, being the finest operator does not imply that it is an excellent operator. A good or a bad operator depends upon the application in the decision-making environment. In high level decision making, usually roughness is not a problem, but relevancy is.

Inference using "and" and "or" in our brain may have different outcomes. This is because our brain can operate very flexibly. One of the possible explanations is that our brain can operate at different levels of strength of "and" and "or" operators.

Yager [13] first presented the idea of the strength of "and" and "or" operators in 1980. He used the idea to measure the strictness of fuzzy operators. In his discussion on the parameters of the operators $\overset{.}{y}$ and $\overset{+}{y}$, he pointed out that p is related to the strength of "and" and "or" operators.

Different fuzzy operators actually reflect different degrees of strength of "and" and "or" operators. For example, here is a fuzzy logic gate "and":

$$
\begin{array}{ccc}
x \longrightarrow & & \\
& \boxed{\overset{.}{*}} \longrightarrow & z \\
y \longrightarrow & &
\end{array}
$$

We shall receive different output if we use different "and" operators. Specifically, take $\overset{.}{*} = \overset{.}{y}$ with $p = \infty$, and let the input be $x = y = 0.999$ then the output $z = x \overset{.}{*} y = 0$. This means $\overset{.}{y}$ is the strictest of all "and" operators and has the highest measure of strength of "and". For the same input, if we switch to other types of $\overset{.}{*}$ operators, the output will be greater than 0; and it reaches the largest output when the operator is $\wedge$. So the $\wedge$ operator is the least strict of all "and" operators and has the lowest measure of strength of "and".

Since "$\overset{.}{*}$" and "$\overset{+}{*}$" have the dual relationship, both operators have the same level of strength, i.e., either both are low or both are high.

Now let us compare the operator $\wedge$ and $\ominus$. Note that

$$x \ominus y \leq x \wedge y.$$

Next we construct two set-valued functions $f, g : [0, 1] \times [0, 1] \longrightarrow \mathcal{P}\ ([0, 1])$ such that

$$f\ (x, y) \overset{\triangle}{=} \{z \mid z = x \ominus y\}$$

and

$$g(x, y) \stackrel{\triangle}{=} \{z \mid z = x \wedge y\}.$$

If we equate the order relation $\leq$ to $\subset$, then we find that $f(x, y) \leq g(x, y)$. That means the surface $z = x \wedge y$ contains the surface $z = x \ominus y$. In other words, the strength of "and" and "or" can be defined as the "volume" in the closed unit intervals.

Let "$*$" be a generalized fuzzy operator that can be either "and" or "or". Denote

$$D(*) \stackrel{\triangle}{=} 1 - \rho \int_0^1 \int_0^1 (x * y)\, dx dy \qquad (9.5)$$

where ρ is a parameter. Since the generalized fuzzy operator $*$ is a bounded, continuous (normally the case), binary function, the above double integral exists. Hence we can use $D(*)$ as a measure of strength for $*$ (i.e., the strength of "and" or "or").

Now we determine the value of the parameter ρ in the expression 9.4. Consider the curve $z = x \wedge y$ (Figure 9.4). We find that the volume of the pyramid K-SOPQ is

$$\int_0^1 \int_0^1 (x \wedge y)\, dx dy = \frac{1}{3} \cdot 1^2 \cdot 1 = \frac{1}{3}.$$

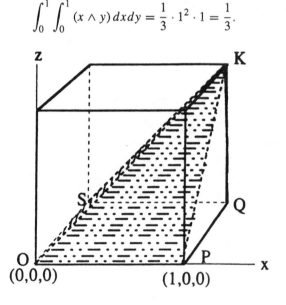

FIGURE 9.4

$z = x \wedge y.$

Therefore, $D(\wedge) = 1 - \rho \cdot \frac{1}{3}$. Since operator $\wedge$ has the lowest strength, we set $D(\wedge) = 0$. Finally, we find that $\rho = 3$.

DEFINITION 21   *Let $*$ be a continuous generalized fuzzy operator. We call*

$$D\left(*\right) \stackrel{\Delta}{=} 1 - 3 \int_0^1 \int_0^1 \left(x * y\right) dx dy \qquad (9.6)$$

the **strength** *of $*$. When $* = \dot{*}$, we call $D\left(\dot{*}\right)$ the strength of "and"; and when $* = \overset{+}{*}$, we call $D\left(\overset{+}{*}\right)$ the strength of "or".*

PROPOSITION 48
$0 \leq D\left(*\right) \leq 1.$

PROOF   Since $D\left(*\right) = D\left(\dot{*}\right) = D\left(\overset{+}{*}\right)$, we can select $D\left(\dot{*}\right)$ to prove the proposition.

Because $0 \leq x \mathbin{\dot{*}} y \leq x \wedge y$, we have

$$0 \leq \int_0^1 \int_0^1 \left(x \mathbin{\dot{*}} y\right) dx dy \leq \int_0^1 \int_0^1 \left(x \wedge y\right) dx dy.$$

This is equivalent to

$$1 - 0 \geq 1 - 3 \int_0^1 \int_0^1 \left(x \mathbin{\dot{*}} y\right) dx dy \geq 1 - 3 \int_0^1 \int_0^1 \left(x \wedge y\right) dx dy.$$

That is,

$$1 \geq D\left(\dot{*}\right) \geq D\left(\wedge\right) = 0.$$

∎

PROPOSITION 49
For the probability operators "$\cdot$" and "$\overset{\wedge}{+}$", then

$$D\left(\cdot\right) = D\left(\overset{\wedge}{+}\right) = \frac{1}{4}. \qquad (9.7)$$

PROOF   For

$$D\left(\cdot\right) = 1 - 3 \int_0^1 \int_0^1 \left(xy\right) dx dy = 1 - 3 \int_0^1 \left(\frac{xy^2}{2} \Big|_0^1\right) dx$$

$$= 1 - 3 \int_0^1 \frac{x}{2} dx = 1 - 3 \left(\frac{x^2}{4} \Big|_0^1 \right)$$

$$= 1 - \frac{3}{4} = \frac{1}{4} .$$

∎

PROPOSITION 50
For the bounded operators "⊕" and "⊖", then

$$D (\oplus) = D (\ominus) = \frac{1}{2} .$$

PROOF   Since

$$D (\ominus) = 1 - 3 \int_0^1 \int_0^1 (x \ominus y) \, dx \, dy$$

$$= 1 - 3 \int_0^1 \int_0^1 \max \{x + y - 1, 0\} \, dx \, dy$$

$$= 1 - 3 \int_0^1 \left[\left(xy + \frac{y^2}{2} - y \right) \Big|_{1-x}^1 \right] dx$$

$$= 1 - 3 \int_0^1 \frac{x^2}{2} dx = \frac{1}{2} .$$

∎

From the above results, we can put Zadeh's operators, probability operators, and the bounded operators in order of the degree of "roughness" as

$$D (\vee) = D (\wedge) < D (\cdot) = D \left(\overset{\wedge}{+} \right) < D (\oplus) = D (\ominus)$$

or

$$x \ominus y \leq x \cdot y \leq x \wedge y \leq x \vee y \leq x \overset{\wedge}{+} y \leq x \oplus y .$$

9.5   Fuzzy Operators Based on the Falling Shadow Theory

There are more than 90 different fuzzy operators proposed for fuzzy set operations today. These operators are, more or less, led by experience. Consequently,
they lack a theoretical basis. A problem that draws attention in the fuzzy set theory
is this: "How do we define fuzzy set operators?"

First we realize that there exists an infinite number of extensions from the traditional set theory to the fuzzy set theory. This is shown in Figure 9.5. In the figure,
$\underset{\sim}{A}(u) \cap \underset{\sim}{B}(u)$ and $\underset{\sim}{A}(u) \cup \underset{\sim}{B}(u)$, viewed as functions of $\underset{\sim}{A}(u)$ and $\underset{\sim}{B}(u)$, can be
defined by any surfaces consisting of four points A, B, C, and D. Naturally, there
is an infinite number of such surfaces.

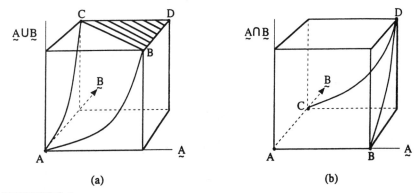

FIGURE 9.5
Extensions of fuzzy set operators.

The problem we have is not so much in developing additional fuzzy set operators.
Instead, we are looking for some sound justifications, if there are any, of how to
select operators for a given application. This necessarily requires a theory that,
under a unified setting, we can develop and explain as many formulas as possible,
and spell the appropriate conditions of applications for each operator. In order
to convey the main ideas of our approach, we omit all of the proofs that require
measure theory. We use the symbol $\mathcal{F}^*(U)$ $(\subset \mathcal{F}(U))$ to restrict the domain of
fuzzy subsets under our discussion.

9.5.1   Falling Shadows and Cut Clouds

Given a measurable space $(U, \mathcal{B})$ and a probability field $(\Omega, \mathcal{A}, P)$, and $u \in U$,
$C \subset U$, denote

$$\overset{\circ}{u} \overset{\Delta}{=} \{B \mid u \in B \subset \mathcal{B}\} \quad and \quad \overset{\circ}{C} \overset{\Delta}{=} \left\{\overset{\circ}{u} \mid u \in C\right\}.$$

If $\overset{\circ}{B}$ is a σ-field on $\mathcal{P}(U)$ and $\overset{\circ}{B}$ contains $\overset{\circ}{U}$, then $\left(\mathcal{P}(U),\overset{\circ}{B}\right)$ is called the **hyper measurable space** on U.

Let the mapping $\xi : \Omega \longrightarrow \mathcal{P}(U)$ be a **random set** on U. For any $\underset{\sim}{A}\in\overset{\circ}{B}$, the following holds:

$$\xi^{-1}\left(\underset{\sim}{A}\right) = \left\{\omega \mid \xi(\omega) \in \underset{\sim}{A}\right\} \in \mathcal{A}.$$

Since $\overset{\circ}{U} \subset \overset{\circ}{B}$, it is implied that for any $u \in U$, $\overset{\circ}{u} \in \overset{\circ}{B}$. Therefore, when ξ is a random set on U, we can compute the probability of its inverse $\xi^{-1}\left(\overset{\circ}{u}\right)$ in $\mathcal{A}$. Denote

$$\underset{\sim}{A}(u) = p\left(\xi^{-1}\left(\overset{\circ}{u}\right)\right) = p\left(\omega \mid \xi(\omega) \in\overset{\circ}{u}\right) = p\left(\omega \mid \xi(\omega) \ni u\right).$$

The set $\underset{\sim}{A}$ is called the **shadow of the random set** ξ, and ξ is called the **cloud** of $\underset{\sim}{A}$ (Figure 9.6).

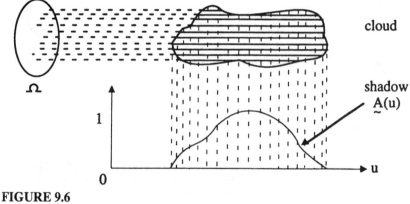

FIGURE 9.6
Cloud and shadow.

For a given fuzzy set (shadow) $\underset{\sim}{A}\in \mathcal{F}(U)$, obviously there are infinitely many clouds having $\underset{\sim}{A}$ as their shadow. A representative cloud, called the **cut cloud**, is a random set defined as follows:

Let $([0, 1], \mathcal{B}_0, m)$ be a probability space. Then $\mathcal{B}_0$ is a Borel field and m is a Lebesque measure. The **cut cloud** is defined by

$$\xi : [0, 1] \longrightarrow \mathcal{P}(U), \quad \lambda \longrightarrow A_\lambda.$$

This cloud will coincide with $\underset{\sim}{A}$ graphically and is the most straightforward one.

9.5.2 The Definition of Fuzzy Set Operations

The idea behind the definition of fuzzy set operations is as follows. First we lift two fuzzy sets to the status of cloud sets, while in the "sky" we find their union and intersection of random sets. Finally, let them fall back.

Let $A, B \in \mathcal{F}^*(U)$, and let their clouds be

$$\xi : I_1 \longrightarrow \mathcal{P}(U), \quad \lambda \longmapsto \xi(\lambda) \stackrel{\triangle}{=} A_\lambda,$$

and

$$\eta : I_2 \longrightarrow \mathcal{P}(U), \quad \mu \longmapsto \eta(\mu) \stackrel{\triangle}{=} B_\mu,$$

where $I_1 = I_2 = [0, 1]$. Although I_1 and I_2 are the same, the two probability fields $(I_1, \mathcal{B}_0, m)$ and $(I_2, \mathcal{B}_0, m)$ should be viewed as different. Therefore, we need to find a common probability field so that both ξ and η are defined under it. Consider the joint probability field $\left(I_1 \times I_2, \mathcal{B}_0^2, p\right)$, where p is the joint probability distribution on $[0, 1]^2$ and satisfies:

$$p(A \times I_2) = m(A), \quad \text{and} \quad p(I_1 \times B) = m(B)$$

for any $A, B \in \mathcal{B}_0$. We call p the **joint scalar distribution**.

Using the same notation, we redefine ξ and η on $[0, 1]^2$ below:

$$\xi : [0, 1]^2 \longrightarrow \mathcal{P}(U), \quad (\lambda, \mu) \longmapsto A_\lambda,$$

and

$$\eta : [0, 1]^2 \longrightarrow \mathcal{P}(U), \quad (\lambda, \mu) \longmapsto B_\mu.$$

The random sets ξ and η allow us to perform union and intersection operations as follows:

$$(\xi \cup \eta)(\lambda, \mu) \stackrel{\triangle}{=} \xi(\lambda, \mu) \cup \eta(\lambda, \mu),$$

and

$$(\xi \cap \eta)(\lambda, \mu) \stackrel{\triangle}{=} \xi(\lambda, \mu) \cap \eta(\lambda, \mu),$$

where $(\lambda, \mu) \in [0, 1]^2$. It can be shown that both $\xi \cup \eta$ and $\xi \cap \eta$ just defined are random sets. Now we are in a position to give a definition of union and intersection operations of fuzzy sets.

DEFINITION 22   *Let* $A, B \in \mathcal{F}^*(U)$. *Define the union and intersection of* A *and* B *as the shadows of* $\xi \cup \eta$ *and* $\xi \cap \eta$, *respectively. That is,*

$$\left(A \cap B \right)(u) \stackrel{\triangle}{=} p\left((\lambda, \mu) \mid A_\lambda \cap B_\mu \ni u \right), \qquad (9.8)$$

and

$$\left(A \cup B \right)(u) \stackrel{\triangle}{=} p\left((\lambda, \mu) \mid A_\lambda \cup B_\mu \ni u \right). \qquad (9.9)$$

Figure 9.7 helps to explain this definition.

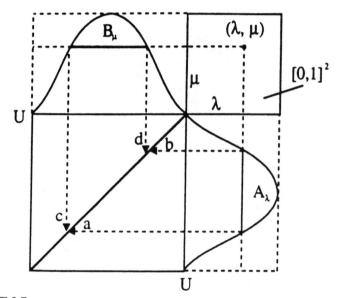

FIGURE 9.7
The Union and intersection of A **and** B.

As shown in Figure 9.8, given $u \in U$, there exists a point $\left(A(u), B(u) \right)$ in $[0, 1]^2$. From that point we divide $[0, 1]^2$ into four regions:

$$E_1 = \left[0, A(u) \right] \times \left[0, B(u) \right];$$

$$E_2 = \left[0, A(u) \right] \times \left[B(u), 1 \right];$$

$$E_3 = \left[\underset{\sim}{A}(u), 1 \right] \times \left[\underset{\sim}{B}(u), 1 \right];$$

and

$$E_4 = \left[\underset{\sim}{A}(u), 1 \right] \times \left[0, \underset{\sim}{B}(u) \right].$$

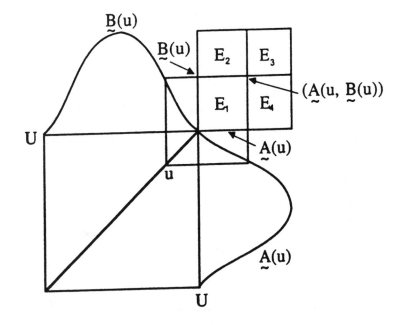

FIGURE 9.8
Graphical illustration of theorem 24.

THEOREM 24
Let $\underset{\sim}{A}, \underset{\sim}{B} \in \mathcal{F}^*(U)$. The fuzzy set operations as previously defined are equivalent to

$$\left(\underset{\sim}{A} \cap \underset{\sim}{B} \right)(u) = p(E_1)$$

and

$$\left(\underset{\sim}{A} \cup \underset{\sim}{B} \right)(u) = p(E_1 \cup E_2 \cup E_4). \tag{9.10}$$

9.5.3   The Joint Scalar Distribution

From the theorem just given, we recognize that the results of fuzzy set operations are dependent upon the choice of p. Here p is a probability distribution of a two-dimensional random variable (λ, μ) on $[0, 1]^2$. The only restriction on the choice of p is that its marginal distribution be a uniform distribution. There are many distributions having this property. We list three such (typical) distributions as follows:

1) p is uniformly distributed on one diagonal line of the unit square $[0, 1]^2$
2) p is uniformly distributed on the other diagonal line of the unit square $[0, 1]^2$
3) p is uniformly distributed on the unit square $[0, 1]^2$

All three cases are shown in Figure 9.9.

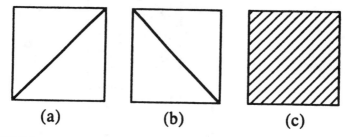

(a)   **(b)**   **(c)**

FIGURE 9.9
Three typical distributions.

We call the first type of distributions the **positively proportional type** (Figure 9.9 a), the second the **inversely proportional type** (Figure 9.9 b), and the third the **independent type** (Figure 9.9 c).

9.5.4   Three Special Operational Forms

In this section, we derive fuzzy set operational forms on the basis of the three types of the joint scale distributions of p we have just discussed.

THEOREM 25
Let $\underset{\sim}{A}, \underset{\sim}{B} \in \mathcal{F}^*(U)$.

1) *If p is a positively proportional distribution, then*

$$\left(\underset{\sim}{A} \cap \underset{\sim}{B}\right)(u) = \underset{\sim}{A}(u) \wedge \underset{\sim}{B}(u) \quad and,$$

$$\left(\underset{\sim}{A} \cup \underset{\sim}{B}\right)(u) = \underset{\sim}{A}(u) \vee \underset{\sim}{B}(u),$$

i.e., Zadeh's operators.

2) *If p is an inversely proportional distribution, then*

$$\left(\underset{\sim}{A} \cap \underset{\sim}{B}\right)(u) = \max\left\{\underset{\sim}{A}(u) + \underset{\sim}{B}(u) - 1, 0\right\};$$

$$\left(A \cup B\right)(u) = \min\left\{A(u) + B(u), 1\right\},$$

i.e., the bounded operators.

3) If p is an independent distribution, then

$$\left(A \cap B\right)(u) = A(u) \cdot B(u) \quad and,$$

$$\left(A \cup B\right)(u) = A(u) + B(u) - A(u) \cdot B(u),$$

i.e., the probability operators.

PROOF   We will only prove the second equation of part 2).

Since p is distributed over the diagonal line segment, a point (λ, μ) is on that segment if and only if $\mu = 1 - \lambda$. Hence,

$$\left(A \cup B\right)((u) = p\left(\{(\lambda, \mu) \mid A_\lambda \cup B_\mu \ni u\}\right)$$

$$= p\left(\{(\lambda, 1 - \lambda) \mid A_\lambda \cup B_{1-\lambda} \ni u\}\right)$$

$$= p\left(\left\{(\lambda, 1 - \lambda) \mid \lambda \leq A(u)\right\} \cup \left\{(\lambda, 1 - \lambda) \mid \lambda \geq 1 - B(u)\right\}\right)$$

$$= p\left(\left\{\lambda \mid \lambda \leq A(u)\right\} \cup \left\{\lambda \mid \lambda \geq 1 - B(u)\right\}\right)$$

$$= p\left(\left\{\lambda \mid \lambda \leq A(u)\right\}\right) + p\left(\left\{\lambda \mid \lambda \geq 1 - B(u)\right\}\right)$$

$$- p\left(\left\{\lambda \mid \lambda \leq A(u)\right\} \cap \left\{\lambda \mid \lambda \geq 1 - B(u)\right\}\right)$$

Now by using the fact that p is uniformly distributed on the diagonal line segment, we have

$$p\left(\left\{\lambda \mid \lambda \leq A(u)\right\}\right) = \text{the length of the interval } \left[0, A(u)\right] = A(u),$$

$$p\left(\left\{\lambda \mid \lambda \geq 1 - B(u)\right\}\right) = \text{the length of the interval } \left[1 - B(u), 1\right] = B(u),$$

and

$$p\left(\left\{\lambda \mid \lambda \leq A(u)\right\} \cap \left\{\lambda \mid \lambda \geq 1 - B(u)\right\}\right)$$

$$= \text{the length of the interval } \left[0, A(u)\right] \cap \left[1 - B(u), 1\right].$$

Case 1.   If $A(u) + B(u) \leq 1$, then $\left[0, A(u)\right] \cap \left[1 - B(u), 1\right] = \Phi$. It follows that

$$p\left(\left\{\lambda \mid \lambda \leq A(u)\right\} \cap \left\{\lambda \mid \lambda \geq 1 - B(u)\right\}\right) = 0.$$

This means

$$\left(\underset{\sim}{A} \cup \underset{\sim}{B}\right)(u) = \underset{\sim}{A}(u) + \underset{\sim}{B}(u).$$

Case 2. If $\underset{\sim}{A}(u) + \underset{\sim}{B}(u) > 1$, then

$$\left[0, \underset{\sim}{A}(u)\right] \cap \left[1 - \underset{\sim}{B}(u), 1\right] = \left[1 - \underset{\sim}{B}(u), \underset{\sim}{A}(u)\right].$$

That is,

$$p\left(\left\{\lambda \mid \lambda \leq \underset{\sim}{A}(u)\right\} \cap \left\{\lambda \mid \lambda \geq 1 - \underset{\sim}{B}(u)\right\}\right) = \underset{\sim}{A}(u) - 1 + \underset{\sim}{B}(u).$$

This implies

$$\left(\underset{\sim}{A}^c\right)(u) = \underset{\sim}{A}(u) + \underset{\sim}{B}(u) - \underset{\sim}{A}(u) + 1 - \underset{\sim}{B}(u) = 1.$$

From both cases, we obtain

$$\left(\underset{\sim}{A} \cup \underset{\sim}{B}\right)(u) = \left(\underset{\sim}{A}(u) + \underset{\sim}{B}(u)\right) \wedge 1.$$

∎

The size of λ and μ reflect the tightness measures applied to the domain of fuzzy sets. If λ is small, then A_λ is large; this means that we loosen the measure on A_λ. Otherwise, we tighten the measure on A_λ. A similar interpretation applies to μ. For the positively proportional type p, the degree of tightness of λ and μ is synchronized; for the inversely proportional type, it is asymmetrical in that when one is tight, then the other is loose, and vice versa; and for the independent type, the degree of tightness is evenly spread out between the two. Generally, for positively correlated concepts such as "body strength" and "body toughness", we should use the positively proportional type of joint scalar distributions; for negatively correlated concepts such as "healthy" and "weak", we should use the inversely proportional type. Under the definition that $\underset{\sim}{A}^c(u) = 1 - \underset{\sim}{A}(u)$, and when $\underset{\sim}{A}$ and $\underset{\sim}{A}^c$ are both present in fuzzy set operations, we should use the inversely proportional type of p, because that will lead to the desired condition: $\underset{\sim}{A} \cap \underset{\sim}{A}^c = U$ and $\underset{\sim}{A} \cap \underset{\sim}{A}^c = \Phi$.

References

[1] Bellman, R. and Giertz, M., On the analytic formalism of the theory of fuzzy sets, *Information Sciences*, 5, 1973, 149–156.

[2] Chen, Y., Research on Fuzzy operators, *Fuzzy Mathematics*, 2(2), 1982, 1–10.

[3] Goodman, I. R. and Nguyen, H. T., *Uncertainty Models for Knowledge Based Systems*, North-Holland (Elsevier Science Publishers B. V.), 1985.

[4] Li, H.-X., *Fuzzy Mathematical Methods in Engineering and Their Applications*, Tianjing Scientific and Technical Press, Tianjing, 1993.

[5] Li, H.-X. and Wang, P.-Z., *Fuzzy Mathematics*, National Defense Industry Press, Beijing, 1994.

[6] Li, H.-X. and Yen, V. C., et al., The Operations of Fuzzy Cardinalities, *JMMA*, 182, 1994, 768–778.

[7] Li, H.-X. and Yen, V. C., Factor spaces and fuzzy decision making, *Journal of Beijing Normal University*, 30(1), 1994, 41–46.

[8] Wang, P.-Z. and Sanchez, E., Treating a fuzzy subset as a projectable random set, in *Fuzzy Information and Decision*, M. M. Gupta and E. Sanchez (Eds.), Pergamon Press, 1982, 212–219.

[9] Wang, P.-Z. and Zhang, N. L., Fuzzy falling shadow space, *Journal of Mathematical Research and Exposition*, 3(1), 1982, 163–178.

[10] Wang, P.-Z., *Fuzzy Sets and Falling Shadow of Random Sets*, Beijing Normal University Press, Beijing, 1985.

[11] Wang, P.-Z., *Fuzzy Engineering — Principles and Methods*, China Productivity Center, Taipei, 1993.

[12] Wang, P.-Z. and Li, H.-X., *Fuzzy Mathematical Theory of Knowledge Representation*, Tianjin Scientific and Technical Press, Tianjin, 1994.

[13] Yager, R. R., On the measure of fuzziness and negation, *Information and Control*, 44(3), 1980, 236–260.

10

Multifactorial Decision Based on Theory of Evidence

10.1   A Brief Introduction to Theory of Evidence

Shafer's theory of evidence [8], also called the Dempster–Shafer theory of belief functions, is primarily used for managing uncertainty. Some results have applications in decision making. For details, one can consult Shafer [8] and Zhang and Wang [12].

From here on we assume Θ denotes a finite set.

10.1.1   Belief Functions

A function $Bel : \mathcal{P}(\Theta) \longrightarrow [0, 1]$ is called a **belief measure** if it satisfies
1) $Bel(\Phi) = 0$, and $Bel(\Theta) = 1$
2) For any positive integer n and any n subsets $A_1, A_2, \cdots, A_n$ of Θ, the following inequality holds:

$$Bel\left(\bigcup_{i=1}^{n} A_i\right) \geq \Delta_{A_i}^{n} Bel, \qquad (10.1)$$

where

$$\Delta_{A_i}^{n} Bel \triangleq \sum_{k=1}^{n} (-1)^{k-1} \sum_{I} \left\{ Bel\left(\bigcap_{i \in I} \mid I \subset \{1, 2, \cdots, n\}, \ |I| = k\right)\right\}.$$

Related to a belief measure is the **basic belief assignment**, also called the **basic probability assignment,** that measures the strength of the argument in favor of a subset A of Θ. A function $m : \mathcal{P}(\Theta) \longrightarrow [0, 1]$ is called a **basic distribution of the degree of belief** if it satisfies

i) $m(\Phi) = 0$

ii) $\sum \{m(A) \mid A \subset \Theta\} = 1$

The following theorem below reveals the relationship between the belief measure and the basic distribution of the degree of belief.

THEOREM 26

A necessary and sufficient condition for a function $B : \mathcal{P}(\Theta) \longrightarrow [0, 1]$ to be a belief measure is that there exists a unique basic distribution of the degree of belief $m : \mathcal{P}(\Theta) \longrightarrow [0, 1]$ such that for any $A \subset \Theta$, the following equality holds:

$$B(A) = \sum \{m(C) \mid C \subset A\}.$$

The proof is omitted.

Intuitively, we can explain the concept of the belief measure this way. First we view any subset of Θ as a proposition. For example, a quantity lies in the domain Θ but its actual value is unknown; this means the quantity can be in any subset of Θ, or equivalently we can put it in a propositional form: "the actual value is in A" for $A \subset \Theta$. Next, we view the concept of evidence as the set of facts or information that are related to the truth or falsehood of the proposition. With these two concepts as a background, a belief measure (conservative) can be interpreted as a measure of strength of belief in the truth of the proposition, or as a measure of approval of the evidence for the proposition. Thus, $m(A)$ represents the degree of belief distributed to the subset A.

10.2 Composition of Belief Measures

Let Bel_1 and Bel_2 be two belief measures on distinct sets of evidence. What will be the belief measure if the two sets of evidence were combined? An answer is that the belief measure is a λ-composition of Bel_1 and Bel_2, where λ is a number between 0 and 1 (usually, λ is set at 1).

Let Bel_1 and Bel_2 be two belief measures on Θ, and $\lambda \in [0, 1]$. We denote Bel_1 and Bel_2 as λ−composable if they satisfy

$$k \overset{\Delta}{=} \sum \left\{ \left(\frac{u(A \cap B)}{u(A)u(B)} \right)^{\lambda} m_1(A) m_2(B) \mid A, B \subset \Theta \right\} \neq \Phi \qquad (10.2)$$

where u is a measure (called the reference measure) selected a priori to reflect our concept of "large" and "small", and m_1 and m_2 are distributions of the degree of belief of Bel_1 and Bel_2, respectively. If Bel_1 and Bel_2 are λ−composable, we denote the composite belief measure by $Bel_1 \lambda Bel_2$ and m to be its distribution of the degree of belief. Assume that for every subset C of Θ, m satisfies

$$m(C) = \frac{1}{k} \sum \left\{ \left(\frac{u(A \cap B)}{u(A)u(B)} \right)^{\lambda} m_1(A) m_2(B) \mid A \cap B = C \right\}. \quad (10.3)$$

Then we can show that λ is commutative and associative. (Note: We define $\frac{0}{0} \overset{\triangle}{=} 0$ in Expressions 10.1 to 10.3.)

It is worth noting here that when $\lambda = 0$, the composition rule becomes the well-known Dempster's composition rule. However, $\lambda = 1$ is used more frequently in applications.

10.2.1   Extensions of Belief Measures

Let $\mathcal{M}$ be a subset of $\mathcal{P}(\Theta)$. We call $\mathcal{M}$ an intersection system if it is closed under the intersection operation $\cap$.

THEOREM 27
[Extension Theorem] Let $\mathcal{M}$ be an intersection system of $\mathcal{P}(\Theta)$. In mapping $Bel_0 : \mathcal{M} \longrightarrow [0, 1]$ with terms well defined and satisfying conditions 1) and 2) for the belief measure defined in Section 10.1.1, Bel_0 can be extended to a belief measure on Θ, and this is the smallest of such extensions.

The proof is omitted.

10.2.2   Direct Products of Belief Measures

Assume Θ_1 and Θ_2 are two finite sets and Bel_i is a belief on Θ_i ($i = 1.2$). Denote $\mathcal{M} \overset{\triangle}{=} \{A \times B \mid A \subset \Theta_1, B \subset \Theta_2\}$ and define $Bel_0 : \mathcal{M} \longrightarrow [0, 1]$ by

$$A \times B \longmapsto Bel_0(A \times B) \overset{\triangle}{=} Bel_1(A) \cdot Bel_2(B).$$

It is clear that $\mathcal{M}$ is an intersection system in $\mathcal{P}(\Theta_1 \times \Theta_2)$, and when each term is meaningful, Bel_0 satisfies the conditions of the belief measure. By the extension theorem, Bel_0 can be extended to a belief measure on $\Theta_1 \times \Theta_2$. The smallest extension is called the **direct product** of Bel_1 and Bel_2, and is denoted by $Bel_1 \times Bel_2$.

For more than two belief measures, the direct product can be defined in two ways: 1) use the method of induction, and 2) use the extension method similar to the case of two measures as just discussed. It is proven that the two approaches are actually equivalent.

10.2.3 A Coincidence Theorem

For a given belief measure $Bel : \mathcal{P}(\Theta) \longrightarrow [0, 1]$. The mapping $pl : \mathcal{P}(\Theta) \longrightarrow [0, 1]$ is called the **dual plausibility measure** of Bel if for any subset A of Θ, A satisfies

$$pl(A) = 1 - Bel(A^c).$$

Let p be a probability measure on Θ. If for every subset A of Θ, A satisfies

$$Bel(A) \leq p(A) \leq pl(A)$$

then p is called the **consistent probability measure** of Bel. We state the following theorem without proof.

THEOREM 28
[Coincidence Theorem] Let Bel be a belief measure on Θ and $\mathcal{M}$ be a subset of $\mathcal{P}(\Theta)$. If $\mathcal{M}$ forms a chain under the set operation "$\subset$", then there exists a consistent probability measure p of Bel such that Bel $|_{\mathcal{M}} = p |_{\mathcal{M}}$.

10.2.4 Integration with Respect to a Belief Function

Let Bel be a belief measure on Θ. Integration of the function $f : \Theta \longrightarrow [0, 1]$ with respect to the belief function Bel is defined by

$$\int_{\Theta} f\, dBel \stackrel{\triangle}{=} \int_0^1 Bel(\{f > x\})\, dx.$$

If m is the distribution of the degree of belief of Bel, then

$$\int_{\Theta} f\, dBel = \sum \left\{ \min_{\theta \in A} f(\theta) \cdot m(A) \mid A \subset \Theta \right\}.$$

Note that $\{\{f > x\} \mid x \in [0, 1]\}$ is a chain, hence

THEOREM 29
Let Bel be a belief measure on Θ and $f : \Theta \longrightarrow [0, 1]$. Then there exists a Bel consistent probability measure p such that

$$\int_{\Theta} f\, dBel = \int_{\Theta} f\, dp.$$

10.2.5   A Class of Generalized Fuzzy Sets

Let U be a universe of discourse, and let α be a fuzzy probability with extension $\underset{\sim}{A} \in \mathcal{F}(U)$. A situation that frequently emerges from applications is as follows: For $u \in U$, because of insufficient understanding on u and α, it is difficult to assign a grade of membership $\underset{\sim}{A}(u)$ of u. If such grades were given, they would most likely be done with reservations or reluctance. For example, if someone asks you "how is Mr. Do?" (i.e., what is the grade of membership of Mr. Do with respect to the concept "well"?), your answer probably would be "It's hard to tell, for we haven't seen each other lately".

On the other hand, when we study the relationship between u and $\underset{\sim}{A}$, we normally start from the positive view by considering the degree of membership of u belonging to $\underset{\sim}{A}$, rarely considered from the opposite view that the degree of membership of u *not* belonging to $\underset{\sim}{A}$. This is a flaw in our approach. If we considered the relationship of u and $\underset{\sim}{A}$ from both positive and negative views simultaneously (i.e., determine simultaneously the degree of membership of u belonging to $\underset{\sim}{A}$ and not belonging to $\underset{\sim}{A}$), then the result would be more realistic, and the content of fuzzy set theory would be greatly enriched.

These discussions motivate us to introduce the concept of a class of generalized fuzzy sets.

DEFINITION 23   *Let U be a universe of discourse. $\Theta = \{\theta_0, \theta_1\}$, and $\mathcal{B}(\Theta)$ be the set of all belief measures on Θ. We call a mapping $\underset{\sim}{A}: U \longrightarrow \mathcal{B}(\Theta)$ a* **generalized fuzzy set** *on U. For any $u \in U$, $\underset{\sim}{A}(u)$ is called the* **membership belief measure** *of u. We define $\zeta\left(\underset{\sim}{A}(u)\right) \overset{\Delta}{=} \underset{\sim}{A}(u)(\{\theta_1\})$ and call it the* **degree of approval** *of $\underset{\sim}{A}$ at u, $\delta\left(\underset{\sim}{A}(u)\right) \overset{\Delta}{=} \underset{\sim}{A}(u)(\{\theta_0\})$ is called the* **degree of denial** *of $\underset{\sim}{A}$ at u, and $\tau\left(\underset{\sim}{A}(u)\right) = 1 - \zeta\left(\underset{\sim}{A}(u)\right) - \delta\left(\underset{\sim}{A}(u)\right) \left(\tau\left(\underset{\sim}{A}(u)\right) \in [0, 1]\right)$ following expression 10.1) is called the* **degree of unknown** *of $\underset{\sim}{A}$ at u.*

From this definition, ordinary fuzzy sets, are generalized fuzzy sets, where the degree of unknown of these fuzzy sets at every point of U is zero.

10.3 Multifactorial Evaluation Based on the Theory of Evidence

In this section, we apply the notion of the theory of evidence to multifactorial evaluation. The general process is divided into three stages.

Stage 1. Find the set of all factors relevant to the evaluation, i.e., find the family of basic factors $\pi = \{f_1, f_2, \cdots, f_n\}$.

Stage 2. Perform the single factor evaluation. For every factor f_i, find a belief measure $Bel_i : \mathcal{P}(\Theta) \longrightarrow [0, 1]$ (hereafter, we assume $\Theta = \{\theta_0, \theta_1\}$); find $\zeta_i \overset{\triangle}{=} Bel_i(\{\theta_1\})$ that represents the satisfaction level or degree of approval on the state of factor f_i; find $\delta_i \overset{\triangle}{=} Bel_i(\{\theta_0\})$ that represents the dissatisfaction level or degree of denial on the state of factor f_i; and $\tau_i \overset{\triangle}{=} 1 - \zeta_i - \delta_i$ that represents the degree of unknown on the state of factor f_i.

The collection of all Bel_i $i = 1, 2, \cdots, n$ on π determines a generalized fuzzy set:

$$BEL(f_i) :\overset{\triangle}{=} Bel_i \quad (i = 1, 2, \cdots, n).$$

For every i, if $\zeta_i = 1$, the object under evaluation is fully satisfied with the state of f_i; if $\delta_i = 1$, the object under evaluation is not satisfied at all with the state of f_i. In these cases, if we regard θ_1 as a belief measure of $Bel(\{\theta_1\}) = 1$ on Θ, then we can interpret θ_1 as the fully satisfied state of f_i; likewise, we can interpret θ_0 as the unsatisfactory state of f_i.

Stage 3. Find the multifactorial evaluation. This is done by deriving a belief measure on Θ through synthesizing all generalized fuzzy sets BEL on π. We outline a procedure for this stage and explain the basic ideas behind it as follows.

First, we find the direct product of belief measures Bel_i $(i = 1, 2, \cdots, n)$:

$$\overline{Bel} \overset{\triangle}{=} \prod_{i=1}^{n} Bel_i : \mathcal{P}(\Theta^n) \longrightarrow [0, 1] \tag{10.4}$$

and assume m is its distribution of degree of belief.

The interpretation of an element $(\theta^1, \theta^2, \cdots, \theta^n) \in \Theta^n$ is similar to the previous case. For example, suppose $(\theta^1, \theta^2, \cdots, \theta^n) = (\theta_1, \theta_1, \theta_0, \cdots, \theta_0)$. This means that the object under evaluation is fully satisfied on the state of factors f_1 and f_2, but that it is unsatisfied with the state of the remaining factors.

Next, for every $(\theta^1, \theta^2, \cdots, \theta^n)$ we determine a number between 0 and 1 that represents the final judgment on the object under evaluation. Letting $(\theta^1, \theta^2, \cdots, \theta^n)$ range over the entire Θ^n, we have the **composition function** $M : \Theta^n \longrightarrow [0, 1]$.

Finally, transform $\overline{Bel} : \mathcal{P}(\Theta^n) \longrightarrow [0, 1]$ to a belief measure on Θ by using the composition function and then determine the final evaluation.

Now we consider some properties that a composition function should possess. For any subset $A \subset \Theta^n$, $m(A)$ is the degree of belief of A. When A is a singleton, i.e., $\{(\theta^1, \theta^2, \cdots, \theta^n)\}$, we can use the product $M(\theta^1, \theta^2, \cdots, \theta^n) \cdot m(\theta^1, \theta^2, \cdots, \theta^n)$ as part of the degree of approval $\zeta = Bel(\{\theta_1\})$ for the result of evaluation. When A is not a singleton, $m(A)$ is likely determined by one of the points in A. Hence, we define

$$\min \left\{ M\left(\theta^1, \theta^2, \cdots, \theta^n\right) \cdot m(A) \mid \left(\theta^1, \theta^2, \cdots, \theta^n\right) \in A \right\}$$

as the contribution of $m(A)$ to ζ. At any rate, we have

$$\zeta \overset{\triangle}{=} Bel(\{\theta_1\})$$

$$= \sum \left\{ \min \left\{ M\left(\theta^1, \theta^2, \cdots, \theta^n\right) \cdot m(A) \mid A \subset \Theta^n \right\} \right.$$

$$\left. \mid \left(\theta^1, \theta^2, \cdots, \theta^n\right) \in A \right\}$$

$$= \int_{\Theta^n} M d\overline{Bel}.$$

Analogous to the above discussion, we have

$$\delta \overset{\triangle}{=} Bel(\{\theta_0\})$$

$$= \sum \left\{ \min \left\{ 1 - M\left(\theta^1, \theta^2, \cdots, \theta^n\right) \cdot m(A) \mid A \subset \Theta^n \right\} \right.$$

$$\left. \mid \left(\theta^1, \theta^2, \cdots, \theta^n\right) \in A \right\}$$

$$= \int_{\Theta^n} (1 - M) \, d\overline{Bel}.$$

Now we have a framework for the evaluation model. Due to mathematical considerations, we define an axiomatic approach to composition functions before specifying the model.

DEFINITION 24 *A function $M : \Theta^n \longrightarrow [0, 1]$ is called a* **composition function** *if it satisfies the following axioms:*

1) $M(\theta_1, \theta_1, \cdots, \theta_1) = 1$, $M(\theta_0, \theta_0, \cdots, \theta_0) = 0$; and

2) Let $S(\theta^1, \theta^2, \cdots, \theta^n) \stackrel{\Delta}{=} \{i \mid \theta^i = \theta_1\}$. For any two elements $(\theta^1, \theta^2, \cdots, \theta^n)$, $(\theta^{1'}, \theta^{2'}, \cdots, \theta^{n'}) \in \Theta^n$, if $S(\theta^1, \theta^2, \cdots, \theta^n) \supseteq S(\theta^{1'}, \theta^{2'}, \cdots, \theta^{n'})$ then

$$M(\theta^1, \theta^2, \cdots, \theta^n) \geq M(\theta^{1'}, \theta^{2'}, \cdots, \theta^{n'}).$$

We now state the **degree of belief model** (π, BEL, M) under the multifactorial evaluation setting.

Step 1. Define the family of basic factors $\pi = \{f_1, f_2, \cdots, f_n\}$.

Step 2. Perform single-factor evaluations, i.e., construct the generalized fuzzy set BEL on π.

Step 3. Design the composition function $M : \Theta^n \longrightarrow [0, 1]$.

Step 4. Find the outcomes of the multifactorial evaluation:

$$\zeta \stackrel{\Delta}{=} Bel(\{\theta_1\}) \stackrel{\Delta}{=} \int_{\Theta^n} M d\overline{Bel},$$

$$\delta \stackrel{\Delta}{=} Bel(\{\theta_0\}) \stackrel{\Delta}{=} \int_{\Theta^n} (1 - M) d\overline{Bel},$$

and

$$\tau \stackrel{\Delta}{=} 1 - \zeta - \delta.$$

To clarify the computational formulas used in Step 4, we need:

LEMMA 2

Let (π, BEL, M) be a degree of belief model in the multifactorial evaluation, p_i, and p'_i $(i = 1, 2, \cdots, n)$ be two sets of probability measures satisfying

$$p_i(\{\theta_1\}) = Bel_i(\{\theta_1\}), \text{ and } p'_i(\{\theta_0\}) = Bel_i(\{\theta_0\}).$$

Then ζ and δ are determined by

$$\zeta = \int_{\Theta^n} M d \prod_{i=1}^{n} p_i \text{ and } \delta = \int_{\Theta^n} (1 - M) d \prod_{i=1}^{n} p'_i. \qquad (10.5)$$

Note that p_i, and p'_i can also be written as

$$p_i(\{\theta\}) = \begin{cases} Bel_i(\{\theta_1\}) = \zeta_i, & \theta = \theta_1 \\ 1 - Bel_i(\{\theta_1\}) = 1 - \zeta_i, & \theta = \theta_0 \end{cases}$$

and

$$p_i' (\{\theta_0\}) = \begin{cases} Bel_i (\{\theta_0\}) = \delta_i, & \theta = \theta_0 \\ 1 - Bel_i (\{\theta_0\}) = 1 - \delta_i, & \theta = \theta_1. \end{cases}$$

PROOF   Since

$$\int_{\Theta^n} M d \prod_{i=1}^{n} p_i = \int_0^1 \prod_{i=1}^{n} p_i (\{M > x\}) dx$$

in proving the first expression of (10.5), it is only necessary to show that for any $x \in [0, 1]$, x satisfies

$$\prod_{i=1}^{n} p_i (\{M > x\}) = \overline{Bel} (\{M > x\}). \tag{10.6}$$

To show this equality, we define a notation $[\theta_1, \theta]$ by

$$[\theta_1, \theta] = \begin{cases} \{\theta_1\}, & \theta = \theta_1 \\ \Theta, & \theta = \theta_0. \end{cases}$$

By the definition of the composition function, for any $x \in [0, 1]$, there exists an index L_x and $A_l = [\theta_1, \theta^1] \times [\theta_1, \theta^2] \times \cdots \times [\theta_1, \theta^{n_l}]$ $(l = 1, 2, \cdots, L_x)$, such that $\{M > x\} = \bigcup_{l=1}^{L_x} A_l$. Hence,

$$\prod_{i=1}^{n} p_i (\{M > x\}) = \triangle_l^{L_x} \prod_{i=1}^{n} p_i = \triangle_l^{L_x} \overline{Bel} = \overline{Bel} (\{M > x\}).$$

This proves the first equality. The second one follows similarly.   ∎

THEOREM 30
Under the conditions given in Lemma 2,

$$\zeta = \int_{\Theta} \cdots \int_{\Theta} M \left(\theta^1, \theta^2, \cdots, \theta^n \right) dp_1 \left(\theta^1 \right) \cdots dp_n \left(\theta^n \right)$$

$$= \sum \left\{ M \left(\theta^1, \theta^2, \cdots, \theta^n \right) \prod_{i=1}^{n} p_i \left(\{\theta^i\} \right) \mid \theta^i \in \Theta, \quad i = 1, 2, \cdots, n \right\},$$

and

$$\delta = \int_{\Theta} \cdots \int_{\Theta} \left(1 - M\left(\theta^1, \theta^2, \cdots, \theta^n\right)\right) dp_1'\left(\theta^1\right) \cdots dp_n'\left(\theta^n\right)$$

$$= \sum \left\{ \left(1 - M\left(\theta^1, \theta^2, \cdots, \theta^n\right)\right) \prod_{i=1}^{n} p_i'\left(\left\{\theta^i\right\}\right) \right.$$

$$\left. \mid \theta^i \in \Theta, \quad i = 1, 2, \cdots, n \right\}.$$

The proof is simple and thus omitted.

This theorem provides the computational formulas of ζ and δ in the degree of belief model of the multifactorial evaluation. We can use them for actual applications. However, in certain cases, these two formulas can be further simplified. In the following section, we give two such special cases.

10.4   Two Special Types of Composition Functions

Composition functions may take a variety of forms. Common among these forms are the additive composition functions and the multiplicative composition functions. These two types of composition functions have very simple computational formulas useful for the results of evaluation.

DEFINITION 25   *A function* $M : \Theta^n \longrightarrow [0, 1]$ *is an* **additive composition function** *if for any*
$\left(\theta^1, \theta^2, \cdots, \theta^n\right) \in \Theta^n$ *and for any* $i_0 \in \{1, 2, \cdots, n - 1\}$, *the following equality holds:*

$$M\left(\theta^1, \theta^2, \cdots, \theta^n\right) = M\left(\theta^1, \cdots, \theta^{i_0}, \theta_0, \cdots, \theta_0\right)$$

$$+ M\left(\theta_0, \cdots, \theta_0, \theta^{i_0+1}, \cdots, \theta^n\right).$$

If M is an additive composition function, and set w_i for $i = 1, 2, \cdots, n$ as

$$w_i \overset{\triangle}{=} M\left(\theta_0, \cdots, \theta_0, \theta_1, \theta_0, \cdots, \theta_0\right)$$

(where the i-th component of $(\theta^1, \theta^2, \cdots, \theta^n)$ is θ_1 and all other components are set to the same value θ_0), then it can be easily shown that

$$M\left(\theta^1, \theta^2, \cdots, \theta^n\right) = \sum \left\{ w_i \mid i \in \left\{ \theta^j = \theta_1, \; j = 1, 2, \cdots, n \right\} \right\}.$$

That is to say, the composition function M is determined by the weight vector $(w_1, w_2, \cdots, w_n)$.

DEFINITION 26 *A function* $M : \Theta^n \longrightarrow [0, 1]$ *is a* **multiplicative composition function** *if for any*
$(\theta^1, \theta^2, \cdots, \theta^n) \in \Theta^n$, *and for any* $i_0 \in \{1, 2, \cdots, n - 1\}$, *the following equality holds:*

$$M\left(\theta^1, \theta^2, \cdots, \theta^n\right) = M\left(\theta^1, \cdots, \theta^{i_0}, \theta_0, \cdots, \theta_0\right)$$

$$\cdot M\left(\theta_0, \cdots, \theta_0, \theta^{i_0+1}, \cdots, \theta^n\right).$$

If M is a multiplicative composition function, and set v_i for $i = 1, 2, \cdots, n$ as

$$v_i \overset{\triangle}{=} M\left(\theta_1, \cdots, \theta_1, \theta_0, \theta_1, \cdots, \theta_1\right)$$

(where the i-th component of $(\theta^1, \theta^2, \cdots, \theta^n)$ is θ_0 and all other components are set to the same value θ_1), then it can be easily shown that

$$M\left(\theta^1, \theta^2, \cdots, \theta^n\right) = \prod \left\{ v_i \mid i \in \left\{ j \mid \theta^j = \theta_0, \; j = 1, 2, \cdots, n \right\} \right\}.$$

A special case of the multiplicative composition function arises when the state of each factor is "serially" related to each other; for example, if it is unsatisfactory on a particular state of a factor, then it will influence and spread to all factors and conclude that the object (under evaluation) is unsatisfactory. In this case, we should set $v_i = 0$ for all $i = 1, 2, \cdots, n$, and the function M is simplified to

$$M\left(\theta^1, \theta^2, \cdots, \theta^n\right) = \begin{cases} 1, & \theta^1 = \theta^2 = \cdots = \theta^n = \theta_1 \\ 0, & \text{otherwise.} \end{cases}$$

In the following, we restrict the multiplicative composition function to the previous type.

For additive composition functions and multiplicative composition functions, the following theorem makes the computation on the results of evaluation explicit.

THEOREM 31

Let (π, BEL, M) be a degree of belief model in the multifactorial evaluation.
1) If M is an additive composition function, then

$$\zeta = \sum_{i=1}^{n} w_i \zeta_i \quad and \quad \delta = \sum_{i=1}^{n} w_i \delta_i.$$

2) If M is a multiplicative composition function, then

$$\zeta = \prod_{i=1}^{n} \zeta_i \quad and \quad \delta = 1 - \prod_{i=1}^{n} (1 - \zeta_i).$$

PROOF We will prove 1) only.
By Theorem 30,

$$\zeta = \int_{\Theta} \cdots \int_{\Theta} M\left(\theta^1, \theta^2, \cdots, \theta^n\right) dp_1\left(\theta^1\right) \cdots dp_n\left(\theta^n\right)$$

$$= \int_{\Theta} \cdots \int_{\Theta} \sum_{i=1}^{n} M_i\left(\theta^i\right) dp_1\left(\theta^1\right) \cdots dp_n\left(\theta^n\right)$$

where $M_i\left(\theta^i\right) \stackrel{\Delta}{=} M\left(\theta_0, \cdots, \theta_0, \theta_1, \theta_0, \cdots, \theta_0\right)$ and, as before, only the i-th component has a value θ_1.
Therefore,

$$\zeta = \sum_{i=1}^{n} \int_{\Theta} M_i\left(\theta^i\right) dp_i\left(\theta^i\right) = \sum_{i=1}^{n} w_i \zeta_i.$$

∎

10.5 The Maximum Principle for Multiple Object Evaluations

Assume $u_1, u_2, \cdots,$ and u_m are m candidate objects for evaluation. For every object u_j, we can always find its evaluation via a degree of belief model. This implies that we, in fact, have a set of three-dimensional elements: $\left(\zeta^{(j)}, \delta^{(j)}, \tau^{(j)}\right)$, $j = 1, 2, \cdots, m$. Our question is "how do we determine the best object from the set of m evaluated objects?" We discuss three possible approaches to determine the best object; they are called the conservative, moderate, and aggressive selection principles.

The **conservative selection principle**: Select u_{j_0} if there exists a

$$j_0 \in \{1, 2, \cdots, m\}$$

such that j_0 satisfies

$$\zeta^{(j_0)} = \max \left\{ \zeta^{(j)} \mid j = 1, 2, \cdots, m \right\}.$$

The special characteristic of this principle is that it uses the degree of approval as the basis of selection. Under this principle, the best object selected has the maximum degree of approval, whereas the sum of the degree of denial and the degree of unknown is at the minimum. In other words, this approach makes no distinction between the degree of unknown and the degree of denial. Hence, it is conservative.

The **aggressive selection principle**: Select u_{j_0} if there exists a $j_0 \in \{1, 2, \cdots, m\}$ such that j_0 satisfies

$$\delta^{(j_0)} = \min \left\{ \delta^{(j)} \mid j = 1, 2, \cdots, m \right\}.$$

This principle utilizes the degree of denial as the basis of selection. Under this principle the best object selected is the one with the minimum degree of denial, whereas the sum of the degree of approval and the degree of unknown is at the maximum. In other words, this approach combines the degree of unknown with the degree of approval. Hence, we call it aggressive.

The **moderate selection principle**: Select u_{j_0} if there exists a $j_0 \in \{1, 2, \cdots, m\}$ such that j_0 satisfies

$$\zeta^{(j_0)} + \frac{1}{2}\tau^{(j_0)} = \max \left\{ \zeta^{(j)} + \frac{1}{2}\tau^{(j)} \mid j = 1, 2, \cdots, m \right\}.$$

Unlike the conservative (the aggressive) selection principle where the degree of unknown was entirely absorbed by the degree of denial (the degree of approval), this principle allocates the degree of unknown equally to the degree of approval and the degree of denial. The concept is similar to the use of a uniform prior distribution in Bayesian statistics.

References

[1] Chen, Y. Y., Liu, Y. F., and Wang, P. Z., Mathematical models of multifactorial evaluation, *Fuzzy Mathematics*, 3(1), 1983, 61–70.

[2] Li, H.-X., Multifactorial fuzzy sets and multifactorial fuzzy degree of nearness, *Fuzzy Sets and Systems*, 19(3), 1986, 291–297.

[3] Li, H.-X., Multifactorial analysis, *Fuzzy Systems and Mathematics*, 2(1), 1988, 9–19.

[4] Li, H.-X., *Fuzzy Mathematical Methods in Engineering and Their Applications*, Tianjing Scientific and Technical Press, Tianjing, 1993.

[5] Li, H.-X. and Wang, P.-Z., *Fuzzy Mathematics*, National Defense Industry Press, Beijing, 1994.

[6] Li, H.-X. and Yen, V. C., et al., The operations of fuzzy cardinalities, *JMMA*, 182, 1994, 768–778.

[7] Li, H.-X. and Yen, V. C., Factor spaces and fuzzy decision making, *Journal of Beijing Normal University*, 30(1), 1994, 41–46.

[8] Shafer, G., *A Mathematical Theory of Evidence*. Princeton University Press, 1976.

[9] Wang, P.-Z., *Fuzzy Sets Theory and Its Applications*, Shanghai Scientific and Technical Press, Shanghai, 1984.

[10] Wang, P.-Z., *Fuzzy Sets and Falling Shadow of Random Sets*, Beijing Normal University Press, Beijing, 1985.

[11] Wang, P.-Z., *Fuzzy Engineering — Principles and Methods*, China Productivity Center, Taipei, 1993

[12] Zhang, L. W. and Wang, P. Z., Multifactorial evaluation models based on theory of evidence, *Journal of Systems Engineering*, 3(1), 1986, 63–73.

Index